The Story of
THE BLUES AND ROYALS

Her Majesty the Colonel-in-Chief signing the visitors book in the
Household Cavalry museum

The Story of
THE BLUES AND ROYALS

(Royal Horse Guards and 1st Dragoons)

J. N. P. WATSON

LEO COOPER
LONDON

First published in Great Britain in 1993 by
LEO COOPER
190 Shaftesbury Avenue, London WC2H 8JL
an imprint of
Pen & Sword Books Ltd
47 Church Street, Barnsley, S Yorks S70 2AS

A CIP catalogue record for this book is available
from the British Library

ISBN 085052 238 2

Printed & Bound by Redwood Books
Trowbridge, Wiltshire

CONTENTS

FOREWORD

by

General Sir Desmond Fitzpatrick, KCB, DSO, MBE, MC

THERE have been several accounts of the careers of the Royal Horse Guards (The Blues) and of the Royal Dragoons (1st Dragoons), covering the period from 1661, during which year both those regiments were formed, until the close of the Second World War. There are none, until now, however, telling the two stories – and, subsequently, the history of the single regiment – from 1945 to the present day, a span of almost half a century.

The accounts we have here not only complete the regimental histories, they also draw together the respective strands of what were once two of the world's most celebrated regiments – one of Household Cavalry, the other from the Cavalry of the Line – from their creation in the year that Britain's first standing army was founded, past the Second World War, through the troubled peace of the 1940s, '50s and '60s, through the amalgamation of 1969, and onto what has proved to be a remarkable success story. Thus Part One of the book summarises the early history (ending with a list of previous regimental writings); Part Two follows, in detail, the separate post-war stories of the two regiments until they were merged; and Part Three records the distinguished annals of the regiment we know today.

What renders this book unique is the fact that it is the only record of a fusion of regiments from different corps, one from the Household Cavalry, one from the Royal Armoured Corps. The Royals – with much thought and sensitivity by both sides –

became part of the Household Cavalry, with its dual role of mounted ceremonial and fighting armour, while by no means losing their original identity. The best qualities of each regiment were drawn together to comprise and create what is generally regarded as something even better than the parent regiments.

In addition to the written word of this comprehensive history of The Blues and Royals we have here a most remarkable collection of illustrations. The paintings give a wonderful evocation of the rich heritage of both regiments, while the black and white photographs provide, by themselves, a complete visual record of the most recent history.

Desmond Fitzpatrick
Colonel
The Blues and Royals

INTRODUCTION

"I was most impressed . . . They did all that was asked of them in great style and were not deterred by anything . . . I found [them all] well mannered, well turned out in all circumstances, calm and collected, which is, if I may say so, what I would expect of Household Cavalrymen."

So wrote Brigadier Julian Thompson, commanding 3 Commando Brigade during Operation 'Corporate', the Falklands campaign – of the two Blues and Royals troops under his command, in a letter to the Regiment's Commanding Officer, Lieutenant Colonel James Hamilton-Russell. I lead with that quote because the troops concerned were not hand picked; they were just about the only ones available for dispatch to the South Atlantic in that momentous spring of 1982. Their conduct and demeanour therefore fairly reflects the spirit, the training, and the courage of the whole Regiment. Most soldiers of the British Army are doubtless diligent, brave and tough. What distinguishes the cavalrymen of The Blues and Royals may be enshrined in those two words "great style".

The professionally stylish examples of the leaders has, in their case, always been emulated by those who are led, and I hope that the quality of "great style" shines through these pages. It comes from a compound of the type of man the Regiment is careful to recruit; from the trooper's basic training, which is that of the Household Division; from his technical training, which, also of a very high standard, is that of the Royal Armoured Corps; and from his dedication and exuberance which is based on outstanding leadership, regimental tradition, *esprit de corps* and squadron and troop comradeship. And those who have enjoyed the advantages of serving as both horse soldiers and armoured cavalrymen invariably add something extra, a certain bonus of

1

loose-limbed confidence perhaps, to the air of The Blues and Royals. In all the armies of the world, the British Household Cavalryman, with his dual fighting and equestrian ceremonial roles, is magnificently unique.

There were, during the late 1960s, many sceptics, members and ex-members of both Regiments, who doubted whether the fusion of the two Regiments – one of Household Cavalry, the other of Line Cavalry, one with a divided role, the other with a single role, each with its subtly different attitudes to soldiering – could be made to work successfully. Those sceptics' reservations were speedily invalidated. I hope I have shown (in Part Three) how well, more or less from the moment of amalgamation in 1969, the new Regiment absorbed the best strands of the two parent Regiments, uniting them to make the fresh career of a Regiment with a character essentially its own. The fact that The Blues and Royals went on to create what is arguably a military élite second to none in the world renders it all the more unfortunate, as I am sure all members of the Association will agree, that they were reduced to two armoured reconnaissance sabre squadrons in the union with The Life Guards in a single service regiment in October, 1992.

Soon after Field Marshal Sir Gerald Templer became Colonel of the Blues in 1963 he remarked on that Regiment's oft-quoted reputation for "family feeling and friendliness". This was a famous characteristic, too, of the Royals. Little wonder, therefore, that the combination of the two produced the remarkably strong warmth of comradeship among both the members and ex-members of The Blues and Royals, and their families, with which we are now so familiar.

When the Regimental Association honoured me with the task of putting these records together it was to cover the years 1945 to 1992. However, on taking my first look at the project, it seemed important to show how closely the early careers of the Royal Horse Guards and the 1st Dragoons ran. And when I refer later to such esoteric matters as the consequence of Lord Granby's wig and hat blowing off at the Battle of Warburg (saluting without headdress) or the Eagle of Napoleon's 105th Regiment, or the death of Second Lieutenant John Dunville VC (black beneath badges of rank); or to such events as the Waterloo and Alamein anniversaries, I felt that readers without some knowledge of the early histories should have a guiding reference. Hence my brief chronicle of the period 1661–1945, represented here as Part One and supported by a colourful collection of pictures and vintage photographs.

The compilation of the "orbats" was fraught with difficulty. Apart from the fact that there were many deficiencies and in-accuracies in the nominal rolls shown in the regimental maga-zines, The Blues had no journal (other than *The Household Brigade Magazine*) until 1963, and, surprisingly, there was no official source from which to check appointments. As for the Royals' journal, *The Eagle*, that carried no nominal rolls in the early post-war years. At one point I nearly despaired of being able to verify names and thought it better to scrap the whole lot. In the end, however, the decision was taken to keep them in spite of the risk of errors. Meanwhile, I much regret the omission of Warrant Officers' initials, but so many were missing from the records that, for the sake of consistency, it was resolved to exclude them in the case of everyone of the rank of Warrant Officer Class II and below.

As regards the illustrations in Parts Two and Three I am only sorry that more of the tantalising photographs reproduced in the various magazines could not be used. But, unless they were very sharp they would not print up well a second time. (Also, repro-duction is extremely expensive). There is an object lesson here: editors ought to maintain a library of originals for posterity! I trust that readers will appreciate that it was not always possible to cross-check the veracity of details – personalities, dates, where-abouts, and so on – written on the back of snapshots, or, indeed, many more formal captions attributed to this or that scene or group. And, as for the maps – for which I am duly thankful to David Notley – any errors that transpire may be attributed to me, not to him.

I need hardly say that a host of Blues and Royals, past and present, have played invaluable parts in the production of this history, several giving up many hours of their time to put me right on a wide variety of detail. My first tribute is to Colonel Jeremy Smith-Bingham, whose inspiration it was to have the Household

Cavalry chronicles brought up to date and who has been most supportive from start to finish. My thanks are due secondly to Colonel Peter Rogers, who launched me into the project and who was at the same time commanding the Regiment and Chairman of the Regimental Association almost throughout the period of my research. I could not have asked for a kinder or more painstaking guide and mentor. Moreover, he made substantial contributions to Part Three of the history, as the reader will see. I am equally grateful to Major Paddy Kersting, the Curator of the Household Cavalry Museum. He showed great patience at my frequent invasions of his domain and demands for magazines and other documents, and coordinated all the photography necessary to complete the illustrations. His assistant, Ted Woodbridge, was also most helpful.

General Sir Desmond Fitzpatrick and Colonel Rogers read through the entire draft and made many useful suggestions; as did Lieutenant Colonel S. E. M. Bradish-Ellames, Lieutenant Colonel B. J. Lockhart and Major General P. D. Reid, the Royals chapters in Part Two (1945–69); and Major General Sir Roy Redgrave and Colonel Smith-Bingham the Blues chapters of that period. I am, in addition, grateful to General Fitzpatrick, Colonel Rogers and Colonel Smith-Bingham for their comments on Part Three. My (necessarily brief) account of the career of the Regiment's detachment in the Falklands campaign was put together with the careful help of the two troop leaders, Lieutenants (now Major) M. R. Coreth and Lord Robin Innes-Ker, and of Colonel J. G. Hamilton-Russell, then commanding the Regiment. Colonel Hamilton-Russell also most kindly undertook to go through the whole book again at a later stage and pointed out a number of discrepancies.

Among the former and serving members of one or other of the Regiments, who either contributed information, lent photographs, or advised on the maps and the orbats I would make particular mention of – apart from those already named – the following: Major the Marquess of Anglesey, Major General G. T. A. Armitage, Major C. V. C. Booth-Jones, Lieutenant Colonel W. S. H. Boucher, Major Sir Rupert Buchanan-Jardine, Mr M. P. T. de Lisle Bush, Lieutenant Colonel D. J. Daly, Lieutenant

Colonel H. W. Davies, Major A. J. Dickinson, Colonel J. B. Evans, Major General Sir James Eyre, Lieutenant Colonel P. B. Fielden, Mr D. Godfrey-Cass, Lieutenant Colonel H. O. Hugh-Smith, Major B. J. Hodgson, Major P. A. Lendrum, Lieutenant Colonel H. P. D. Massey, Lieutenant Colonel P. Massey, Captain J. W. Matthews, Mr J. Neill, Capt the Earl of Normanton, Mr J. L. Ovens, Brigadier A. H. Parker Bowles, Major E. L. Payne, Colonel J. H. Pitman, Colonel D. de C. Smiley, Mr P. F. Smith, Major W. A. Stringer, Major General D. J. St. M. Tabor, Major P. J. Tabor, Lieutenant General Sir Richard Vickers, Brigadier the Duke of Wellington, and General Sir Richard Worsley.

I greatly appreciate the help given me by Colonel Jonathan Salusbury-Trelawny and his assistants when I quarried their photographic library in the Household Division Public Relations offices; by the staff of *Soldier Magazine's* library at Aldershot, and by those of the Hulton Deutsch picture library for allowing me to carry out similar exercises on their premises.

Above all my thanks are for my wife, Lavinia. She not only typed the manuscript, captions and index, along with all the plethora of correspondence connected with this history, but also mastered the idiosyncrasies of a word processor expressly for the task. There cannot be a greater act of devotion than that!

Pannett's Shipley,   *J.N.P.W.*
Horsham.
November, 1992

Part One

FROM HORSE TO ARMOUR

1661–1945

The Colonel of the Regiment. General Sir Desmond Fitzpatrick, KCB, DSO, MBE, MC; Commanding Officer, the Royals, 1952–53; Colonel of the Royals, 1964–69; Deputy Colonel, The Blues and Royals, 1969–79; Colonel and Gold Stick since 1979. *Portrait: Carlos Sancha*

King Charles II. It was under King Charles's auspices that both the Royal Horse Guards (The Blues) and The 1st Royal Dragoons were raised in 1661. *Portrait: after Lely*

Aubrey de Vere, Earl of Oxford, The Blues' first Colonel. *Portrait: after Kneller*

STATUS OF THE HOUSEHOLD CAVALRY

On 29 March, 1969, The Royal Horse Guards (The Blues), the second regiment of Household Cavalry, and the Royal Dragoons (1st Dragoons), the oldest Regiment of the Cavalry of the Line, were amalgamated to form a single new Regiment of Household Cavalry, The Blues and Royals (Royal Horse Guards and 1st Dragoons).

The Corps of Household Cavalry has two principal roles, one as the Sovereign's mounted guards (and frequently dismounted, too), the other as fighting armoured cavalry. The status of the corps is enshrined in the court offices of the Gold and Silver Sticks-in-Waiting, the former appointment being now shared, on an equal footing, between the Colonels of The Life Guards and The Blues and Royals, while the latter appointment is held by the officer commanding the whole corps, who may delegate to any Household Cavalry field officer. The Sovereign's wishes regarding the Household Cavalry are made known to the regimental commanders through one of the two Gold Sticks and the Silver Stick. Until 1820 these posts were officially filled only by the Colonels and the Commanding Officers of The Life Guards.

Gold and Silver Stick date from the supposed threat, in 1678, of an uprising by "Popish recusants". The Life Guards had been, since their inception, honoured with the primary obligation and exclusive responsibility of maintaining a constant watch over King Charles II (and, from 1662, the Queen), whose escort, when travelling, usually consisted of 180 "private gentlemen", sixty from each of the three troops. In 1678 Charles II's eldest illegitimate son, the Duke of Monmouth, who was then Colonel of The Life Guards and Captain of the King's Troop of that Regiment, (as well, incidentally, as Lord-General of the Army) persuaded his father to let him, or one of the other two troops captains, "attend on the King's person on foot, wheresoever he walks from his rising to his going to bed, immediately next to the King's own person before all others, carrying in his hand an ebony staff or truncheon with a gold head, engraved with his Majesty's cipher and crown ... Near him also attends another principal commissioned officer with an ebony staff and silver head, who is ready to relieve the captain on all occasions".

The Royal Regiment of Horse, or the Earl of Oxford's Regiment of Horse, as The Blues were known during those early years, was the sister regiment of The Life Guards (named during their early history as the Horse Guards), often supporting them in their roles of finding Royal guards and escorts and more often than not riding alongside them on active service. Although The Blues were essentially a "Guards regiment", their elevation to Household Cavalry was gradual. At least by early in the 18th century they were loosely recognized, to all intents and purposes, as such by the general public; but it was not until after the Napoleonic wars that they were ultimately honoured. During their sojourn at the Cavalry Barracks, Windsor, which were built especially for them, their Colonel and Commanding Officer were called upon to act as Gold and Silver Stick to George III when he was in residence at the Castle.*

Then, in 1807, a further move towards The Blues' incorporation into the Household Cavalry was made when they were instructed to draw their Standards, as The Life Guards had been drawing theirs, from the Lord Chamberlain's department. Finally, on 1 March, 1820, the Duke of Wellington, then Colonel of The Blues, received a letter from the Duke of York, the Army's Commander-in-Chief, as follows:

"Taking into consideration the distinguished conduct of the Royal Regiment of Horse Guards Blue and being fully aware of the partiality which His late Majesty ever entertained for the Corps, His Majesty conceives that he is only fulfilling the intention of His late Majesty in granting to that Regiment the same honours and privileges in every respect as are possessed by the two regiments of Life Guards, and, in consequence of which it is His Majesty's gracious intention that your Grace should roll with, and take your share of your duty as Gold Stick with, the Colonels of those two Regiments; and also that the Field Officers of the Horse Guards should take their share of the duty of Silver Stick."

---

* The King was on quite familiar terms with the Blues officers. Appearing, unexpectedly, at breakfast-time in the officers' mess one morning, he is on record as exclaiming: "Look – abundant breakfast! Excellent breakfast! Cold beef, venison, pastry, ham and game. Tea, coffee, eggs, beefsteaks. Ay, ay; excellent breakfast!" And he joined them in a hearty meal.

Thus, by the bestowal on their Colonel of the office of Gold Stick, The Blues' final and formal inclusion in the Household Cavalry was consummated. And since The Blues were now on precisely the same level as The Life Guards the Regiment shared the London duties. Consequently, in July, 1821, they moved from Windsor to Regent's Park Barracks. As a further matter of interest, although the Foot Guards became a part, with the Household Cavalry, of the Household Brigade, and subsequently the Household Division, the term "Household" was in the military context, reserved exclusively for the Household Cavalry until quite late in the 19th century, the Household Brigade being, in the old days, essentially the collective description of the First and Second Life Guards and The Blues.

From the beginning The Blues had, too, much in common with the Royal Dragoons and, henceforward, this regimental biography will concentrate on the careers of those two regiments.

17th CENTURY

The Royal Horse Guards (The Blues) find their origin in a Parliamentary cavalry regiment raised and commanded by an officer called Unton Crook. Following the demise of the Commonwealth and the return of Charles II, the restored monarch kept Crook's Ironsides on as his Royal Regiment of Horse, with the royalist Daniel O'Neal as commanding officer. But the new Parliament, with memories of Cromwell's heavy-fisted Major-Generals and their henchmen, not to mention Charles I's private army, fresh in its collective mind, would not sanction a regular armed force and, in December, 1660, O'Neal and his men were paraded in Bath, summarily disarmed and sent home.

However, the rising of the "Fifth Monarchy" dissidents in the following year, albeit speedily quashed, gave the King a good excuse for raising a permanent standing army such as his greatly admired cousin, Louis XIV, commanded. Hence, in addition to his personal bodyguard, The Life Guards (the Life Guard of Horse, or Horse Guards), he resurrected, along with the Grenadiers and the Coldstream, the Royal Regiment of Horse, with that veteran campaigner, Aubrey de Vere, Earl of Oxford,

11

as Colonel, and O'Neal as Commanding Officer. The Royal Regiment of Horse – mustered at Tothill Fields, London, on 16 February, 1661 – had worn dark blue coats in their Cromwellian days; it so happened that was also the colour of Lord Oxford's livery.

That summer English envoys arrived in Portugal to negotiate arrangements for the marriage between their King and Princess Catherine of Braganza (who was then incarcerated in a nunnery). Since the North American trading post and fortress of Tangier was a portion of the Portuguese princess's dowry a mounted troop (then the equivalent of an independent cavalry squadron) was raised as part of the English garrison. Hence the Tangier Horse mustered at Southwark on 21 October, 1661, and sailed for the stark Moroccan port the following January. The Tangier garrison was almost constantly at war with its Arab neighbours and, in 1684, the English government decided to evacuate that expensive, inhospitable and generally unrewarding station. We next meet the Tangier Troop at home, enlarged and reconstituted as Our Own Regiment of Dragoons, and proud of their first battle honour – TANGIER.

Dragoon? The word originates from the French musket known as a *dragon* which bore a carving of a dragon and was carried by Louis XIV's horsed infantry. And that is how the English dragoons were to be trained to fight – to ride to their battlegrounds in sections of four, three men then dismounting and advancing with their muskets while the fourth stood back holding the horses.

And dragoon guards? During the 18th century the three additional regiments of horse, which had been raised in 1685 to meet the threat posed by the Western Rebellion, were allotted the dragoon role. In 1746 they were redesignated "dragoon guards" to compensate for the loss of the superior status of "Horse". They were never guardsmen as such, nor Household troops. Incidentally, the Horse Grenadier Guards, an adjunct of the Horse, or Life, Guards were effectively "dragoons", since their operational task was to dismount and engage the enemy with grenade, musket and bayonet. But, in 1788, they were absorbed into the 1st and 2nd Troops (later Regiments) of The Life Guards in the *arme blanche* role.

It was at the zenith of the Western Rebellion, the Battle of Sedgemoor, that The Blues and the Royals first fought together, the former under Sir Francis Compton, the latter under Lord Cornbury, son of the former Lord Chancellor, Clarendon. It was a Blues patrol that sounded the alarm of Monmouth's night approach. And, at a critical juncture in the fight, John Churchill, the future Duke of Marlborough, who was then Colonel of the Royals, put himself at the head of one of their troops. Charging as cavalry, rather than dismounting as dragoons, they overwhelmed the rebel artillery.

After the "Great Revolution" of 1688 both Regiments sailed with William III to drive James II out of Ireland and were together at the Battle of the Boyne in 1690. The Royals went on to fight the French in Flanders for three years (1694–97) alongside The Life Guards, while The Blues enjoyed an interim of looking after The Life Guards' commitments at home.

During William III's reign the Royal Regiment of Horse Guards was unofficially referred to as the "Oxford Blues", after their former Colonel, to distinguish them from the new Monarch's Dutch Blue Guards, with whom they and The Life Guards alternated on the sentry boxes close to Whitehall Palace, comprising a pair of boxes by the Banqueting Hall, another pair on what is now Horse Guards Avenue and a third pair about where the present boxes stand.

18th CENTURY

With Queen Anne on the English throne and Louis XIV attempting to establish Bourbon power in Spain Her Majesty's Royal Regiment of Dragoons played their part in the War of the Spanish Succession, serving in Portugal and Spain from 1703 to 1710. Their next active service with The Blues was when England resumed her quarrel with France, this time on behalf of the Empress Maria Theresa in the War of the Austrian Succession, the campaign in which George II rode at the head of the British Army. At the Battle of DETTINGEN (1743) The Blues faced and subdued the French Household Cavalry, the Maison du Roy. And, after the victory, the Royals, who had routed the French Black Musketeers – and captured their Standard, centered by a bunch of nine arrows, tied with a wreath and carrying the motto *Alterius Jovis Altera Tela* – celebrated by adopting that Regiment's black plume as their own. In the same campaign both Regiments were at bloody Fontenoy (1745), The Blues being in the Household Cavalry Brigade (with the Third and Fourth Troops of Life Guards and the Horse Grenadiers).

In 1756 England was in conflict once more, this time going to the aid of Frederick of Prussia who was threatened simultaneously by France, Austria, Saxony and Sweden. Frederick invaded Saxony thus starting the Seven Years War. Blues and Royals now found themselves under command of the Blues' Colonel, the redoubtable Marquis of Granby, and they would eventually share in the 1760 battle honour of WARBURG, the event from which The Blues' tradition of other ranks saluting without hats is derived – from Granby's wig and hat flying off in the charge, he "going bald-headed for it" and saluting the Commander-in-Chief hatless. Warburg was very much a cavalry action, twenty-two squadrons being involved, and in particular a Blues and Royals triumph. While Granby led the frontal attack at the head of The Blues, the Royals broke the last French resistance from the flank. The Blues were then occupied in the final rout and pursuit of the enemy. They were stationed, on their return home, at Northampton where they built the Army's first riding school, and where they remained until the Cavalry Barracks at Windsor was ready for them in 1804.

The posturing of a hostile Franco-Spanish fleet saw the Royals up in Scotland from 1781–1784 and subsequently in Worcestershire. Brigaded with the Inniskilling Dragoon Guards, the Royals and The Blues sailed for Flanders again in the summer of 1793 to meet France's new revolutionary army, which was to be on the warpath for more than 20 years. Both Regiments were to add the names of another two great cavalry exploits, WILLEMS and BEAUMONT, to their tally of battle honours.

Napoleon's Peninsular ambitions had to be frustrated, and the Royals were among the troops sent, with that objective, to Portugal in 1809. They were positioned behind the Lines of Torres Vedras and won their next battle honour at FUENTES D'ONORO. The Duke of Wellington was full of admiration: "I think that I have never seen a finer regiment," he informed the British cavalry commander; "they are very strong, the horses in very good condition and the Regiment apparently in high order." The Blues, brigaded with The Life Guards, joined the expeditionary force three years later and, like the Royals, fought all through the remainder of Wellington's Peninsular campaign. They were engaged in the battles of Salamanca and Vittoria, among many lesser encounters. Guards regiments, that is to say the three of Household Cavalry (First and Second Life Guards and Blues) and the three of Foot (Grenadiers, Coldstream and Third Guards), were still only obliged to salute their own officers. And it is amusing to recall that, soon after Wellington was appointed to the Colonelcy of the Royal Horse Guards (on 1 January, 1813) he was duly gratified on passing a party of Foot Guards who saluted him with their muskets. "Thank God," exclaimed the Iron Duke, "I've got a 'present' out of the Guards at last!"

In June, 1815, the deposed French Emperor, Napoleon Buonaparte, having escaped from his island of exile, Elba, massed his Grand Army behind him once more and deposed the Bourbons. He was determined to defeat the armies of England and Prussia, and to be supreme in Europe again. He was marching towards Brussels.

For the Waterloo campaign Wellington's cavalry were grouped under command of the Earl of Uxbridge, afterwards Marquess of Anglesey, Colonel of The Blues. The Royals were with the Inniskillings and Royal Scots Greys in Sir William Ponsonby's Union Brigade. Two squadrons of the Royals helped to cover the withdrawal from Quatre Bras. On the great day, 18 June, Uxbridge ordered both the Union Brigade and Lord Edward Somerset's Household Cavalry Brigade, in which the 1st King's Dragoon Guards were brigaded with the two regiments of Life

Senior NCOs of the Royals during the Crimean campaign.
Standing: RSM Wilson and Troop Sergeant-Major Tripp;
sitting: Troop Sergeant-Majors Clements, Feldwick and Norris

Guards and The Blues, to charge simultaneously in extended line, to stem the advance of Marshal D'Erlon's divisions. And that they all did with great gallantry and to decisive effect. It was now that Captain Clark and Corporal Styles, of the Royals, captured the Eagle of Napoleon's 105th Regiment, the emblem of which would be adopted as the Royals cap badge, which was to be absorbed in The Blues and Royals crest and which is worn on the left sleeve of all members to this day.

Before 1829 Britain deployed no police force as such and, until quite late in the century, it was a small, quite primitive organization. The Blues, notwithstanding the additional ceremonial duties to which they were now committed as fully fledged Household Cavalrymen, were busy from time to time keeping public order. It was in earnest, for example, that they were called out to quell the Chartist riots of 1848 and the Reform Movement demonstrations of 1866, to name but two such responsibilities in support of the civil power.

Meanwhile the Royals came out of the Crimean War with fresh laurels. They sailed from Liverpool in May, 1854, some 300 sabres strong, and five months later were embattled against the Russians. They were fortunate to be in General Scarlett's Heavy Brigade, with the Inniskillings and 4th and 5th Dragoon Guards and the Royal Scots Greys, rather than in Lord Cardigan's ill-fated Light Brigade. Scarlett used them to victorious advantage and with few casualties. The sounds of the voice of the Royals' commanding officer, Colonel Yorke, shouting "By God the Greys are cut off! Gallop! Gallop!", the subsequent cheer from all ranks, and the trumpeter sounding "the gallop" when the Russians were seen surrounding the Royals' sister-regiment, the Royal Scots Greys, were to be long remembered and cherished in the Heavy Brigade. By May, 1855, the Royals were back at Portsmouth, and so to Aldershot with the prospect of BALA-CLAVA and SEVASTOPOL being sewn to their guidons. The following year found them in Ireland, where they remained until 1861, and to which they returned in 1867.

The Blues' next dramas were staged in North Africa during the 1880s. Britain, holding the largest investment in the Anglo-French Suez Canal, greatly influenced the way in which Egypt was governed. But an anti-British rebellion was growing, a movement of "Egypt for the Egyptians". Ahmed Arabi, generally known as Arabi Pasha, amassing a dissident army, threatened to overthrow the Khedive, a danger which prompted the British government to dispatch an expeditionary force under General Sir Garnet Wolseley; this included a Household Cavalry composite regiment, The Blues squadron being under command of the regimental Second-in-Command, Colonel Milne Hume. They

The room occupied by Captain Allan Maclean, the Royals, Dublin 1872. Captain Maclean, nicknamed "Rocky", joined the Royals in 1862 and commanded the Regiment in the late 1880s

Colonel F. G. Burnaby, Royal Horse Guards. Killed at the Battle of Abu Klea, 1885

reached Cairo on 14 August, 1882, and were in action along the Sweetwater Canal within a week. Then, with the rebels advancing on Kassassin, the Household Cavalry played a central role in the celebrated "Moonlight Charge" and the pursuit that followed it, with only two Blues fatal casualties being recorded. On 12 September, Wolseley decided to attack Arabi's stronghold at Tel-el-Kebir at dawn on the 13th, and the Household Cavalry hunted down the fleeing dissidents. Cairo was occupied, Arabi captured and TEL-EL-KEBIR duly found a place on The Blues' Standards. Wolseley wrote home to the Duke of Cambridge that

"These men of the Household Cavalry are teaching me a lesson, and that is that it would pay us well as a nation to obtain men of a better stamp for our Army than those we now enlist, by offering double the pay we now give. We suffer from this system of paying the soldiers badly for our ordinary Regiments, whilst the Household Cavalry have such good men that crime is unknown amongst them."

Both The Blues and the Royals were among the ten regiments finding detachments, each of about three officers and forty-five men, for the Heavy Camel Regiment which accompanied Colonel Stewart's abortive expedition in 1884 to relieve General Gordon, who was besieged at Khartoum by the Mahdi and his dervishes. When the expeditionary force reached the wells at Abu Klea, following a forced march of 150 miles (the cavalry riding their detested camels) scouts warned of an estimated 16,000 tribesmen massing to fight. The British formed a *zeriba*, or defensive square, with the camels lined up in its centre; and this little desert stronghold withstood wave upon wave of ferocious assault.

In the hand-to-hand fighting, following one of the fanatical dervish rushes, that most colourful of Blues officers, Colonel Frederick Burnaby, who would have taken over from Stewart had the latter been put out of action, was killed. And it was said that Corporal Mackintosh – also of The Blues, also killed – would have earned the Victoria Cross, had he lived, for his gallantry in attempting to save Burnaby. These two were The Blues' only battle casualties; the Royals lost Major Gough and thirteen other ranks. The expedition continued to Khartoum, reaching the town on 28 January, 1885, where they received the news of its capture by the Mahdi, and the death of Gordon.

The Boers' demand of independence for the republics of Transvaal and the Orange Free State – widely regarded, throughout the western world, as being a premature request, but which had been simmering with growing anger and impatience during the 1890s – boiled over when Kruger gave his ultimatum and declared war on the British Empire in the autumn of 1899, and the Boers invaded Natal. Troops, wearing khaki for the first time, were at once dispatched from Britain; these included the Royal Dragoons, under Colonel Burn-Murdoch, very soon to be promoted brigadier-general, and a Household Cavalry composite regiment, its Blues squadron being commanded by Major H. T. Fenwick. Both Regiments arrived at Cape Town before the close of the year and both were already in action in January, 1890, against the wily horsemen, adept field craftsmen and crack shots of which the opposition was composed. This three-year conflict

Blues machine-gun crew, 1890. The officer on the right is Lieutenant
A. V. H. Vaughan Lee

was one of many long and arduous marches and of many sharp
encounters. A young Blues officer (Lieutenant Hon A. Meade)
kept a tally of the distances covered by the Household Cavalry
between 11 February and 28 August, 1900: a total of 1,592 miles
in 161 days.

One of the Household Cavalry's most prized reputations, one
shared with the Royals, was that of their constant success in
keeping their horses in better condition than nearly all the other
mounted units involved in the campaign – despite the dreadful
circumstances, in particular the pathetically small corn ration and
lack of grazing.

20th CENTURY

After the Boers' organized resistance collapsed, by the late
summer of 1900, The Household Cavalry sailed home; but the
Royals remained in South Africa for a further two years. Taking
on the desperate semi-independent patrols that were all that was
left of the Boer army, they rode from Natal into Transvaal, up to
the Olifant's River and on to Delagoa bay before embarking for

Southampton in October, 1902, with many decorations waiting to be pinned on their chests. In addition to the battle honour SOUTH AFRICA the Household Cavalry won RELIEF OF KIMBERLEY and PAARDEBURG for their Standards, while the Royals added RELIEF OF LADYSMITH to their guidon.

King Edward VII disliked seeing the word "Private" inscribed on the Boer War campaign medals of the soldiers of that status in the Household Cavalry. He had the rank altered to "Trooper", which was to remain exclusive to The Life Guards and The Blues until the First World War.

The "heavy" cavalry of the line had, like the Household Cavalry, been exempt from foreign service in peacetime, but the tactical distinction between "heavy" and "light" being now almost a thing of the past, the Royals were earmarked for their first tour of duty in India. They set sail for Bombay under command of Lieutenant Colonel Lord Basing, in January, 1904, much to the annoyance of the German Emperor, Kaiser Wilhelm, who had been their Colonel-in-Chief since 1894. He objected to his Regiment being so far away, but was somewhat mollified on being informed that King Edward's own regiment, the 10th Hussars, took their turn of Indian service. Growing strife in South Africa was met with a demand for quick reinforcements, among them the Royals who left India for Cape Town in November, 1911. And, in the following month, on the bleak and comfortless feature known as Roberts Heights, near Pretoria, they were celebrating the 250th anniversary of the raising of the Tangier Troop. Stark living conditions, coupled with violent riot control and routine policing, proved an unpleasant contrast to the joys of India.

WORLD WAR ONE

Come the Great War they were shipped home to take their place in the 3rd Cavalry Division on Salisbury Plain. By October, 1914, still with their South African ponies, they were on the Western Front, a squadron being in action at Ypres. On the night of 25

21

October they relieved the Household Cavalry in the trenches at Zandvoorde.

The Blues began their First World War career with a squadron, under command of Major Viscount Crichton, in the Household Cavalry Composite Regiment which steamed out of Southampton for Le Havre on 16 August, 1914, and so to General Allenby's Cavalry Division. By 1915 The Blues formed their own regiment, and that summer, during the Second Battle of Ypres, they were entrenched adjacent to the Royals. Here is an extract from a letter home by a Royals officer (Captain Hon Julian Grenfell, DSO) who died of his wounds on 27 May of that year: "I adore war. It is like a big picnic without the objectlessness of a picnic. I have never been so well or so happy. Nobody grumbles at one for being dirty. I have only had my boots off once in the last ten days, and only washed twice." (Grenfell was author of that fine poem *Into Battle* and many other verses).

In the context of this history the following excerpt from Sir George Arthur's account of the Second Battle of Ypres is interesting:

"Zero hour (2.30) approached and The Blues and the Royals stood waiting to make what must have seemed an almost hopeless attempt. 'Fix bayonets and dry your butts!' (A very necessary precaution when cold steel meets the human body). Old Blues will always look back to that moment and conjure up the picture of their Colonel, Lord Tweedmouth, thinking with gratitude of the example he set them. He stood calm as ever, watch in hand, ready to launch his attack. He dropped his watch back into his pocket. 'Advance!' Off they went, steadily and in open files towards the German lines. Six hundred yards had to be covered, the chief support coming from the Brigade's own machines gunners ... Arrived at the German position the two regiments closed their files and converged to take the enemy in force. The attack succeeded ... Alastair Leveson-Gower reached the objective with only two of his troop unwounded. He himself was hit in the thigh, and will long be remembered surveying calmly the situation, a small unwounded German beneath him, and an immense cigar in his mouth. Afterwards, as he was delighted to narrate, he was carried back by two good friends, both corporals, by name Coffin and Churchyard".

Eventually The Blues were converted to Number 3 (Royal Horse Guards Blues) Battalion of the Guards Machine Gun Regiment. The Blues and Royals between them scored nearly all the battle honours awarded from the Western Front, mutual being MONS, YPRES, LANGEMARCK, FREZENBURG, LOOS, ARRAS, SCARPE, HINDENBURG LINE, CAMBRAI, FRANCE AND FLANDERS.

Among the very large number of decorations won the highest was Second Lieutenant John Spencer Dunville's Victoria Cross. In June 1917, Dunville led a patrol, accompanied by a Royal Engineers detachment, which was part of a Royals assault group of about a hundred men. They were attempting to make a path through barbed wire with a Bangalore torpedo. When the torpedo failed to explode the Sappers, covered by Dunville's patrol, began cutting the wire by hand. The Germans in the opposing rifle pits were alerted and a fire-fight began. With the success of the breach operation looking doubtful, Dunville, though seriously wounded, placed himself between the Germans and the Sappers, from which position he could engage them more effectively. Owing to his gallantry the gap was cut through and the advance made possible. He died next day in hospital.

Both Regiments were continuously in action to within a fortnight of the Armistice. The Royals remained with the Army of Occupation until August, 1919, then enjoying a brief spell in England where the international polo player, Lieutenant Colonel H. A. Tomkinson, assumed command, and, in April, 1920, he took them to Ireland. There, in the dark days before independence, they had their first angry disputes with the IRA. From the spring of 1922 the Royals divided their time between Hounslow and Aldershot before sailing, first to Egypt, then to troublesome India. After that they were only home for another two years, 1936 to 1938, when they were sent to Palestine and given another tricky, and almost impossible, role, that of attempting to keep the peace between Arabs and Jews.

The pictures shown here, from Egypt and India, were sent to me by Mr J. L. Ovens, who served in the Royals between 1926–32. They were accompanied by the following memoir:

Jumping display (Corporal Gloyn up), by the Royals, Egypt, 1929.
RSM Mander on the right

"... regret only four photos, I found it impossible to remove the others
after nearly 60 years. It was a pity as I had snaps of the Regiment's horses
all picketed out in the maidan, tied to long ropes and a peg securing one
hind leg, via ankle strap. We slept out in the open at first on the
manoeuvres of Feb '31 in the area of Shamirpet. These exercises were
tough and HQ Squadron lost three horses through exhaustion.

"In 1932 the same area was used by Brigade and the Nizam's private
army was the enemy as before.

"Lt T. G. Hardy was killed in a polo match on Dec 15th, 1930, a great
loss to the Regt.

"Around June 1931 the temperature averaged 110° going up to 117°
and the local people were dying of heat stroke and lack of water at the
rate of 120 a day. Very hot winds and dust storms didn't help the
situation. In 1930 and '31 leave parties were sent south to Wellington
Barracks, up in the Nilgiri Hills some 7,000 ft high. The final part of the
trip was on a mountain railway with a racked track going up very steeply
on a small shelf, so you had solid rock on the inside and a sheer drop on
the outside, really hair-raising. Once there, it was marvellous, wonderful views over the mountains, cool fresh air and fresh salads and fruit.

The Royal Dragoons, *c* 1825. *Portrait: T. Ivester Lloyd*

Captain John Thoyts, Royal Regiment of Horse Guards Blue. Cornet 1800; Served as captain with the Regiment through the Peninsular campaign; Captured after his horse was shot under him at Waterloo; Major and Brevet Lt-Colonel, 1815; Retired 1820. *Portrait: Davis*

Captain Clarke and Corporal Styles, of the Royals, capturing the Eagle of the French 105th Regiment at Waterloo. The Eagle remains the emblem of The Blues and Royals. *Artist: M. Wood*

Everybody got a great boost and was sorry to return to the plains after six weeks of bliss.

"In early 1932 the Regt won a lot of trophies, the Cavalry Cup for football, all-India machine gun trophy, Southern Command Revolver championship and two champions at the all India boxing. L/Cpl Crease at heavy-weight; Tpr Bogey Marston, welter-weight. The Regt received high praise from top brass in Delhi."

Both The Blues and the Royals were fortunate to escape amalgamation with other cavalry regiments under the "Geddes Axe" of 1922, which saw so many merged, including The First and Second Life Guards, amongst whom there had, hitherto, been the hottest competition. Instead, The Blues went intact after the War to Regent's Park Barracks, and, following the fusion of the two Life Guards' regiments, they alternated with them between Windsor and Hyde Park. It was not until 1940, in Palestine, that they found themselves alongside their old comrades in the Royals again.

The Royals Drum Horse, India, 1930. Sergeant Barnes and Coronet

The Blues on the road between London and Pirbright, 1933

King Edward VIII – with
Lieutenant Colonel Lord
Forester, RHG (Silver Stic
crossing the road from Hy
Park Barracks in 1936, pri
to inspecting the Regimen

Regimental Corporal Major W. Twidle and Corporal of Horse G. Lowman, at Horse Guards in the 1930s

WORLD WAR TWO

Mobilization, in 1939, saw the Household Cavalry with a composite horse regiment and a training regiment, both at Windsor, and a composite reserve regiment at Hyde Park Barracks. In February, 1940, the composite service regiment, including two Blues squadrons, set sail for Palestine where they joined the Royals, the Greys (the only two Line Cavalry regiments left with horses), the Wiltshire Yeomanry, the Warwickshire Yeomanry and a battalion of the Essex Regiment, in the Cavalry Division. Nearly all cavalrymen were now aware that the days of the horse in war were past and were applying to "go mechanized". The Household Cavalry Regiment (soon to become 1HCR) marched for the last time with their horses up to the Syrian frontier at the end of the year and, during the ensuing weeks, were busy reorganizing and converting to the internal combustion engine.

King George VI with "B" Squadron of the Household Cavalry Composite Regiment at the Royal Ascot Hotel, 1939

In May, 1941, as truck-borne infantry, in ancient lorries, they and the Royals were on their way with Habforce to prevent the Iraqis seizing Habbaniya from the RAF garrison there and thus annexing the oil city of Baghdad. That achieved and their baptism of fire received, the Household Cavalry returned to Syria where they helped take the heavily fortified town of Palmyra off the Vichy French. After Hitler declared war on Stalin, whose troops were promptly sent into Persia, 1HCR advanced on Teheran with the 9th Armoured Brigade from the opposite direction, remaining there for ten days in August, 1941, and establishing an important liaison with their new Russian allies.

Meanwhile the Royals, under command 4th Armoured Brigade, had been busy mopping up in Syria, ending at Aleppo where they bivouacked on the aerodrome, and where much good sport was to be had in off-duty hours, game shooting and flighting. The Royals lost their horses at about the same time as 1HCR, but they secured armoured cars, the South African Marmon-Harrington Mark III being the vehicle issued, a little earlier. Lieutenant Colonel Reggie Heyworth, who had taken over command in May, 1939, applied in the autumn of 1940 for the Regiment to be a member of the Royal Armoured Corps, with reconnaissance as the chosen role. And, as soon as the horses went, Heyworth had his men replace their equestrian forage caps with distinctive grey berets. In December, 1941, having been trained as armoured car men by the 11th Hussars, the Royals joined the 8th Army in the Western Desert and on Christmas Day they entered Benghazi.

At the tail-end of 1940 the Household Cavalry formed a second regiment, which was to become 2HCR. Major Henry Abel Smith, who had been commanding a squadron of 1HCR, flew home during the Iraq campaign to take over command of this second regiment from his fellow-Blue, Lieutenant Colonel Lord Forester. 2HCR had been earmarked to be a motor battalion with the Guards Armoured Division. However, Abel Smith, being informed that it was not to have armoured cars, requested that, in the interests of training and the provision of reinforcements, the whole of the Household Cavalry should be armoured car-based. Consequently, in the spring of 1942, a team from the 11th Hussars arrived with 1HCR, now back in Palestine, to assist with their conversion to the armoured reconnaissance role.

In adopting Marmon-Harringtons 1HCR reduced from four squadrons to three, so there were a lot of good men available for other work. In February, 1942, an interesting little group, about 120 strong, under Captain G. A. Murray-Smith, Royal Horse Guards, left Jerusalem for attachment to the 8th Army. Officially named 101 Tank Regiment, but known informally as "Smithforce", this party was issued with dummy tanks to be used in a deceptive role. They managed to keep a high proportion of enemy armour busy while our own armoured forces deployed in comparative safety behind minefields. At one point, owing to receipt during April of an incorrect map reference from divisional headquarters, they were sent astray. "On decoding it," wrote 1HCR's historian, "they were somewhat surprised as it [sent them] in front of our forward troops. However, theirs not to reason why, and they set off, eventually reaching the Royals armoured car outpost where their arrival caused considerable astonishment." German Stukas, sent to bomb them, bombed the Italians by mistake. (Murray-Smith described this as "the finest hour of Smithforce"!)

During Rommel's counter-offensive early in 1942, when the Royals were acting as flank and rearguard for the withdrawal to the Gazala line, the greatly loved and admired Colonel Heyworth was hit by a splinter from a Stuka bomb and died that night at the Advanced Dressing Station. Major A. H. Pepys, handing over "A" Squadron to Major R. St G. B. Gore then took command until Major R. Joy, who had been wounded by the same missile, returned to relieve Pepys a few days later. The Regiment was now poised for Montgomery's Alamein offensive.

EL ALAMEIN is perhaps the most cherished of the Royals' battle honours. Auchinleck's Alamein defensive line was hinged on the Mediterranean in the north and the Qattara depression in the south. It was from this firm base that Montgomery, who succeeded in command of Eighth Army in the summer of 1942, determined to launch an offensive that would see the Axis forces out of North Africa. The Royals, replacing their Marmon-

Harringtons with the thicker-armoured, harder-hitting Daimlers and Humbers, were to work forward of General Lumsden's 10 Corps on the northernmost sector of the line. Their commanding officer was now once again Colonel Tony Pepys. Colonel Ronnie Joy, having received an immediate DSO for his gallant and judicious handling of the Regiment at Gazala and during the Battle of Knightsbridge, had been promoted to be second-in-command of a brigade.

The Royal Dragoons moved up, cleared tracks through the minefields and into their assembly area on 22 October for D-day on the 23rd. The leading squadrons, "A" (Major Hon John (Jack) Hamilton-Russell) and "C" (Major Roddy Heathcoat-Amory) advanced through the night. Daylight found them deployed widely behind the enemy lines. During the first week of November, when they were busy raiding the enemy supply columns, they accounted for some fifty of his guns and over 200 vehicles, including several tanks.

The Regiment was among those armoured car regiments that spent the next seven months leading the victorious army, hot on the enemy's tail, via Benghazi to Tunis. Lieutenant Colonel Humphrey Lloyd assumed command in January, 1943. They spent that summer training and resting in Tunisia, with the exception of "A" Squadron which proceeded to Sicily (where the gallant Major Hamilton-Russell was killed) to be the eyes and ears of the 50th Division. This squadron led on into Italy, where they were later joined by the remainder of the Regiment in the valley north of Lucera. Within a month of that the Royal Dragoons were ordered home to prepare for the Second Front.

In terms of military glory 1HCR were less fortunate in the Western Desert than the Royals. Having spent the spring and early summer of 1942 training in Cyprus and going into action for the first time with their armoured cars at the Battle of El Alamein they were, so to speak, thrown in at the deep end. They formed part of the armoured reconnaissance screen at the south end of the Alamein line, but, although they had a good share of the fighting and took many prisoners, instead of advancing with the follow-up campaign, they were taken out of the line.

At the end of 1942, about the time that Colonel Andrew

Ferguson relinquished command of 1HCR to Major Eric Gooch, also of The Life Guards, the Regiment was dispatched to Syria again, with the mission of patrolling the Turkish frontier, the objective being to prevent Turkey contributing to the Axis cause. That was their task until April, 1944, when they departed for Italy. They were then continuously in action for most of the remainder of the Italian campaign, returning, six months later, to Britain and thence to North-West Europe. From Italy came the red-and-white "Mermaid of Warsaw", worn on the sleeve of all 1HCR ranks, an honour conferred by their admirer, General Anders, commanding the Free Polish troops.

2HCR, which was always somewhat stronger in Blues than Life Guards, and had been training with their new armoured cars, Humbers and Daimlers, under the indefatigable Colonel Abel Smith, since July, 1941, landed across the Normandy beaches just three years later. Their officer-led reconnaissance patrols, the eyes and ears of the Guards Armoured Division, then proceeded to play hide-and-seek with the German tanks and snipers through the trappy Bocage country. At the end of August, "it was vitally important", wrote 30 Corps Commander, Lieutenant General Sir Brian Horrocks,

"to prevent the Germans establishing a defensive position along the River Somme. The only people available to "bounce" a crossing were 2HCR, so the unfortunate leading squadrons, who had already had a long hard day, received instructions at 0100 hours, to seize these bridges which were given the code names of Faith, Hope and Charity. It was a pitch black rainy night and the roads were blocked with enemy transport, including tanks. It must have been a nightmare drive, but the squadron pushed on steadily. They not only captured the bridges intact but also succeeded in immobilizing the local French pro-German movement which enabled them to hold Faith, Hope and Charity for four hours ... It was a truly remarkable performance."

On 3 September the Regiment's leading patrols were the first British troops into Belgium; and, a week later, after heavy fighting, another troop reconnoitred and occupied the vital Escaut canal crossing by Neerpelt, over which Montgomery's army drove into Holland. The Regiment, among a host of other adventures, took a major cooperative part in Operation "Market Garden", the abortive Arnhem attempt. And then, with the Germans still resisting tenaciously, 2HCR showed Guards Armoured the way over the Rhine, and ended the war by entering the German naval base at Cuxhaven on VE day.

1HCR, after nearly five years' campaigning in the Mediterranean region, left the Italian front for home in October, 1944, and in March, 1945, followed their fellow-Household Cavalrymen of the 2nd Regiment into Belgium, where they immediately took over a section of the south bank of the River Maas from the 11th Hussars. Colonel Gooch "spoke to them of the forthcoming campaign [says the 1HCR historian] as the next hunt, and said that in the present instance he would probably do no more than take them to the meet." And that was so. Handing over to Colonel Walter Sale (RHG) at the end of the month, Gooch returned to London to plan the reconstitution of the Household Cavalry on a fresh peacetime basis, with Life Guards and Blues each having an armoured car regiment, and each a horsed squadron at Hyde Park Barracks, an organization which, as we shall see, was achieved gradually during the late 1940s.

The 1st Regiment, also coming under command Guards Armoured, were in touch with 2HCR for the first time in the fourth week of April near Fallingbostel. They were in contact with the enemy right up to the final week of the war, hunting down the last pockets of resistance, SS troops, Hitler Youth and "Werewolves" in the German hills. After the surrender 1HCR moved to Goslar in Northern Germany, while 2HCR advanced south to Brühl, near Cologne. 1HCR was reformed entirely with Life Guards personnel and 2HCR entirely with Blues, thus beginning a very different chapter in the story of the Household Cavalry.

The Royals, still with Colonel Lloyd commanding, followed 2HCR into Normandy at the end of July, 1944, heading 12 Corps, to the left of 30 Corps, in which the Guards Armoured Division, with 2HCR, were operating. They fought on through Falaise towards the Seine. The following passage in Pitt-Rivers's account of the Royals' progress illustrates just one of the hazards in armoured reconnaissance in that campaign:

"In a series of encounters the armoured cars expanded their bridgehead [over the River Lys] against a determined enemy. [He] was unsupported by tanks or anti-tank guns (other than such as the German infantry were wont to possess) but fought cunningly, making great use of snipers. Two car commanders fell in this way during the day [Sept 6] and a third, Sergeant Howarth of "C" Squadron, received a wound in the back from an automatic when he overran an infantry position. In operations against infantry there came always the moment when the armoured cars were at a disadvantage. As long as they stood back they could effectively subdue their opponents, but when they moved in among them to accept their surrender they exposed themselves to the risk of being taken on in a helpless position. Among the total list of casualties a good handful can be scored to the action of those enemies who surrendered and then thought better of it."

In September the Royals were transferred to XXX Corps and played a decisive part in Operation "Market Garden". Early in 1945 Lieutenant Colonel Tony Pepys reassumed command, despite having lost a foot in the Desert campaign, and led the Regiment up to the Maas, just south of Grave, where, for 10 days, they came under command of 2HCR. Then they returned to 12 Corps, moving down to Belgium. They devoted the early part of March to preparations for the assault crossing of the Rhine and began trooping over the river before dawn on the 30th. On 1 May they were over the Ems and next day brought in some 10,000 prisoners. On 7 May they crossed the Danish frontier. Colonel Pepys wrote home as follows:

"The next day, May 7th, was another unforgettable [one]. We left Plon at first light and, in glorious sunshine, drove northwards through the lovely country of Schleswig-Holstein. We drove through Kiel. Ninety-eight per cent of the houses and other buildings of the city were destroyed or severely damaged by our bombing. The civilians lined the streets and stared dumbly at us as we passed through. Meanwhile streams of forlorn and dejected looking German soldiers were moving in the opposite direction. Some were walking, some on bicycles or on horseback and others were piled and packed tight in battered, worn-out-looking lorries and horse-drawn transport of every kind, including hansom cabs. It was a dismal, almost incredible spectacle. What an end of the glorious armies of the Fatherland!"

The Royals remained in Denmark until November, when, like the Household Cavalry, they moved into Germany. In their case it was to Eutin in Schleswig-Holstein.

Let General Horrocks, writing a quarter of a century later, have the last word on the Household Cavalry and the Royals in 1944–45 and after:

"I first got to know [the Royals] during the breakout from the bridge-head in Normandy, when 30 Corps advanced from the Seine to Holland, covering 250 miles in six days against scattered German opposition. Our advance was preceded by a screen of superb armoured car regiments; from right to left the 2nd Household Cavalry Regiment, the Inns of Court, the 11th Hussars and the Royals ... The Royals have like many others, lost their individual identity and have ... joined the Household Cavalry, and become Royal by amalgamation with The Blues. It would be difficult to imagine a better combination than these two splendid regiments, The Blues and Royals ...

Field Marshal Montgomery (commanding the 21st Army Group) with Lieutenant Colonel A. H. Pepys, DSO (commanding the Royals) at Asten, Holland, 1945. Colonel Pepys is wearing the regimental grey beret, which was introduced by Lieutenant Colonel Heyworth in 1941

"After the war it ... fell to my lot to give many lectures to both military and civilian audiences, and I always said this: 'If you are walking down Whitehall in London you will pass two magnificently equipped mounted sentries in the full dress of the Household Cavalry. They are not just relics of some byegone age or showpieces to attract tourists. Those men serve in a Regiment that did more, far more than its share, to win the last war. So take your hats off to them – they deserve it!.'"

However, as this narrative has only reached the year 1945, the two regiments, The Blues and the Royals, have another 24 years of independence and individuality to run. Let us see where those years were to lead them.

FURTHER READING

Since this account of the earlier history of the two Regiments does little more than scratch the surfaces readers may wish to refer to one or more of the following books:

AINSLIE. Gen de. *Historical Record of The Royal Regiment of Dragoons.* (Chapman and Hall, 1887)

ALEXANDER, Michael. *The True Blue* (Rupert Hart-Davis, 1957) A most entertaining biography of Colonel Frederick Burnaby, Royal Horse Guards, the explorer, politician, balloonist (and altogether colourful personality) who commanded The Blues in the early 1880s. 210 pages

ANGLESEY, Marquess of. *A History of the British Cavalry, 1816–1913.* (4 vols so far, Leo Cooper 1973–1992) The definitive history of the horsed cavalry by a descendant of the 1st Lord Anglesey, the general who commanded the cavalry at Waterloo and who went on to be Colonel of the Blues. The author was, as Lord Uxbridge, a Second World War officer in The Blues and 1HCR (1) 336pp (2) 519pp (3) 478pp (4) 565pp

ARTHUR, Sir George. *The Story of the Household Cavalry* (3 vols, Constable, 1909 and Heinemann, 1926) The first volume of this very comprehensive history covers the period 1660–1743 in 400 pages; the second volume, comprising 366 pages, continues the saga up to the close of the South African War; and the third volume concludes with the Edwardian era and the First World War, in 254 pages.

ATKINSON, C. T. *History of the Royal Dragoons, 1661–1934* (Maclehose, University Press, Glasgow) Written in a little over 500 pages this account of the early Royals history is both scholarly and most readable.

CANNON, Richard. *The First or Royal Regiment of Dragoons* (Longman Orme, 1840).

CLARKE-KENNEDY, A. E. *Attack the Colour!* (Research Publishing, 1975). A good account of the Royals in the Waterloo campaign.

CROFTON, Sir Morgan Bt *The Household Cavalry Brigade in the Waterloo Campaign* (Sifton Praed, 1912) 50 pages

DAWNAY, N. P. *The Standards, Guidons and Colours of the Household Division, 1660–1973*. (Midas Books 1975) 262 pages

de CHAIR, Somerset. *The Golden Carpet* (Faber, 1943) Reminiscences of a Blues officer who was I.O. on the Brigade staff during 1HCR's campaign in Iraq and Syria. 216 pages

FIELDEN, Philip. *Swings and Roundabouts* (Privately published 1991). The author joined the Royals in the 1930s, served through most of the Second World War with them, and afterwards commanded the Regiment in Germany, Aden and Malaya.

HEATHCOAT AMORY, Roderick. *Reminiscences*. (Privately published, 1989). More memories from a former Royals Commanding Officer.

HILLS, R. J. T. The author of three contributions to Leo Cooper's *Famous Regiments* series, each some 100 pages. Published 1970–72. *The Life Guards, The Royal Horse Guards* and *The Royal Dragoons*. Colonel Hills was a Life Guards Quartermaster between 1939–49.

MAYS, Spike. *Fall out the Officers* (Eyre and Spottiswoode, 1969). An amusing pen-portrait including some reminiscences of the life of a trooper in the Royals between the Wars. 220 pages

MILLAND, Ray *Wide Eyed in Babylon* (Bodley Head, 1976) Including the actor's memoirs as a Blues trooper in the 1930s.

ORDE, Roden. *The Household Cavalry at War*: *Second Household Cavalry Regiment*. (Gale and Polden, 1953). This long and engrossing account of 2HCR's fortunes from 1940 to 1945, by a wartime Blues officer, is liberally illustrated and well supplied with maps. It runs to over 600 pages.

PACKE, Edmund. *An Historical Record of The Royal Regiment of Horse Guards, or Oxford Blues, Its Services and the Transactions in which it has been engaged, from its First Establishment to the Present Time* (William Clowes, 1834) 150 pages

PITT-RIVERS, J. A. *The Story of the Royal Dragoons, 1938–1945* (William Clowes). A very nicely written account of the Royals in the Second World War. Capt Pitt-Rivers was Signals Officer. About 150 pages.

ROCKSAVAGE, Earl of. *A Day's March nearer Home* (Privately published, 1947). The Second World War memories of a Royals troop leader.

WRIGHT, Thomas. *The Life of Colonel Fred Burnaby* (Everett 1906) 300 pages

WYNDHAM, Col. Hon. Humphrey. *The Household Cavalry at War: First Household Cavalry Regiment*. (Gale and Polden, 1952). This companion to Major Orde's book traces the career of 1HCR from its foundation at Windsor in 1939 to its disbandment in Germany in 1945. It contains a wide range of photographs and maps. About 180 pages.

Lieutenant-General Sir John Elley. He began his soldiering in 1789 as a private in the Blues, and, in 1790, purchased a troop quartermastership in the Regiment. By 1808 he was a Lt-Colonel; AAG Cavalry in Spain; AG Cavalry at Waterloo; retired as Lt-General, KCB; MP for Windsor during Sir Robert Peel's premiership; died 1839. *The portrait is listed as from the Spanish School*

Under command of Colonel Yorke at Balaclava, 25 October 1854. The Royals charging the Russian cavalry with the Heavy Brigade. The Regiment embarked for the Crimean Campaign at Liverpool in May, 1854, disembarking at Portsmouth in May, 1855. *Artist: Walker*

A Blues Guard leaving Horse Guards *c* 1830. The crested helmets were adopted in 1812; cuirasses were reintroduced in 1821 for the Coronation of King George IV. *Artist: A. S. Boult*

The Royals on Chobham Ridges, *c* 1870. *Artist: R. Simkin*

Part Two

POMP, CIRCUMSTANCE AND
PEACEKEEPING

(1945–1969)

Three officers – after taking part in the Sovereign's escort for the wedding of HRH Princess Elizabeth to Lieutenant Philip Mountbatten, RN – caught by the photographer at the back entrance to their mess at Hyde Park Barracks. *Left to right*: Lieutenant the Marquess of Blandford (LG), Major the Marquess Douro, MC (RHG) and Lieutenant the Earl of Westmorland (RHG)

Sovereign's Escort, 1947. Their Majesties The King and Queen driving to the Guildhall shortly after their visit to South Africa. The King is fulfilling the ceremony of touching the sword at Temple Bar. The Blues Officers, on the left, are Lieutenant J. B. Seyfried and (*right*) Captain A. R. J. Buchanan-Jardine. *Daily Graphic*

Chapter I

THE PAGEANTRY REVIVED

(1945–1953)

In the opening chapter of Colonel Humphrey Wyndham's history of the First Household Cavalry Regiment he recalls Winston Churchill visiting his (Churchill's) cousin, Lord Blandford, then a subaltern in Wyndham's company of the First Life Guards Battalion of the Guards Machine Gun Regiment, on the Western Front in 1918. Churchill remarked to Wyndham that "it would have been better if we [the Household Cavalry] had been turned into tank units instead of machine-gun units."

"When one looks back on it now," says Wyndham, writing in 1950, "in our present knowledge that the essential State duties of the Household Cavalry can be carried out by a self-contained unit found from both Regiments, leaving the Regiments themselves free to be organized as two armoured car regiments, one cannot help feeling that Mr Churchill was right, and that it would have been very wonderful if the present organization could have been adopted twenty years sooner. Then The Life Guards and The Blues would have led the way in the mechanization of the cavalry, instead of being made to follow it as they did."[1]

One wonders whether Colonel Wyndham went so far as to envisage the Household Cavalry between 1919–39 interchanging between horses in London and tanks at Windsor. That makes an interesting hindsight flight of fancy in view of the current organization. Anyhow let us see what did happen when the Household Cavalry ceased for ever to keep horses in their peacetime service regiments, but revived mounted elements for state duties.

With the Allies on the certain road to victory in 1944, Colonel Gooch, as Silver Stick,[2] handed over 1HCR in Belgium to his fellow Life Guard, Colonel "Boy" Wignall, and returned to

Troopers' dining hall, Hyde Park Barracks, 1948

Windsor to take command of the Household Cavalry's Regimental Headquarters and Training Regiment, with the special mission of preparing the peacetime organization. What he proposed, after due consultation and as soon as hostilities ceased, was that 1HCR should be reconstituted as The Life Guards, and 2HCR as the Royal Horse Guards, both to be permanently with armoured cars and, contrary to the pre-war principle of never serving abroad in peacetime, to proceed to wherever they might be required, at home or abroad. His second plan was that each Regiment should, as soon as possible, maintain a mounted squadron at Hyde Park Barracks to fulfil the traditional state ceremonial functions.

Meanwhile the minimum height for Household Cavalrymen

was restored to the pre-war 5' 10", having been reduced for the war to 5' 7".

The post-war mounted contingent began duty at Hyde Park Barracks with a single composite Squadron consisting of two troops from The Life Guards and two from The Blues, on detachment from the Household Cavalry Training Regiment at Combermere. The men were mostly ex-1HCR; the first horses were selected from the best of those that returned from the Middle East in 1941–42. The Squadron was almost immediately busy furnishing the King's Life Guard, Blues alternating with Life Guards on a daily basis. So in the early post-war years the orders that had resounded in Knightsbridge at 10.30 am each day in the 1930s, rang out once more: *Take order march! Escort to receive the Standard – walk march! Royal Salute – carry swords!* But until late in 1947 that was in khaki service dress, much to the indignation of the anonymous civilian who sent a postcard to the adjutant at Combermere Barracks bearing an old photograph of a pre-war Guard changing, with the message, "It is time, sir, that you dressed the Guard correctly once again!"[3] Doubtless that injunction reflected the broad sentiment of Londoners.

The accommodation at Hyde Park Barracks was still most uncomfortable. The barracks had been the home of the Household Cavalry Depot until the end of 1941. When 2HCR moved to Bulford (under command Guards Armoured Division) the Depot and Training Regiment were re-established at Windsor. Hyde Park Barracks was then occupied by the Royal Army Service Corps. In 1945 the composite Mounted Squadron found the barracks full of damp and leaks and rot and the forge suffering from bomb damage.

Between 1945–51 the Household Cavalry Training Regiment gave all recruits four weeks basic military instruction, conscripts then proceeding to armoured car trade training, while regulars were sent on to undergo their 20 weeks riding school at Knightsbridge. This arrangement continued until 1951 when an armoured car training regiment (67th Training Regiment, Royal Armoured Corps) was established near Carlisle, to cater for basic driving, wireless, gunnery and assault trooper instruction and trade testing. The Household Cavalry were to be strongly represented on the permanent staff there.

Back at Knightsbridge, in the summer of 1946, the composite Squadron found its first substantial escort, a captain's escort,[4] to accompany the King and Queen to the saluting base for the Victory Parade. Mounted Squadron strengths had been steadily building. The horse strength increased from 31 July, 1946, when, in a ceremony in the forecourt of Buckingham Palace, thirty Dutch blacks, a present from Queen Wilhelmina of the Netherlands, were handed over to the Household Cavalry. "All these horses were in perfect condition," a Mounted Squadron representative reported, "and after a few days' grooming at Knightsbridge, looked very well on the day of the ceremony."[5] However, they did not, for the most part, prove popular with those to whose care they were committed![6]

A group of Polish officers had been training the remounts, but now members of the Squadron's own rough riding staff were beginning to return from the Royal Army Veterinary Corps courses at Melton Mowbray. By the end of the summer the numbers of men at Knightsbridge had increased sufficiently to split into a Life Guards and a Blues squadron. When that happened the new Silver Stick, Colonel Henry Abel Smith, moved Regimental Headquarters up from Windsor to Knightsbridge, the organization at Hyde Park Barracks now being known as "RHQ and Mounted Squadrons", while those left at Windsor went under the title "Household Cavalry Training Regiment and Depot". Things were looking up in London: "A television set has been installed

at Horse Guards and the canteen refurnished and a billiard table provided. The married quarters have now nearly all been repainted and are occupied by our own married families. A troopers' visiting room has been furnished where the old hospital used to be and the troopers' dining hall and NCOs' Mess have been painted and decorated by an industrious squad of German prisoners-of-war, who have also repainted the stables and the barrack rooms and are steadily working round the whole of the barracks and removing the dirt that has accumulated through six years of war-time neglect."[7]

Four o'clock inspection, Horse Guards, 1947. The Guard
Commander, Captain A. R. J. Buchanan-Jardine, MC, is
accompanied by Corporal-Major Burnham, the Master Saddler.

The return to full dress came about by slow degrees. It was first
worn, in 1947, to assist in the making of three separate films, *All
the King's Horses*, *The Courtneys of Curzon Street* and *An Ideal
Husband*. That year the first post-war Trooping the Colour was
in khaki, for both the Household Cavalry and the Foot Guards;
in August the musical ride went into full dress for the Liverpool
tattoo; but the Sovereign's escort for the State Opening of Parliament was again a service dress affair. In September the King gave
permission for full dress to be worn for the wedding of Princess
Elizabeth to Lieutenant Philip Mountbatten RN. And from that
day forward the King's Life Guard was also in full dress. As
regards the wedding day the Adjutant wrote that: "Our difficult-
ies will be appreciated when it is realized that only ten days'
notice was received that we should be wearing full dress and that
only about ten per cent of the escort had ever worn full dress

before. However, we have received numerous letters of congratulations."[8]

In 1951 it was decided to reorganize the command structure on a more flexible basis. The Silver Stick, who had been commanding at Hyde Park Barracks, moved his headquarters to Horse Guards, while "the Mounted Squadrons" became "the Household Cavalry Mounted Regiment."[9]

Earlier in the same year the Blues' Gold Stick, Field Marshal Lord Birdwood, died. He was succeeded by Major General Sir Richard Howard-Vyse,[10] who, popularly known as "Colonel Wombat", had commanded the Regiment during the 1920s.

Meanwhile, in 1950, the King, on hearing of the proposal that the Household Cavalry should come under command of the Inspector-General of Cavalry, soon to be the Director, Royal Armoured Corps, gave instructions that The Life Guards and The Blues be welded with the Foot Guards into "the Household Brigade", thereby putting them directly under command of the Major General in London. The General at this time was Major General Julian Gascoigne. This is what he says of the subject in his recent memoirs:

"At my first interview with the King, on taking over London District, he gave me a task of great significance in the history of the Brigade of Guards.

"For generations the Household Cavalry had been one of the two bodies closest to the Crown, the Brigade of Guards being the other. The Household Cavalry had never had much to do with the Brigade of Guards and the Brigade of Guards never thought much of the Household Cavalry. They never made friends or anything like that. The Household Cavalry did not belong to the Guards Club. We knew each other, but basically did not like each other much. When the King sent for me when I took over he said that the cavalry was going to be re-organized and the Household Cavalry was going to come under the command of the Inspector-General of Cavalry, and "I cannot possibly have that," he said. "The first thing you have got to do as Major-General is to arrange to bring the Household Cavalry under your command in the same way as the Brigade of Guards is." So I duly brought them into the Household Brigade, which was later renamed the Household Division. It has taken 18 years before we had the first Major-General from the Household Cavalry in Desmond Langley, to be followed by Jim

48

Eyre, also Household Cavalry. The Brigade of Guards had better look to their laurels!"[11]

The King's Life Guard, a composite Household Cavalry guard, preparing to leave Horse Guards, 1947. The Standard is carried by Regimental Corporal Major Maxted, MM, RHG

NOTES AND REFERENCES

1. Wyndham, 2–3
2. The Gold Sticks at this time were Major General the Earl of Athlone (LG) and Field Marshal Lord Birdwood (RHG)
3. *Household Brigade Magazine*, Spring, 1946
4. This first notable post-war escort was commanded by Captain A. R. J. Buchanan-Jardine, RHG, who had been awarded the Military Cross and the Dutch Order of the Bronze Lion after his daring and invaluable scout car excursion across the Dutch border and behind the leading German tanks in September, 1944. The Life Guards

division was under Lieutenant M. M. G. Naylor-Leyland who was shortly to win the MC in Palestine, while the Blues division was commanded by Lieutenant Lord Burghersh, a former 2HCR troop leader who was then about to become (as Captain the Earl of Westmorland) the Household Cavalry's first post-war equitation officer. He was Master of the Horse until 1990. The Standard was carried by Regimental Corporal Major Maxted, RHG, who had been awarded the Military Medal for gallant and distinguished conduct in Syria, in 1941.

5. *Household Brigade Magazine*, Autumn, 1946
6. "They were very heavy common horses and some were totally unsuitable. They were very uncomfortable to ride." (In a letter from Major Sir Rupert Buchanan-Jardine)
7. *Household Brigade Magazine* Winter, 1946–47
8. Ibid
9. The Mounted Regiment's first Commanding Officer was Lieutenant Colonel Viscount Dillon, RHG
10. Major General Sir Richard Granville Hylton Howard-Vyse KCMG, DSO. Joined The Blues in 1904; Western Front, 1914–17; Brig-Gen, Palestine, 1917–18; comd RHG, 1922–26; Inspector of Cavalry, 1930–34; Colonel RHG and Gold Stick, 1951–63
11. Julian Gascoigne, *Memoirs* (ed by Bamber Gascoigne). Awaiting publication at the time of writing

Chapter II

ARMOURED CARS IN POST-WAR GERMANY

(1945–1952)

Except for the second half of 1945, when the Royals enjoyed the advantage of being in Denmark, both they and The Blues spent the next five years with their armoured cars in the British Army of the Rhine. The Wehrmacht being totally defeated and unconditional surrender having been imposed on the German nation, Rhine Army was at first "the British Liberation Army", then an army of occupation in a Germany whose cities and towns had been largely reduced to rubble by the Allied air and invasion forces, and whose people were in a state of hunger and humiliation, desperation and despair. The Allies – the Americans, Russians, British and, several months later, the French – had divided Germany into four zones. The Soviets held the Eastern zone, their western demarcation line running south from Lübeck on the Baltic down along a stretch of the Elbe, then way south again through the Harz Mountains to Folda, turning east to meet the western point of Czechoslavakia in the Thuringer Forest. Berlin, which was within the Russian zone, was also divided between the four powers. The Americans had the south-eastern zone, containing Frankfurt, Stuttgart and Munich; the French were against their own frontier in the south-west on the Rhine next to Alsace-Lorraine.

The British zone, which was in the north, reached from the North Sea, the Baltic and Schleswig-Holstein, southwards over the Ruhr and the Rhine to a little way south of Bonn. It included Hamburg, Hanover, Brunswick, Cologne and Dusseldorf, and it contained a much longer share of the border with the Soviet zone than that for which our American Allies were responsible. To

51

Senior NCOs of The Blues, 1946. Standing: (left to right): Corporals of Horse Jarman, Hopkins, Cosgrove, Slade, TQMC Smith, Corporal of Horse Burgess, SQMC Evans and Corporals of Horse Emery, Harrison and Clarke. Sitting: (left to right): Corporal of Horse Coles, AQMS Foster (REME), SQMC Copps (with SQMC Neill, below), RCM Maxted MM, SQMC Flaxman, SCM Lacey and Corporals of Horse Brown, Humberstone, Burton and Farrance

begin with there were curfews to be imposed, a displaced persons and refugee problem to be solved, a thriving black market to be curbed and a great deal of violent theft, in both town and countryside, to be quelled. But, with Russia flexing her imperialist muscles and intent upon bringing about a quick German reunification, and, if possible, forging that into a communist satellite, the British and Americans were soon transferring their attention from internal security duties to organizing the defence of Western Germany against the military posturing of the Soviet Union. The hot war of 1939–45 was more or less immediately followed by the cold war.

For some twenty years from 1945 the two regiments of Household Cavalry and the Royals, along with the King's Dragoon Guards, the 11th Hussars, the 12th Lancers, the 13th/18th Hussars, the 15th/19th Hussars and the 16th/5th Lancers were to remain in the armoured car role, the Royal Tank Regiment and the other cavalry regiments of the line being always equipped with tanks in those days. Armoured cars were very well suited to the Rhine Army: they were useful in the early years of policing the country; they were ideal in the role of border patrolling, and, while the North Atlantic Treaty Organization grew stronger and more sophisticated, armoured reconnaissance units, the ground eyes and ears of Rhine Army, played a vital role in preventing a European war.

THE ROYAL HORSE GUARDS

Following the disbandment of the Guards Armoured Division in June, 1945, the 2nd Household Cavalry Regiment moved south to Brühl near Cologne, coming under the wing of the Foot Guards again, the new dismounted Guards Division. On 17 July, the last of the Regiment's Life Guards personnel having driven east to join 1HCR, the 2nd Regiment was reconstituted as the Royal Horse Guards (The Blues). And what a very different guise this represented from The Blues of 1939! Not only had armoured cars replaced the horses, which meant that it was a highly technical, and a much larger, Regiment, but it was also full of conscripts – the war emergency personnel, who comprised over half

The British Zone, showing the principal stations of The Blues, the Royals and the present Regiment

54

the strength, giving way, in 1947, to National Servicemen. For the next 15 years fewer than half the subalterns would be regulars, while several of those who were then captains had joined only for the war and would, in the very near future, be released. It could be said that the corporal majors and senior corporals of horse who had volunteered in the 1930s formed the backbone of the Regiment. For the next 15 years the regulars' working time would be largely spent in training intake after intake of National Servicemen, most of whom were counting off the days on the calendars before the happy moment of their demobilization. The following, sung to the tune of *The British Grenadiers*, was not an unusual refrain to be heard wafting from German barrack rooms occupied by Blues troopers in the late 1940s:

> *Oh, we didn't choose*
> *We were given the Blues*
> *As anyone 'ere can see-ee*
> *With a tow-row-row-row-row*
> *To the 'Ousehold Cavalr-ee!*

Corporal W. A. Stringer out with the Blues hounds in 1948. He was to be a co-founder of the Blues and Royals Weser Vale Hunt. *Soldier Magazine*

The verses that followed, invariably of a less mild and more directly personal nature, do not perhaps bear repeating. These were the days of that indignant little caricature figure "Chad", with whom so many soldiers had a fellow feeling, who peered over a brick wall complaining of shortages: "Wot, no this? Wot, no the other?" But, despite the fact that fraternization with German girls was still forbidden, that is certainly not to say that conscripts were miserable in their work. They enjoyed plenty of variety in it, and plenty of play too, and morale was high. By 1947 most married men were accompanied by their wives, although married officers under 25 or other ranks under 21 received no accommodation. Here is part of a report home for the first three months of 1946:

"Routine guards – at the great transformer station at Brauweiler, through which the current generated at Knapsack passes to the Low Countries and Western Germany, and at the synthetic petrol factory and dump at Wesseling – absorb nearly the whole strength of each week's duty squadron. In addition, there are routine patrols to catch, or check, the curfew-breaker, the black marketeer, and the armed night raider of farms.

"Trains and the Rhine are two channels through which a large proportion of the contraband from the countryside, other zones, and even other countries, passes into Cologne, which is our nearest great city, where it is said that ten thousand of the population are "living black", without registration cards or ration cards. They are the main demand which the black market must supply. Ration cuts may increase this illegal demand, so checks on rail and river traffic are done frequently and with some success.

"A rail check is a tiresome business demanding tact, patience and some detective ability. A crowded train stops and pours out the station's quota of impatient passengers, each of whom has to be searched closely, even intimately. The average female responds indignantly or by giggles and the results are usually small. But now and then the man with thousands of cigarettes sewn into his coat is found, or the suitcase of a girl is discovered to hold 20,000 "Camels", the working capital of an *entrepreneur* trading with the American Zone.

"All this is a drab and dirty proceeding; a check of the Rhine barges is a far more pleasant thing. The river at Cologne runs strongly between the grey and dun rubble of the ruined bankside houses, and its current is

Officers of the Royal Horse Guards Blue at Regent's Park Barracks, in 1850. (*Left to right*) Captain Francis Sutton, Lieutenant James Shafto, Cornet Philip Bennett, Lieutenant (QM) Herbert Turner, Cornet E. J. M. Hayward, Captain Francis Fitzhardinge Berkeley, Major Richard Howard-Vyse, Lt-Colonel Hon. Cecil Weld-Forester, Captain Duncan Baillie, Captain Hugh Baillie, Captain William Sutton, Lieutenant William Gambier, Lieutenant Owen Williams, Lieutenant James Baillie, Captain Thomas Baillie, Cornet Lord Garlies, Captain Sir Robert Sheffield Bt. *Portrait: Richard Dighton*

'Royal Dragoon: Boer War'. *A bronze by Jonathan Knight*

HIM Kaiser Wilhelm II, Colonel-in-Chief of the Royals, 1894–1914. *Portrait: after Arthur Stockdale Cope*

The Blues parading at Regent's Park Barracks for their departure to Egypt in 1882. *Artist: R. Simkin*

checked by the twisted light green girders of at least four blown bridges. Passages, marked with red buoys, have been blown into the wreckage, and through these squat paddle tugs with a train of deeply loaded barges fight their way up river to Strasburg or Basle or, with less effort, sweep rapidly and buoyantly downstream to Holland and the sea. It was said that these pleasant floating houses were dens of black market vice, so a small party boarded a naval patrol boat and went from barge to barge, searching the living quarters and cargo space. Very little was found, but surprise checks like this must prevent the too easy use by smugglers of what must be a most convenient channel of supply. The searchers were compensated, however, for their blank draw by a day on the river in the sun, on board a small grey shapely boat, whose speed upstream made the thrusting Rhine seem more like the placid Thames, and which went down river like a fresh horse...

"We are soon to leave the Guards Division and this part of the world. Units have been slipping away to the north one by one; next month we move to Menden in Westphalia, and become Corps troops. We regard the future with mixed feelings; we are very sorry to be posted from the Division. We hear that the countryside to which we are going is beautiful, that the woods are filled with game and the rivers with fish; we also hear that the barrack roofs leak. Experience will prove whether the change is for the better or the worse. Like Lycidas we will arise

"... *and twitch our mantles blue*
Tomorrow to fresh woods and pastures new."[1]

Leaving Brühl, where they handed over to the Belgians, and the Guards Division, the Regiment duly moved north to the fringe of the Ruhr, to Menden, in April, 1946. "Our commitments seem oddly opposed," runs the next report:

"Locally, we merely control the town of Menden which includes the guarding of various small supply units located there. Otherwise, we have the run of the entire Corps District, an area of some 41,000 square miles. For this duty, squadrons make long recces lasting anything from one to three days, and they visit in particular those areas of the District not occupied by troops. In some of the more countrified areas this is quite frequent so that the squadrons have a very fair range and it would appear to make a pleasant change from the routine inside barracks.

"Troop training goes on as before, and the journey was made to Paderborn ranges where all squadrons fired during the first week in June."[2]

The Germans were well used by now to seeing a squadron or a troop on the move, or in a leaguer area, or just brewing up their tea by the roadside. An armoured car regiment still consisted, as it had done during the North-west European Campaign, of a head-quarters squadron which received and distributed the ammunition, rations and equipment, and provided the main technical assistance to four sabre squadrons, which, in The Blues, were reduced to three, because of manpower shortage during the summer of 1946, and would stay so reduced thereafter. The sabre squadrons were composed of five armoured car troops, each of those having two Daimler armoured cars, with a turret-mounted two-pounder gun and a besa machine gun, and two turretless armoured scout cars, or "dingos", whose weapon was a bren gun; a sixth, so-called heavy, troop, with AEC Matadors, mounting 75 millimetre guns, and besas; and a seventh, or support troop, whose strength was five dismounted sections, carrying small

The Commander-in-Chief BAOR, General Sir Charles Keightley, inspecting "A" Squadron RHG, Wesendorf, 1948. (*Left to right*) Cornet J. Douglas, Captain A. J. Dickinson, Captain H. S. Hopkinson (adjutant), RCM Berrisford, Major Viscount Dillon, Lieutenant Colonel Sir Peter Grant-Lawson, Bt. (Commanding Officer), and the C-in-C.

arms, and conveyed in armoured half-track personnel carriers, which were often deployed among the sabre troops. The Daimler armoured car, the Regiment's principal vehicle, which was relatively silent and could be moved backwards as fast as forwards, was fashioned for a crew of three, a commander, a gunner and a driver, all of whom should have been qualified operators on the standard radio, the 19 set.

During the winter of 1947-48 "C" Squadron put in a four-month stint in Berlin where the political struggle, fomented by the Russians, led to frequent riots and a mood of unrest. In violation of the Allied agreements, the Russians, now claiming that Berlin was an integral part of their zone, began a programme of disruption and restrictions which culminated in June, 1948, with their blockade of the city, an outrage lasting until May, 1949. During that time the British armour in the city was furnished by a squadron of the Royals. The Americans and British defeated the blockade by air-lifting supplies to the Allied garrisons and Berlin's 2.2 million people. The Blues provided the escort for the first post-blockade road convoy. Major General Sir Roy Redgrave, then a captain and Regimental Intelligence Officer, remembers:

"It was left to us to decide what the convoy should consist of and what cargo ought to be carried. We soon agreed that one jeep and three three-ton lorries would be sufficient to prove the point. . . . There was much talk, too, about what stores should be carried by the convoy, something that the garrison really needed such as medical supplies, radios, ammunition, spare vehicle parts? Every suggestion we made was gratefully acknowledged by Headquarters British Sector Berlin, who replied that they had already received all they needed in the Allied airlift. Eventually we heard that our two armoured car squadrons, which had been in the city throughout the blockade, had an urgent request – could we send some fodder for polo ponies? So it was that the trucks were loaded to the brim with hay harvested off the disused airfield from our camp at Wesendorf.

"I accompanied the convoy as far as Helmstedt where I was required to set up my radio next to the international autobahn control police post . . . As a French Gendarme raised the red-and-white barrier, I watched the jeep and the trucks, shedding little bits of hay, drive towards the Russian check point . . . The mandatory time allowed to drive from

Helmstedt (Check Point Alpha) to Berlin (Check Point Bravo) was two hours, which ensured that Allied vehicles did not break the speed limit, deviate or stop. On this special occasion I am sure there were Heads of State sitting beside their telephones in Bonn, Paris, London and Washington, anxiously following that plucky convoy's progress. Was the blockade of Berlin over at last? Had the Cold War eased a little? Could the Allies now end the incredibly costly airlift? But radio contact with the convoy was lost when they reported that they were twenty miles east of Magdeburg and two hours later neither we in Helmstedt nor West Berlin could speak to them on the radio.

"The Russians were most upset when we asked them to explain what they had done with our men. Their concern was genuine and they agreed to accompany an Allied Military Police search party. It did not take long to locate them, because there, parked in a lay-by, were three unattended British trucks. After all who wants to steal a load of hay? Just beyond them were five Russian lorries. Sitting on a grassy bank in the sunshine was a happy band of warriors who had obviously been assessing the respective merits of Russian vodka and Scotch whisky.

"I thought it was a really good omen and it increased my faith in human nature, but sadly rather like the incident in 1914 between the shell-torn trenches in Flanders when British and German soldiers fraternized, the High Command on both sides of the Iron Curtain took a deplorably unimaginative view of this delay in the arrival of the first Allied convoy into West Berlin. However, they had driven through the Red Army ring, origin of a unique shoulder flash, which was worn by British troops in Berlin until 1990, a black circle ringed with a red band and 'Berlin' inscribed above – known affectionately as 'The Flaming Arsehole'."[3]

In February 1950, "A" Squadron of The Blues began a Berlin tour and they were reinforced for a time by "C" Squadron.

A great deal of energy was consumed in the Rhine Army in sport and it may be fairly claimed that, in those stirring times, The Blues were second to none in this field. They were superior in skiing, fencing and athletics; they put together the champion rugby team, not to mention three members of the BAOR XV, including its captain.[4] They boasted the theatre's heavyweight boxing champion.[5] They were regularly carrying off rosettes from the various formation and regimental horse shows. They produced two Olympic horsemen[6] and it was from the regimental turf club (the Severn Club) and the racecourses of

Corporal Worrall, Blues – and Army – heavyweight champion, with a straight left. *Soldier Magazine*

Hamburg, Hanover and Dortmund, that Rhine Army's champion jockey emerged.[7] There was, too, a regimental pack of hounds, which provided an extremely popular form of recreation at weekends. There was a good supply of horses, used for training volunteers for the Mounted Squadron.

Meanwhile, towards the end of 1948, The Blues, now under command of Lieutenant Colonel Sir Peter Grant-Lawson, of pre-war steeplechasing fame and The Blues' fourth commanding officer since the war,[8] had left Menden for Wesendorf,[9] which was close to the Russian zone border and a little way from the historic town of Celle. Consequently, a new formation sign, the White Horse of Hanover, was sewn on to the battledress sleeves of all ranks. Those busy Wesendorf days – packed with gunnery, driving and wireless training and the trade testing that followed;

Saluting without headdress, Wesendorf, 1949. The officer taking the salute (*right*) is Captain H. S. Hopkinson, adjutant. *Soldier Magazine*

zonal border patrols; manoeuvres, with nights spent under canvas; sport, skiing expeditions, and many improved opportunities for other forms of recreation – were probably the happiest of The Blues' first Rhine Army sojourn.

Owing to the increased threat posed by the Russians, a decision was taken, in 1949, to strengthen Rhine Army with an additional armoured division; and, as part of the resultant redeployment, the Royal Horse Guards were ordered, towards the end of 1950, to move to Lower Saxony, to Wolfenbüttel, near Brunswick, "A" Squadron driving there direct from Berlin. "This move was most unwelcome," they declared that winter,

"but we are now settled in and have already made various improvements. We hope that, over the next few months, some more works projects will be carried out, including a coat of paint throughout the barracks ... With the extra six months' National Service we have been able to reach our establishment in men ... The amenities of Brunswick and Wolfenbüttel are better than Celle and many more men go out in the evenings ... The WVS lady helpers entertain a very large number of men who attend the games and amenities they organize so well in the NAAFI rest rooms."[10]

THE ROYALS

It was the Royal Dragoons that The Blues relieved at Wolfenbüttel. And it is to the Royals, whom we left in Denmark, in 1945,
that we now return. The Regiment entered Denmark on VE day
and they must have been much sadder to leave that pleasant
country the following November than The Blues were to be
uprooted from Wesendorf. There was flighting, racing and
draghunting in Denmark, lovely beaches, bright lights, bright
Danish faces and many Royals' romances concluding in marriage.
"In Copenhagen [we] were billeted in the Kastellet or Citadel, the
old home of the Danish Army," the composer of "C" Squadron's
letter to the regimental magazine wrote, "and we were extremely
comfortable there and looked forward to a pleasant winter. But
this was not to be. The "D" Squadron representative stated that
"we left Denmark to the unanimous sorrow of all ranks". Here is
an extract from "B" Squadron's buoyant letter:

"Although we worked day and night, we still managed to find time to
enjoy ourselves and to take part in the almost continuous celebrations of
victory which the Danes organized on our behalf. By the time we left the
frontier on 16 May we had effectually disarmed and passed into Germany over 175,000 German troops. Not bad going for a week's work . . .
    "As in all the Danish towns we had been through, the population of
Aalborg turned out in great strength to greet us. The local resistance
movement had organized a great reception for us and had even arranged
and advertised a football match against us for that very afternoon! In
spite of being tired after their long drive, the squadron football team
played a good game to win 3–2 before a very large crowd . . .
    "During our stay in Aalborg each troop was given the opportunity of
'liberating' at least one Danish town in the area; those are never-to-be-
forgotten days. Everywhere we went we were given the same tremendous reception."[11]

"Came the return to Germany," sighed the "A" Squadron reporter, "on our arrival at Eutin there was a notable absence of
rejoicing . . . Then began the monotonous routine of soldiering in
the army of occupation".[12] Eutin, some 25 miles south-east of
Kiel, in Schleswig-Holstein, was indeed a rather drab place in

Major (QM) C. W. J. Lewis, MBE. Enlisted in the Royals, 1924; RSM, 1940; Lieutenant (QM), 1942; retired 1961. *Barr (Photographer)*

those days, but the Royals, good cavalrymen that they were, were determined to make the best of it. ("It was clear from the start that something had to be done to relieve boredom, and, accordingly, a part of the Schloss Hotel was taken over, a meagre supply of beer was installed, and the Eagle Club came into being, an institution for the nourishment and diversion of the men of the Royal Dragoons."[13])

They did not realize how fortunate they had been at Eutin, with its skating, bathing and sailing, and easy access to old Danish haunts, until posted, early in June, 1946, to Gifhorn, about 20 miles north of Brunswick, with a couple of squadrons at Boden-teich, which according to "D" Squadron, "is situated in a pine forest miles from anywhere, and has as its immediate neighbour a large ammunition dump . . .

The ammunition has almost been removed – the dump remains. Our life here has been one of [vehicle] maintenance, rifle shooting and patrolling the British-Russian frontier by day and night". "B" Squadron decided that "no, Eutin was not such a bad place after all", while "A" reported, from Gifhorn, that 'our patrol duties on the Russian frontier entail quite a lot of night work and we have achieved a lot of success in catching Germans and others who have been attempting to cross. It has not been easy to meet our opposite numbers on the other side who unfortunately seem to regard us with the deepest suspicion'."[14]

Conversely, "C" Squadron recorded that "just over the border is a good swimming pool, and, with the kind permission of the Russians and the gracious blessings of the Kremlin our chaps are allowed to use it after duty".[15]

In September, 1946, the Regiment was posted somewhat closer to Brunswick, to Dedelsdorf, a former Luftwaffe aerodrome, where, owing to rapid demobilization and lack of reinforcements, "A" and "D" Squadrons were amalgamated to form "X" Squadron and "B" and "C" to make up "Y". But, with the extension of National Service, they were able to return to a basis of four sabre squadrons the following June. In February, 1947, "X" Squadron enjoyed a four-months tour in Berlin, and that was the first of several Royals experiences of the troubled "island city", including, as we have seen, a squadron there throughout the blockade. The programme of the 1947 Berlin tattoo contained a musical ride, the Royals being one of four cavalry regiments contributing to it. The others were the Greys and the 7th and 10th Hussars.

The lives the Royals led in Rhine Army were very similar to those of their comrades in The Blues. They were pushed on yet again, later in 1947, this time it was to Wolfenbüttel, where, incidentally, both regiments were last stationed in 1761 as part of Granby's cavalry force. They took over their barracks from the 13th/18th Hussars and contrived to put in at least as much sport as any other cavalry regiment in the British zone. In 1948 alone they won the Rhine Army ski team races; they reached the hockey semi-finals; they fielded a good rugby team (but couldn't beat The Blues!); their formidable cricket side included two in the Rhine Army team; they were fourth in the BAOR swimming

"A" Squadron, the Royals, 7-a-side rugby team at the Olympic Stadium, Berlin, 1949. (*Left to right*): Corporal Davison, Trooper Soper, Lance Corporal Mitchell, 2nd Lieutenant Brewster, Captain J. A. Dimond, MC, 2nd Lieutenant Roe and Major E. T. Greaves

contests; their triumphant association football team, which carried off the 7th Armoured Division inter-unit cup at the Hindenburg Stadium, Hanover, found the captain of the BAOR combined services team[16]; they produced a good half-dozen successful jockeys, including four who would be prominent names in the racing world in civilian life,[17] a success due, in great measure, to the talent and vigilance of their stud groom.[18] And they distinguished themselves in no fewer than 26 different gymkhanas, one of the most successful riders there being Major Heathcoat-Amory, who succeeded Lieutenant Colonel Pepys as Commanding Officer in January, 1949. In July that year they staged a combined horse show with The Blues. ("An admirable course," they said, "was designed by Major Rook near the airstrip at Wesendorf"[19].) There were a great many exercises including, in the summer of 1950, one in the American zone called

Exercise 'Rainbow', of which the Royals were the only British unit taking part. The signal troop reported that:

"On the operational side 'Rainbow' was one of the most realistic and well-laid-on schemes we have ever been on, and on the less operational side we enjoyed the various American forms of entertainment, including Bingo. We enjoyed working with the Yanks, and we hope we contributed a little to further improve the already excellent Anglo-American relations. Even though the precious dollars sometimes ran short a fair ration of steak disappeared down the Signal Troop throats. Sgt. Bradley caused quite a stir in one snack bar when he asked for fried tomatoes with his steak. Apparently the Americans have never heard of fried tomatoes, so they still have something to learn from the 'old world'."[20]

Now it is November, 1950, and time for the Royals to hand over their Wolfenbüttel barracks to The Blues. For they were under orders to move to Egypt, via Chester, where we shall meet them next. And here, to end this account of the Royals' five-year sojourn in Germany is a generous and comradely message of farewell that summer from the sergeants:

"Although we had to 'whistle' in a rather quickly arranged function with our great friends and neighbours, The Blues (owing to exercises, manoeuvres and dates for moves) we held a supremely enjoyable function with them here. We have had many a pleasant time together in the past three years, particularly at their place, and it was unanimously agreed that we should give them a party solely in their honour. The day began with a cricket match. The result – almost unbelievable, is we made 98 (R.Q.M.S. a fine 53), wanting one run to win. Jones, last man, made a ginny swipe and was out, the fool. The match was exactly drawn, which was, after all, just what was wanted. At a most enjoyable dance in the evening a presentation was made to them of a horse's head in bas-relief on a plaque, as a souvenir of our comradeship.

"RSM Morgan, in his speech presenting the plaque, said that The Blues would always be honoured guests in our Mess, and RCM Berrisford in reply said they would not wish to have a better Mess 'lay alongside'."[21]

NOTES AND REFERENCES

1. *The Household Brigade Magazine* (Spring, 1946). The quote is from Milton's poem *Lycidas*.
2. Ibid (Summer, 1946)
3. In a letter from Major General Sir R. Redgrave
4. Captains A. J. Dickinson and R. M. F. Redgrave and Lieutenant D. Kingsley
5. Corporal Worrall, who was, in due course, Army heavyweight champion
6. Major A. L. Rook and Lieutenant M. A. Q. Darley
7. Cornet G. T. Coombs
8. The others were: H. Abel Smith, 1945–46; E. J. H. Merry 1946–47; W. M. Sale, 1947–49
9. "A" Squadron (Major D. J. St M. Tabor) had been at Wesendorf since autumn, 1948. It was at that time that Cornet Richard Sale, the Commanding Officer's son, was captured and briefly imprisoned by the Russians.
10. *The Household Brigade Magazine* (Winter, 1950–51)
11. *The Eagle* (Spring, 1946)
12. Ibid
13. Ibid (Autumn, 1946)
14. Ibid
15. Ibid
16. Sergeant Edwards
17. Majors V. H. McCalmont, M. J. P. Starkey and P. B. Fielden, and Lieutenant H. T. Jones
18. Corporal Beeforth
19. *The Eagle* (December, 1949)
20. Ibid (June, 1950)
21. Ibid

RHG

1948

Commanding Officer: Lieutenant Colonel Sir Peter Grant-Lawson Bt
2 i/c: Major Viscount Dillon
Adjutant: Captain H. S. Hopkinson
RSO: Lieutenant M. A. Q. Darley
IO: Captain R. M. F. Redgrave MC
RCM: WOI Berrisford
Chief Clerk: WOII Harrison

A Squadron
Sqn Ldr: Major A. L. Rook MC
2 i/c: Captain A. J. Dickinson
SCM: WOII Offen

B Squadron
Sqn Ldr: Major Hon J. Berry
2 i/c: Captain A. R. J. Buchanan-Jardine MC
SCM: WOII Sallis

C Squadron
Sqn Ldr: Major C. G. M. Gordon
2 i/c: Captain A. F. L. Hutchison
SCM: WOII Colley

HQ Squadron
Sqn Ldr: Major J. C. Jenkins
MO: Surgeon Captain G. Ledgard
Technical Adjutant: Captain A. C. N. Medlen
Quartermaster: Captain (QM) C. E. Firth
RQMC: WOII Ruff
SCM: WOII Neill

Mounted Squadron
Sqn Ldr: Major Marquess Douro MC
2 i/c: Captain J. H. R. Shaw MC
SCM: WOII George

Band
Director of Music: Captain D. McBain
Trumpet Major: WOII Waters

1st ROYAL DRAGOONS

1948

Commanding Officer: Lieutenant Colonel A. H. Pepys DSO
2 i/c: Major E. F. Gosling
Chief Instructor: Major R. Heathcoat-Amory MC
Adjutant: Captain B. J. Hodgson
IO: Lieutenant A. C. Barker
RSO: Lieutenant A. J. A. Cubitt
RSM: WOII H. Morgan MM
Chief Clerk: WOII Kelly

A Squadron
Sqn Ldr: Major P. B. Fielden MC
2 i/c: Captain E. T. Greaves
SSM: WOII Butterworth

B Squadron
Sqn Ldr: Major A. Graham MC
2 i/c: Captain E. C. Winstanley
SSM: WOII Ireland

C Squadron
Sqn Ldr: Major M. J. P. Starkey
2 i/c: Captain S. W. E. Carter
SSM: WOII Austin MM

HQ Squadron
Sqn Ldr: Major J. C. Parkhouse
2 i/c: Captain H. D. Head
Technical Adjutant: Captain N. H. Ellis
Quartermaster: Captain (QM) C. W. J. Lewis
RQMS: WOII Old
TQMC: WOII Hill
SSM: WOII Maguire

Band
Bandmaster: WOI Trythall

Chapter III

DRAGOONS v EGYPTIANS

(1950–1954)

Having said goodbye to Northampton Barracks, Wolfenbüttel, on 8 November, 1950, the Royal Dragoons proceeded en route to Egypt, via Dale Barracks, Chester, where they were preoccupied with two priorities, the first being the inspection of the Regiment by their Colonel-in-Chief, King George VI, on 5 December; and the second Christmas and New Year leave. That winter was extremely cold and the troopers appear to have spent almost as much time, during the first week of December, sweeping snow from the barrack square as they did on drill parades, kit cleaning and rehearsals. On the great day the inspecting party, which was led by the Commanding Officer, Colonel Roderick Heathcoat-Amory, with the King, also included GOC Western Command and Colonel Frank Wilson FitzGerald (Colonel of the Regiment).[1] Brigadier General Sir Ernest Makins[2] (Colonel Wilson FitzGerald's predecessor as Colonel) and Brigadier W. T. Hodgson, who led the Old Comrades, "said that this was the best turnout they had witnessed," related a regimental diarist, "and who should be better qualified to judge?"[3]

The solemn occasion was not without its amusing "asides", including one recorded by Major Fielden, commanding "C" squadron. "When [the King] got to my Squadron he stopped at Trooper Chant who looked after the NAAFI canteen and came ... from deepest Cornwall. 'Where do you live?' the King asked. Chant replied, as he usually did, entirely unintelligibly. As we walked on down the line of soldiers, His Majesty asked me what Chant had said. I replied: 'I'm afraid, Sir, I simply couldn't hear'. 'I never hear a word these chaps say,' His Majesty commented."[4] However, after George VI died, 18 months later, his Royals' obituarist wrote of the King's "careful inspection of the parade,

The Colonel of the Royals and the Commanding Officer greeting King George VI prior to his inspection of the Regiment at Chester, 1950 (*Left to right*) HM, Colonel Frank FitzGerald, Captain Viscount Althorp, Royal Scots Greys (Equerry) and Lieut-Colonel R. Heathcoat-Amory, MC. *Liverpool Daily Post and Echo.*

his meeting with the Old Comrades, with each of whom he conversed personally, his evident pleasure in visiting the sergeants' mess, and later his luncheon in the officers' mess. His keen interest in regimental pictures and trophies showed a deep knowledge of regimental history and traditions, and he conversed freely with young and old alike and impressed all by his evident enjoyment at being with his Regiment.

"On conclusion of his visit His Majesty expressed congratulations on the high standard shown by all ranks on and off parade, which was in every way worthy of the Royals."[5]

For the unveiling of the regimental war memorial, which was done by Colonel Wilson FitzGerald that afternoon, the Royals paraded on three sides of a square, the Old Comrades filling in the fourth side and the service being conducted by the Rev S. B. Wingfield Digby, who had been their regimental chaplain in the Western Desert.

With leave behind them the attention of all ranks turned east, and the Quartermaster, the stalwart Major "Spud" Lewis, fitted everyone out with khaki drill. It was next noted that "for embarkation on the busy and faithful old troopship, *Empire Ken*, the band played a stirring farewell from the drab gloominess of Southampton and we thank Bandmaster Trythall for an entertaining and tuneful programme." And subsequently that "on board ship the hammock and sundeck were alternately in favour, but we did also learn something of desert navigation, and listened to lecturers telling us to what a depressing place we were going".[6] (There was a good deal of envy for those who had secured places at home, in the 67th Training Regiment, for example, or in the Royals' Territorial affiliation, the Fife and Forfar Yeomanry!) Many had scarcely occupied their tents at Fayid before they found themselves out on a series of exercises – "Sandpiper", "Desert Lark" and "Sand Grouse". A commentator from "C" squadron was to remark that "since the advent of conscription in 1946,

some 600 National Service soldiers have become Royals. Some of these men will have been with us for as long as 20 months; others, for varying reasons, have served a much shorter time. Today there are just under 300 NS Soldiers in the Regiment, all of whom have served or are serving their apprenticeship in "C" Squadron – the Training Squadron."[7]

It was not long, however, before "C" converted to a sabre squadron and just in the nick of time; for there was something more urgent in the air even than training. Under the Anglo-Egyptian Treaty of 1936 British forces were to garrison the country for a period of 20 years, with our special interest in the Suez Canal recognized and respected. In 1945 the Egyptians, finding the terms humiliating, demanded a revision of the agreement; and, in an atmosphere of national unrest, that demand grew into an insistence that all British troops be withdrawn forthwith. The situation was already so tense by 1947 that our forces were withdrawn from Cairo and Alexandria. In October, 1951, the Egyptian government declared the treaty null and void and put its army on a war footing, at the same time encouraging guerrilla activity. From 15 October for the next four months the Regiment

The King inspecting Major Fielden's squadron. *Liverpool Daily Post and Echo*

was employed on Internal Security duties. With its strong traditions, pride and high ideals, the Royals, a superbly trained armoured car regiment, was tailor made for the job in hand.

All those on leave were recalled and "A" and "B" Squadrons (respectively Major K. F. Timbrell and Major G. T. A. Armitage) were dispatched, in turn, to Ismailia to assist with riot control, while "C" Squadron (Major E. T. Greaves), now with two sabre troops formed, went to support the force blocking the path of the Egyptian army along the Cairo-Suez road. In mid-November all married families were hurried into the confines of their guarded unit camps while the hazardous state of affairs prevailed. To

Egypt, showing
stations in the
Canal Zone

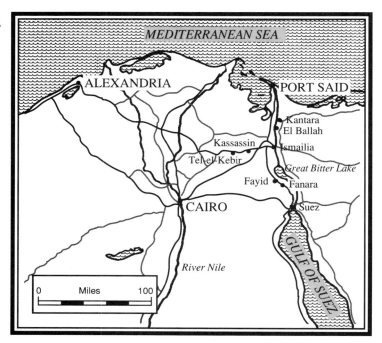

relate a series of typical incidents: on the night of 17 December,
after a bomb was thrown killing a Military Police officer and
destroying his jeep, and heavy fire was, at the same moment,
directed on the security forces by members of the Egyptian
police, an "A" Squadron troop was ordered to rescue the
wrecked vehicle and report on the situation:

"Heavy firing was directed at the troop until silenced by besa and 2 pdr,
directed against the Caracol. The jeep was then recovered and, after an
exchange of fire, the troop withdrew...

"Another troop was sent out to rescue an RAF convoy which was
under fire along the Tel-el-Kebir road. A short encounter ensued using
2 pdr. and besa and the convoy was escorted to safety. During this
encounter the fitters were en route to assist and, passing through
Ismailia, fire was directed at them from a mosque. This was returned
with two bren guns which silenced the snipers completely. Damage to
the building testified to their accuracy.

"Major Timbrell, during a recce around Ismailia, came across a large

Guidon Party, 1953. (*Left to right*) Squadron Sergeant Major Vowles, RQMS Old and Squadron Sergeant Major Jones

crowd of Egyptians setting fire to an unattended three-tonner. He charged the crowd in his Land Rover and put them to flight.

"On 13 January there was an organized attack on HQ BTE [British Troops Egypt] and the Squadron was called out and fired their besas for some period before quiet was restored."[8]

One of the most thankless tasks was that of "line patrols" which consisted of touring and scanning the cable routes, endeavouring to prevent the Egyptians digging them up, partly to sell them, partly to interfere with Canal Zone communications. Less mundane were search operations. On 15 January a "B" Squadron troop cooperating with a battalion of the Foot Guards came under fire during a village search near Tel-el-Kebir, but the operation resulted in only one Royals casualty, a Daimler armoured car driver slightly wounded, in contrast to the capture and disarming of 140 Egyptian police, including a police major-general "who had unwisely chosen that day to come up from Cairo to inspect the unit". A Queen's Commendation (for bravery under fire) went to a "B" Squadron man, Trooper Hesketh, of 3 Troop.

On 19 January another "B" Squadron troop accounted for three Egyptians who exploded a bomb concealed in a street barrow on a bridge, "and later in the afternoon," says the report, "an armoured car was damaged by a bomb thrown from the convent in which Sister Anthony had been murdered by an Egyptian just previously". In the search operation that followed twelve Egyptians terrorists were killed or captured. All the Egyptian police were then disarmed in "Operation Eagle". Referring to the devotion of the Royals' regimental headquarters, signals troop and REME light aid detachment, a chronicler stated that "only by working long hours and frequently at night was it possible to keep all squadrons on the road. The Regiment at times was split from Suez to Port Said, with squadrons under command of two separate divisions, so that the Colonel had to cover a large area."[9]

January, 1952, was a critical time at which to change commanding officers, but that is when it happened. Lieutenant Colonel Heathcoat-Amory,[10] whose command had started shortly before a period of industrial unrest affecting the Regiment in Germany, in January, 1949, ended his tour in the middle of that critical Egyptian winter of 1951–52. "Everything the Regiment has undertaken whilst under his command has been crowned with success, not least our operations in the Canal Zone," was part of the Royals' farewell message to him. Lieutenant Colonel Desmond Fitzpatrick succeeded him,[12] but his command was abbreviated. In September, 1953, he was promoted to take up a staff appointment at the headquarters of NATO's Northern Army Group. Lieutenant Colonel Paddy Massey then assumed command of the Regiment.

With the Egyptian dissidents mostly cowed and the Security

Champion Polo team, Egypt, 1953. (*Left to right*) Lieutenant A. J. A. Cubitt, Major G. T. A. Armitage, Lieutenant W. R. Wilson FitzGerald and Major K. F. Timbrell, MC. *Army PR*

Forces very much in control, Colonel Fitzpatrick had set about re-forming "D" Squadron[13] by diverting troops from the other three; and, although internal security precautions were maintained with routine road blocks and anti-sabotage patrols, training now became the Regiment's first business. Leisure time was well filled too. There were facilities for sports and games of most kinds. In 1952–53 the Regimental football team, trained by Major (QM) Lewis and Regimental Sergeant Major "Skip" Edwards, won several trophies, including the Army Cup.

There was sailing, bathing and fishing in the Great Bitter Lake and at Suez; there was flighting on the lakes near El Ballah and snipe and quail shooting south of Kassassin. ("Fun for all", comments one of the officer-guns, "except the mess staff who have to pluck them!") There was skiing in Lebanon and sight-seeing in Cyprus and Jordan; and there was polo – at which the Royal Dragoons triumphed. There was rejoicing, too, in the Regiment, in March, 1953, on hearing that Major Fielden, from a staff job in London, had won the Grand Military Gold Cup on his horse Atom Bomb. It was the Royals' third win of that coveted Sandown trophy.[14] Next day a former Royal, Captain P. B. Browne, won Sandown's "Past and Present" Steeplechase on Knuckleduster.

Having handed over their accommodation and their responsi-bilities to The Life Guards in Egypt early in 1954, the Royals embarked once again in the *Empire Ken*, this time for home and on leave straight from the boat. And, rather as they had assembled at Chester in 1950 and immediately prepared for the King's visit, now they re-assembled at Tidworth to smarten up for the presen-tation, on 27 April, of a new Guidon by the Chief of the Imperial General Staff, Field Marshal Sir John Harding, on behalf of the

The Royals camp at Fanara with a sabre troop of Daimlers and Dingos in the foreground. *Soldier Magazine*

Queen. "This Guidon will be with you," the Field Marshal told them,

"to remind you of your splendid inheritance of fame and glory; to encourage you to emulate the deeds of your forebears, and to inspire you in your duty. Guard it closely; preserve the great spirit and tradition of your Regiment that it symbolizes; and may it always be to you a source of strength and courage, and a constant reminder of your duty to your Queen and Country."[15]

Of the important happenings on the Royals' calendar in 1954 the most notable were perhaps the retirement from his Colonelcy of Colonel Frank Wilson FitzGerald, the appointment he had held since 1946, and the advent of his successor, Brigadier Tony Pepys.[16] In the spring of that year, soon after the Guidon parade, the Regiment was posted to Rhine Army, to the same spot on the

Regimental Sergeant-Major N. H. Morgan, MM. *Soldier Magazine*

North German plain, 80 miles or so south of Hamburg which had been occupied by their comrades in The Blues five years before – Combermere Barracks, Wesendorf. The Royals were to remain in Germany for the next five years.

NOTES AND REFERENCES

1. Colonel F. W. W. Wilson FitzGerald DSO, MC. Joined the Royals in India, 1908; adjutant, 1913–17; comd Royals, 1931–35; Colonel Royals, 1946–54.
2. Brigadier General Sir Ernest Makins, KBE, CB, DSO. Joined the Royals in 1892; comd, 1910–13; Brig Gen 1914–18; Colonel, 1931–46
3. *The Eagle*, July, 1951
4. P. B. Fielden *Swings and Roundabouts*, p. 79
5. *The Eagle*, June, 1952
6. Ibid, July 1951
7. Ibid
8. Ibid
9. Ibid
10. Brigadier R. Heathcoat Amory, MC. Joined the Royals in India in 1930; comd "C" Sqn El Alamein; comd 15 Scottish Recce Regiment and North Irish Horse, 1945–6; comd Royals, 1949–52; comd 8 Armd Bde, TA, 1954–56
11. *The Eagle*, July, 1951
12. General Sir Desmond Fitzpatrick, KCB, DSO, OBE, MC. Joined the Royals in 1932; IO Palestine, 1938–39; adjutant, 1940; BM 2 Armd Bde, then GSO2 1 Armd Div Western Desert 1942; comd 8th Hussars, 1944–46; comd Royals, 1952–53; Chief of Staff, BAOR, 1964–65; GOC-in-C Northern Ireland, 1965–66; Vice CGS, 1966–68; C-in-C BAOR and Northern Army Group, 1968–70; Deputy Supreme Allied Commander Europe, 1970–73; Colonel, Royals, 1964–69; Deputy Colonel, Blues and Royals, 1969–79; Colonel, Blues and Royals, since 1979.
13. Disbanded, October, 1953
14. The previous wins were those of Lieut. Burn-Murdoch on Larva in 1893, and Lieut R. B. Moseley on Slieve Grien in 1931.
15. *The Eagle*

16. Brigadier A. H. Pepys, DSO. Joined the Royals in 1924; ADC to GOC Egypt, 1927; ADC to Viceroy of India, 1929; adjutant, Royals, 1935; comd Royals, 1942, 1945–46 and 1947–49; comd 22 Armd Bde, 1949–51; Colonel, Royals, 1954–64

1st ROYAL DRAGOONS

June 1954

Commanding Officer: Lieutenant Colonel P. Massey MC
2 i/c: Major J. C. Parkhouse
Adjutant: Captain J. B. Evans
RSO: Lieutenant W. R. Wilson FitzGerald
RSM: WOI J. Edwards
Chief Clerk: Sergeant J. Titmarsh

A Squadron
Sqn Ldr: Major K. F. Timbrell MC
2 i/c: Captain R. H. D. Fabling
SSM: WOII Bradley

B Squadron
Sqn Ldr: Major G. T. A. Armitage MBE
2 i/c: Captain B. J. Hodgson
SSM: WOII Joyce

C Squadron
Sqn Ldr: Major E. T. Greaves
2 i/c: Captain P. P. Davies-Cooke
SSM: WOII W. Woods

HQ Squadron
Sqn Ldr: Major A. B. Houston MC
2 i/c: Captain J. A. Dimond MC
Quartermaster: Major (QM) C. W. J. Lewis MBE
RQMS: WOII Jones
SSM: WOII Vowles

Band
WOI A. F. Trythall

Chapter IV

THE BLUES COME HOME

(1952–1956)

Another fifteen Rhine Army months remained for the Royal Horse Guards following their takeover of Northampton Barracks, Wolfenbüttel, from the Royal Dragoons in November, 1950. They were to look back on their first sojourn in post-war Germany with considerable satisfaction. Given the realistic regimental and formation training which the Army of the Rhine offered, coupled with the obligation of patrolling the zonal border – and despite the handicap of the seemingly endless succession of National Service drafts to be trained – they became increasingly confident in their skill as an armoured car regiment. Like the Royals, they had served in four different stations since the war, with squadrons detached on several occasions in Berlin; they had witnessed Western Germany's dynamic transference from ruin to prosperity, while their own role had changed from that of occupier to defender. To the veterans their old experience of manning a horsed regiment, and one always in Britain, seemed like a bygone age (of long ago), although it had passed little more than a decade before.

The facilities for sports and games in Germany were perhaps second to none in the world, and this most sporting of regiments took full advantage of them. The Blues were paramount, in particular, in the fields of rugby, athletics, skiing and fencing, and their show riders could always be relied upon to take more than their share of the laurels. The Regiment continued, to the end, to produce Rhine Army's champion jockey and the captain and three other members of the theatre's rugby team; and their pack of hounds, from which a regimental point-to-point emerged,

The Blues champion fencing team, 1952. (*Left to right*): Lieutenant C. R. W. Sale, Captain H. S. Hopkinson, Corporal of Horse Loving, MM, Lieutenant Colonel D. de C. Smiley, OBE, MC, and Lieutenant C. V. C. Booth-Jones. *Army PR*

gained a wide reputation for showing consistently good sport. Major General Sir Richard Howard-Vyse returned from his first visit to the Regiment in his capacity as Colonel and Gold Stick, in October, 1951, to report in the most glowing terms of their high morale and general success.

Sir Peter Grant-Lawson having relinquished command and left to take up a staff appointment in Malta, it was Lieutenant Colonel David Smiley[1] who led the Regiment home in the spring of 1952. There, with the Blues' Gold Stick and others to meet them on the quayside at Tilbury, were most of the officers and warrant officers of the Mounted Squadron, the members of which, from their antiquated barracks on the south side of Hyde Park, had spent the last six years fulfilling, with The Life Guards, the time-honoured duties of providing the King's Life Guard, furnishing Royal escorts, taking their part in the Household Cavalry musical ride, parading annually at Windsor for the Garter Ceremony, and many other State functions, but still finding time to camp in Surrey every August for their field exercises and musketry tests; and, at other times, taking a lead in Britain's equestrian life.

The Cavalry Barracks, Windsor – Combermere[2], antiquated, too, but to be renewed much sooner than those at Knightsbridge – were the true and traditional home of the Royal Horse Guards. (The Life Guards were inclined to be treated as tenants!) And how delighted The Blues were to be installed there again after fourteen years away, the Regiment's longest absence from Windsor since the reign of George III. But, for most of them, there would be frequent and protracted tours away from the barracks

Household Cavalry officer sentinels at the Catafalque of King George VI, Westminster Hall, 1952. Lieutenant Colonel Viscount Dillon (RHG), Colonel E. J. S. Ward, MC (LG) and Lieutenant Colonel D. de C. Smiley, OBE, MC (RHG) are in evidence

during the four home years lying ahead. To name one or two of the commitments: "A" Squadron had scarcely taken over their vehicles in 1952 than they were dispatched to Kirkcudbrightshire where they spent the summer helping to train a succession of five yeomanry armoured car regiments; then, early in the autumn, they spent a fortnight driving south, engaging a variety of units on schemes, finishing with one against the remainder of the Regiment who defended the Thames bridges. That summer, too, "C" Squadron established a camp at Walton-on-the-Naze, in Essex, for large numbers of reservists, territorials and Army Cadet Force boys. A training season never passed during these years in which squadrons failed to exercise on Salisbury Plain, at Pirbright or at Stanford, in Norfolk.

Then there were the less military tasks, some quite congenial, like providing wireless communications for county shows and equestrian events, and others more bizarre such as staying in bleak accommodation on the Essex coast to fill sandbags and carry them to reinforce the sea wall against the floods of early 1953 (a summons involving some 300 members of the Regiment); or to provide drivers, mates and distributors of mail following the ASLEF rail strike of 1955; or drivers for the dock strike. And early in 1954 the Mounted Squadron found themselves at Wool-wich, dressed as early 19th-century Light Dragoons, alongside Peter Ustinov and Stewart Granger, for the filming of *Beau Brummell*.

Those four years, spring 1952 to spring 1956, which began with the death of King George VI, were to be among the most dashing and glamorous in the Regiment's three-centuries-long career. But Coronation year began sadly, for Queen Mary, whose special affection for The Blues was widely known, died a few months before the great event, and a dismounted party from Knights-bridge took part in the funeral procession on 29 March. "The death of Her Majesty Queen Mary is mourned by all mess members," wrote a member of the Warrant Officers and Cor-porals of Horse mess at Combermere

"and reminds us of her unfailing remembrance of us at Christmas time each year. Never did she forget the Christmas card, addressed in her own beautifully neat handwriting 'to the Warrant Officers and

The Parade for the Presentation of New Standards, Windsor Home Park, 1953

Corporals-of-Horse of the Blues', which yearly was the first and most treasured prize in the draw on New Year's Day. The card, for 1950, now framed, is a poignant reminder of her friendship towards the Regiment which began before any serving member can remember."[3]

The first parade the new Queen attended, following the end of Court mourning for her grandmother, was that for the presentation of new Regimental and Squadron Standards to the Household Cavalry, in the lovely setting of the Home Park, with Windsor Castle as backdrop, on 28 April, 1953. This colourful occasion – with the Mounted Squadrons flanking the parade, the dismounted contingents facing the dais, in their new number one dress, and armoured car crews filling in the corners – provided a cogent reminder for young Blues of the Household Cavalry's closeness to the Crown and the fact that their Standards, being Royal Standards, were supreme over all other inanimate things to which the British Army paid respect. In the case of The Blues the old Standards were borne, on this occasion, by Regimental Corporal Majors Maxted (from Knightsbridge) and Sallis (from Windsor), assisted by Corporal Majors Kelly and Mumford, while the new Standards were taken from their places on the silver kettle drums by the Quartermasters, Captains Firth and Robarts, for the Queen to present to the Commanding Officer. Her Majesty, whose 27th birthday had been celebrated in the previous week, then addressed the Regiment in her very clear voice as follows:

"I am glad in this my Coronation year to come before you, as your Sovereign and Colonel-in-Chief, to present new Standards to your charge. I pray that they may be to you reminders not only of the honour of your Regiments but also of the special association that, since the Restoration, has existed between the Sovereign and the Household Cavalry. For four centuries your Colonels and Commanding Officers, as Gold Sticks and Silver Sticks, have waited closely upon the persons of their Sovereigns – a mark of the trust which successive monarchs had in them and in those under their command.

"The long and glorious story of your Regiments over the centuries has been one of devotion and zeal to your Sovereign and your country, and the battle honours that you have won may be seen emblazoned on your Standards. From Dettingen to France and Flanders the courage and glorious deeds of your forbears should fill with pride all who serve in your Regiments and who hold dear their honour and their fame. In the last war the First and Second Household Cavalry Regiments won further renown in the deserts of the Middle East, in Africa, Italy and North-West Europe.

"The dying words of one of your officers in the First Great War – 'It is all in the day's work' – express the willingness with which you have cheerfully and successfully undertaken a variety of tasks. You have fought on horses and on foot, in armoured vehicles and from trucks, on camels and on one occasion even on board ship.

"Now, while your two Mounted Squadrons alone remain to recall to us the glory of the original British Cavalry, the armoured car regiments of The Life Guards and The Blues, one abroad and the other at home, take their place at the head of my armoured regiments."[4]

The Blues drum horse, Pompey

By the autumn of 1952 preparations for the Coronation had begun, one of the more urgent of those preparations being the Riding Master's task of seeing forty additional remounts trained. The event was the most significant piece of pageantry of the post-war years. It served, more than anything else, to teach a new generation, who had been brought up in a wartime and post-war world of drabness and austerity, the meaning and value of tradition; to teach them, too, about the Throne as the symbol of a

Laying up of Standards, Guards Chapel, 20 May 1954. (*Left to right*) Padre Fitzpatrick (Chaplain to the Household Brigade), Lieutenant Colonel D. de C. Smiley, MVO, OBE, MC (Commanding Officer), Colonel E. J. S. Ward, MVO, MC (Silver Stick) and Squadron Corporal Major Evans (commanding the escort)

thousand years of history; about the Monarch as the constitutionally supreme being of Britain and the then still close and vibrant Commonwealth and Empire.

When the Queen succeeded her father as Colonel-in-Chief of the seven Regiments of the Household Brigade in 1952, she addressed them as follows: "Whilst each Regiment possesses its own individuality and its own customs, an unshakable bond embraces them all; it is founded, I know, upon devotion to their Sovereign and service to their country, and I am proud indeed to become Colonel-in-Chief of this great fraternity".[5] It was in this spirit that the Queen surveyed her Household Troops at her Coronation and in the same affection that she has held them ever since. Her Majesty was accompanied on her great day, 2 June, 1953, by a Royal Horse Guards Sovereign's escort under Colonel

Smiley's command, with RCM Maxted carrying the Royal Standard, while, at the head of the dismounted column, contingents from The Life Guards and The Blues marched, twelve abreast, wearing number one dress and carrying swords, closely followed by the Royals detachment.

Other exciting things were happening in those Combermere years of the early 1950s. In 1953, and again in 1954, the Household Cavalry Training Cadre, which was also ensconced in the barracks, put together thirty recruits under regular NCOs and a National Service officer and entered them for the Household Brigade Young Soldiers' Platoon competition, a section of the London District Rifle Association Meeting. This involved an inspection in field service marching order and a forced march of five miles, followed by a fire-and-movement test with rifle and

The winning Cavalry Cup team, 1955. Standing: (*left to right*) Troopers Hitchin and Houseley, Corporal Durham, Lance Corporal Mickleborough, Trooper McCorkindale, Corporal Warnock and Troopers McKenna and Shutt. (*Kneeling*): Troopers Mountford, Charlton (Capt.), Thompson, Robbins and Brocklehurst

bren gun, from 400 yards down to one hundred, on the Pirbright ranges. Trained by a Blues captain at Stoney Castle Camp, next to Pirbright, the team won on both occasions, each time defeating six or seven suitably strong entries from the Foot Guards. Trying once more in 1955, they were second to the Scots Guards. That was still a splendid achievement.

In 1954 the Major General commanding the Household Brigade decided that Household Cavalrymen should be eligible for the Guards Independent Company of the Parachute Brigade, a unit of some 120 airborne pathfinders; until then they only recruited from the Foot Guards. The first volunteers, a captain and four other ranks, all from the Royal Horse Guards, completed their training early in 1955. The following year they flew to Cyprus with the 2nd Battalion the Parachute Regiment, against the mounting crisis in the Middle East, and were to take part in both anti-EOKA operations and the Suez campaign of November, 1956.

Here a sad incident of 1953 must be recalled. That was the death, at the age of 19, of the Blues' most imposing and most beloved drum horse, Pompey, on 1 July, a little while after he had fulfilled all his Coronation duties. Foaled in 1934, in Holland, skewbald Pompey was a great favourite with the public and was one of the first equine television stars.[6] The Regiment received messages of sympathy from the Queen, the Prime Minister and the Secretary of State for War. Two replacement drum horses were then purchased, Hadrian from Holland and Hannibal from Shropshire.

Turning to sport, it was as though the playing fields, gymnasiums, ski slopes and equestrian arenas of Westphalia and Lower Saxony had been, for The Blues, the rehearsal grounds for Britain's great athletic tests, because the Windsor years of 1952 to 1956 go down in the annals of the Regiment as being crowned with unparalleled success in their diversity. Shortly after returning from Germany Captain M. A. Q. Darley won the Badminton three-day event on his mare Emily Little, a descendant of the Darley Arabian progenitor of the Thoroughbred, imported by his own 18th-century ancestor. Captain Darley was promptly selected for the Irish Olympic team. In the following year The

Blues' other Olympic horseman Major A. L. Rook, having competed with the British team at Helsinki in 1952, was Victor Ludorum at Badminton on Mrs Baker's horse, Starlight; and he went on, with the same mount, to win the King's Cup at the Royal Tournament.

The Household Cavalry pentathlon teams gave an excellent account of themselves in 1954 and 1955, with, in particular, Corporal Hudson, Royal Horse Guards, twice winning the swimming event with record-breaking times. Corporal Goldsmith, a champion high jumper, received his Army athletic colours, along with Corporal-of-Horse James and Corporal Brooman, while the names Smiley, Sale, Hopkinson, Booth-Jones, Loving and Norris were invariably in the limelight with their foils, épées and sabres. The rugby fifteen, who had nearly always been second to none in Germany, won the Household Brigade Prince of Wales Cup three times out of four during the years 1952–55.

And, glory of glories, the association football squad carried off the highly coveted Cavalry Cup in 1955, beating the Royals on Easter Monday on the Hindenburg Stadium ground at Hanover by four goals to three in extra time. All The Blues' goals were scored by Trooper Thomson. The Royal Dragoons came through to the finals after beating the 3rd Hussars, 3–1, in the semis, while the Royal Horse Guards had fairly easily disposed of the 9th Lancers. The Blues' greatest asset for victory was their centre-half and captain, Trooper Jack Charlton, later an all-England player and brother of all-England Bobby Charlton who was a member of his country's World Cup winning team. This was the Regiment's first win of the Cavalry Cup since 1898.

Officers of the Royal Horse Guards were largely instrumental in the founding of the Household Brigade Polo Club, which absorbed the old Household Cavalry Polo Club (established 1901) in 1954, and which is now, as the Guards Polo Club, one of the two largest centres of the game in Britain. Chukkas were played on Major Archie David's grounds at Henley until the Queen, encouraged by the Duke of Edinburgh, gave permission, in 1955, for Smith's Lawn, Windsor Great Park, to be the seat of

Farewells at Victoria
Station en route for
Cyprus, January 1956

Regimental Corporal Major
J. Sallis

Major D. J. St M. Tabor, MC,
with Sam

Corporal of Horse Stanton. *Sport and General Press Agency*

the club. Major David then agreed to transfer his club to merge with the Household Brigade in the Park.

The replacement of the Victorian Cavalry Barracks began with the removal of the Regiment's greatly cherished lawn in the late summer of 1954. "We have been invaded," wrote their diarist,

"by reconstruction engineers, who have for ever torn up the lawn in front of the Officers' Mess. They are now felling our beloved trees which are at each end of the lawn and square. Ceaseless relays of lorries, bricks and workmen stream in and out of barracks – excavators have removed 2 ft. of earth from the lawn to build foundations for the new square, and much to everyone's surprise, in the middle of the excavations, an enormous well measuring 12ft. in diameter and 20ft. in depth was discovered. The engineers were taken by surprise. We feel that this will not be the only surprise discovery that will be encountered during the rebuilding programme."[7]

Then again, a few months later:

"The hazards of Territorial and cadet camps and all our other military commitments of the summer had only just been cleared up by mid-

October, and this left us with very little time to prepare for the Annual Administrative Inspection. Our drill practices were not made easier by the knowledge that we would have to parade for the Major-General on our new square for the first time; for the Engineers had warned that they would only hand the square over to us the day before the inspection."[8]

It was also recorded that Corporal-Major Cosgrove found in the builders' spoil a George III coin, which he presented to the Household Cavalry museum.[9]

Towards the end of 1954, too, Colonel Smiley left to be Military Attaché at Stockholm, his successor being his Second-in-Command, Major Marquess Douro.[10] By that time the Regiment was aware that they could not have much more than another year of those rosy Windsor days. It seemed to them very like an augury for active service when, late in 1955, they saw the new Saladin and Saracen armoured cars and the new Ferret Scout car put through their paces. Their minds' eyes were urged to turn towards the Orient, first to Tripoli. Then they learned that, owing to the increasing turmoil in the Middle East, their destination would in fact be Cyprus. And when they said goodbye to Comberemere it was to be for nearly three and a half years this time. The advance party reached Famagusta in SS *Lancashire* on 17 January, 1956, and the main party in SS *Devonshire* on 15 February.

Most Blues greeted the promise of a change of scene and of new adventure with great relish. One young officer[11] who was with the advance party welcomed the posting for a different reason. It was a means of escape. Borrowing his soldier-servant's greatcoat and forage cap he tucked himself in the ranks until the boat was clear of Liverpool. The bailiffs had been hard on his tail!

NOTES AND REFERENCES

1. Colonel D. de C. Smiley LVO, OBE, MC and bar. Joined The Blues, 1936; 1HCR, 1940–42 (despatches); Special Forces, Balkans, 1943–44; Force 136 (Far East), 1945; comd RHG, 1951–54; MA, Stockholm, 1955–58; comd Sultan's Armed Forces Muscat and Oman, 1958–61

2. Named after Field Marshal Sir Stapleton Cotton Bt, 1st Viscount Combermere (1772–1865)
3. *The Household Brigade Magazine*, Spring, 1953
4. Ibid, Coronation Number, 1953
5. Ibid
6. Pompey's hooves, shod with silver-plated shoes were sold, or given, as ink wells. It was later discovered that "he must have had five feet"!
7. *The Household Brigade Magazine*, Autumn, 1954
8. Ibid, Winter, 1954/55
9. The very comprehensive new museum, which was built in 1964, stands opposite the guard room by the front gate at Combermere. In the old barracks the collection, such as it then was, was housed in a barrack room. Strong representations were made for the new museum to be either in the more publicly accessible Windsor Castle or at Hyde Park Barracks, but were of no avail.
10. Brigadier Marquess Douro (Duke of Wellington) KG LVO, OBE, MC. Joined The Blues, 1938; 1HCR, 1940–45; comd RHG, 1954–58; Silver Stick, 1959–60; comd 22 Armd Bde, 1960–61; comd RAC, 1 (Br) Corps, 1962–64; MA Madrid, 1964–68.
11. Captain Hon B. C. Wilson, an ardent foxhunter whose establishment at Melton Mowbray was somewhat beyond his means!

RHG
1953

Commanding Officer: Lieutenant Colonel D. de C. Smiley, MVO, OBE, MC
2 i/c: Major Marquess Douro MVO MC
Adjutant: Captain Hon E. L. Jackson
RSO: Captain P. A. Lendrum
RCM: WOI J. Sallis
Chief Clerk: WOII Harrison

A Squadron
Sqn Ldr: Major N. L. Brayne-Nicholls
2 i/c: Captain C. V. C. Booth-Jones
SCM: WOII Kelly

B Squadron
Sqn Ldr: Major C. G. M. Gordon
2 i/c: Captain A. J. Dickinson
SCM: WOII Neill

C Squadron
Sqn Ldr: Major A. C. N. Medlen
2 i/c: Captain M. A. Q. Darley
SCM: WOII Colley

HQ Squadron
Sqn Ldr: Major A. L. Rook, MC
Technical Adjutant: Captain M. A. J. Smallwood
Medical Officer: Surgeon Major E. W. Hayward
Quartermaster: Captain (QM) C. E. Firth
RQMS: WOII Mumford
SCM: WOII Smith

Mounted Squadron
Sqn Ldr: Major Hon J. Berry
2 i/c: Captain F. W. Brogden
SCM: WOII Whennell.

Band
Director of Music: Captain D. McBain
Trumpet Major: WOII Walters

Chapter V

RHG v EOKA

(1956–1959)

The Royal Horse Guards were destined to spend a little over three years in Cyprus in the counter-insurgency role, although that fact was far from certain at the time they arrived (January, 1956) on that beautiful, though troublesome, island. Their advance party was split between Famagusta and Port Said, the role of the Port Said element being to collect some vehicles left behind by The Life Guards when they sailed back from the evacuated Canal Zone; and also a number of polo ponies, which had been bought from two or three different regiments leaving Egypt, and which were transferred to Tripoli, that being The Blues' expected destination. (Fortunately for the regimental polo players, when it was certain they would not be going to Tripoli, the Bays bought the ponies for the same prices.)

The Regiment was faced with the prospect of being mounted in vehicles left behind by The Life Guards. These vehicles, Daimler armoured cars, Daimler Scout cars (dingos) and Land Rovers, were – through no fault of The Life Guards – so old and in such a bad state of repair as to be scarcely roadworthy. (One NCO recognized, without any doubt, an armoured car in which he had ridden with 1HCR during the Italian campaign.) By a great piece of good fortune, however, the Secretary of State for War, Mr Antony Head, flew out to the island at that juncture to stay with the Governor, Field-Marshal Sir John Harding, to review the emergency situation and to talk to commanders. When the Secretary of State visited The Blues, accompanied by General Keightley, the Commander-in-Chief Middle East, Lord Douro complained that he only had sufficient vehicles for two squadrons, and many of those vehicles were not fit for duty.

101

Mr Head was annoyed that such a proud and highly trained Regiment should have been sent on internal security duties without the tools to do the job. He turned to Lord Douro, requesting that, within the next four days, at the end of which the Secretary of State was due to fly home, he should draw up an ideal vehicle establishment for the task in hand. The Commanding Officer and Major David Tabor, his Second-in-Command, decided that the Regiment should be based on the then new Ferret scout car, and drafted their established accordingly. The desired vehicles were shipped out within two months and the Ferret became the classic armoured reconnaissance vehicle for the island, not only to

Driving past at the Queen's Birthday Parade, Nicosia, 1957 Corporal of Horse Godfrey-Cass (who was to become the first RCM, Blues and Royals) with (*behind*) Cornet the Hon. C. S. Fox-Strangways, who was shot and killed by EOKA terrorists within a year of this photograph

combat EOKA, but also for most mobile scouting purposes on the island since then.

Yet at first the Regiment was scarcely given a feeling of permanence in Cyprus. "On arrival it was soon found," ran their first report, "that good progress had been made on the camp sites, although the Regiment was to be treated as an internal security unit and was thus entitled to a much lower scale of accommodation."[1] Regimental headquarters, "A" Squadron and Headquarters Squadron were allotted a rocky camp site, which, in honour of the Colonel-in-Chief, they called Camp Elizabeth, some three miles from Nicosia, while "B" Squadron pitched their tents close to Limassol and "C" near Famagusta. They had arrived at a moment when the terrorist situation was about to warm up to boiling point and good Blues very quickly learned to regard all Greek Cypriots with a wary eye. It was to be three years of almost continuous and constant anti-terrorist *cave*, the regimental episodes related in this chapter being confined only to a few of the most dramatic.

Cyprus measures about 140 miles east to west, while, at its broadest point, it extends 60 miles or so north to south. Towards the west there is the great massif of the Troodos Mountains (6,400ft); to the north stands the range of the Kyrenia Mountains (3,500ft); in the centre, where the capital, Nicosia, lies, is the broad Mesaorian plain; while at the eastern end stretches the 60-mile long Karpas peninsula, nicknamed "the panhandle". In its long history the island has been ruled by many different races, but never by Greece. Before the British were invited on the scene, as protectors, in 1878 (it was to be annexed by Britain when Turkey declared war in 1914), Cyprus had been under Ottoman domination for three centuries. However, by the 20th century, the Greek Cypriot population had grown to over 75 per cent, the Turks were reduced to fewer than 20 per cent, the rest being mixed, for the most part Armenians, Jews, Maronites, and Britons.

Intellectual Greeks, as well as Greek Cypriots, regarding the romantic Hellenic heritage of the island as being of overriding importance to its future, had long dreamed of a fulfilment of Enosis, "union with Mother Greece"; and, in the early 1950s two principal champions of that cause helped to translate the dream into an armed struggle. One was a retired colonel of the Royal Greek Army, George Grivas (codename "Dighenis") a native of Cyprus, a ruthless leader and one of fascist inclination. The other was the Ethnarch, the head of the Greek Cypriot church, Archbishop Makarios. By the autumn of 1955 Grivas, himself concealed in a Troodos hide, strongly assisted on the propaganda front by Athens radio, and, with his terrorist organization, EOKA,[2] well briefed and deployed, set about his campaign to force the British off the island.

That autumn it was deemed appropriate to relieve the Governor, Sir Robert Armitage, and replace him with a soldier, the aforementioned Field Marshal Sir John Harding,[3] who had just relinquished the appointment of Chief of the Imperial General Staff. Following a wave of atrocities the Field-Marshal declared a state of emergency and, before long, the size of the security forces had increased to over 25,000. But recognizing that independence would have to be granted sooner rather than later, the Governor attempted to negotiate terms with Makarios. However, the Archbishop, while refusing to condemn terrorism, also refused to recognize any rights for the Turkish minority, and beyond that, could do nothing but demand a referendum, which, he was confident, would result in a majority vote for Enosis. The Field Marshal replied that Britain, in view of her membership of the Baghdad Pact, her commitments under the Anglo-Jordan Treaty and the Tripartite Agreement, particularly having just lost the Canal Zone, needed Cyprus, for the time being, as a strategic base. But that did not encourage Makarios to soften his line. Shortly after the advent of The Blues on the island a bomb was found in the Field Marshal's bed, and harmlessly exploded outside.

The fact that the Archbishop was a vital power behind EOKA, and that he was heavily involved in the terrorist campaign, was to be proved in the summer of 1956 on the discovery, through information secured from three terrorists captured by a Blues patrol, of Colonel Grivas's diaries. Meanwhile the Field Marshal had Makarios and the equally treacherous Bishop of Kyrenia deported to the Seychelles. Grivas, an intensely religious and

Troop patrol from "B" Squadron taking a break near Limassol on Christmas Day, 1956. (*Left to right*) Trooper Greenwood, Lance Corporal Kersting and Trooper Bingley

patriotic man, regarding the exile as a gross sacrilege, intensified the terrorist activity and his incitement of civil disobedience, while the stream of lies about the British poured out from Athens radio more loudly than ever. The EOKA leader was still issuing his orders from the Troodos hide at that time; soon afterwards he moved to a house in Limassol.

The Blues were responsible, for the most part, for providing patrols, cordons for areas subject to search operations, road blocks, raiding parties, observation posts and escorts, including, for the Field Marshal, a permanent escort troop based on the Government House compound. The troops, initially comprised of a Daimler armoured car and three Ferret scout cars (a subaltern, a corporal of horse and seven other ranks), and later of four Ferrets, supported by dismounted sections carried in Saracen armoured cars, were first deployed, in the case of "A" and Headquarters Squadrons, effectively under the orders of the Commanding Officer, Lord Douro, and in the case of "B" and

"C" Squadrons, as instructed by their brigade commanders, respectively in the areas of Limassol and Famagusta. While all ranks were kept almost permanently on their toes outside camp, off duty relaxation had to be extremely restricted since all the towns were out of bounds. Virtually the only times when soldiers did not carry weapons out of camp was when bathing from the beaches set aside for the security forces and closely guarded. Sustained vigilance and a suspicious mentality, often despite weeks on end without the smallest anti-terrorist coup, was the key to success. "First blood, in the operational sphere," says the same regimental report, "went to "C" Squadron

when Cornet J Butler stopped and searched a car in a 'snap' road-block. One of the occupants of the car was found to be carrying a case containing six charged drain-pipe bombs. In another such check Cornet J. Eyre[4] successfully debagged a man carrying sticks of dynamite tied to his legs with a length of safety fuse tied round his waist."[5]

While EOKA incidents were on the increase in 1956, so, too, a little way across the Mediterranean, the grey clouds of the Suez crisis were thickening and darkening, a fact of which the Royal Horse Guards were reminded, not only by the activity of the Anglo-French airborne forces on the island, but more closely by the instalment in Camp Elizabeth of the Guards Independent Parachute Company (including several Blues), whose purpose turned increasingly from internal security to preparations for the invasion of Egypt as autumn approached.

Meanwhile the Regiment suffered its first disaster. Their doctor, Surgeon Captain Gordon Wilson, was murdered. He was shot in his car while visiting regimental families in a Nicosia suburb. And, adds a Blues chronicler, "not one Cypriot, of whom there were many within a hundred yards, went to his aid."[6] Which was not surprising considering the EOKA leader's threats under which all Greek Cypriots cowered. It transpired that the criminal was Nikos Sampson, the principal assassin of Nicosia, who, though eventually caught by a Blues patrol and locked up, was to win a reprieve.

In mid-winter 1956–57 intensive operations in the snow-clad Troodos Mountains, for which The Blues provided cordons and road blocks, resulted in the defeat of the principal gangs, which thus broke the back of EOKA as a hard-nosed guerrilla force. In March Makarios, released from the Seychelles, based himself in Athens. The terrorist campaign was now reduced more to a poisonous propaganda, stab-in-the-back, rebellious village affair, with Grivas's courier service growing in efficiency and no Greek Cypriot daring to proclaim himself anything but a militant member of the EOKA brotherhood. The Blues as, so to speak, the island's watchful and superbly armed and equipped mobile police force, were ideally suited to thwart the EOKA leader's modified strategy.

A good example of Blues vigilance occurred in 1957, shortly after "B" and "C" Squadrons were withdrawn into Camp El-izabeth and "A" Squadron was sent to relieve "C" at Famagusta, under command of 51 Brigade. Trooper Murray, a 19-year-old

"A" Squadron donkey patrol. Surprise, which was often lost with vehicles, was generally achieved with donkeys, at the approach of which the village dogs usually refrained from barking. Several EOKA couriers were intercepted in this way. The patrol commander here (with binoculars) is Corporal of Horse Hill

"A" Squadron scout car driver, was not missing a movement as he watched a party of schoolchildren stepping off a bus at a road block set up by his troop leader on 22 October. He observed two boys stuffing something down the lining of the seat they had occupied. While the troop leader had the boys placed under guard Murray went straight to the seat, from which he extracted two sellotaped paper packets. It transpired that these contained copies of Grivas's island-wide orders for rebellious activity during the celebrations on Oxi day, 29 October, the date on which the Greeks refused, in 1941, Mussolini's surrender terms. These were the only copies of the EOKA leader's orders for that occasion discovered by the security forces. Entirely owing to Murray's alertness realistic preventive measures were taken on 29 October and EOKA's plans misfired.[7]

That month the Field Marshal handed over the Governorship of the island to Sir Hugh Foot, who, in a brave attempt to take the steam out of the conflict, got word through to Grivas asking for a truce; and while the winter of 1957–58 passed relatively quietly and the United Nations debated the future of Cyprus, The Blues accomplished some much needed individual and squadron training. But, in February, 1958, Grivas, fulminating against what he called "Foot the Deceiver", put the wheels of his violent campaign in motion again, which this time included more strictly enforced disciplines for the Greek Cypriot population ("no alcohol, no gambling, no frivolity until victory is won"). And it was not long before a Blue was recording that "it would be fair to say that the Regiment has been more operational and has covered more miles during the past three months than at any time since the war".[8]

Perhaps the chief blind spot of the Greek Cypriot leaders was their failure to recognize any rights for the Turkish minority, who, naturally, abhorred the notion of Enosis. What they wanted in the event of independence, was *Taxim*, or partition, and that is what the Macmillan Plan envisaged. Meanwhile, on 27 January, 1958, the Turks in Nicosia had staged a riotous demonstration to draw attention to talks on the future of the island then proceeding in Ankara. "During the afternoon," went The Blues report, "it [the riot] was out of hand. By the following morning it became very ugly and "C" Squadron were called in to cordon the gates leading into the old city . . . They had a very nasty morning, being stoned by the mob and repeatedly having to use tear gas to keep the crowds back. At times troops were surrounded, but managed to extricate themselves . . . It was during this morning that Major Booth-Jones, commanding "C" Squadron, received a well-aimed brick on the nose, thereby breaking it and causing its owner to appear covered in blood on the newsreels and television news in England. Fortunately, in the late morning, rain and the efforts of the Turkish political leaders stopped the riots."[9]

Lieutenant Colonel the Hon Julian Berry,[10] succeeding Lord Douro in command at Camp Elizabeth in March, was soon to have a variety of infantry units placed under his direction from time to time – the 3rd Battalion of the Grenadier Guards, the 1st Battalions of the Suffolks, the East Surreys and the Royal Berkshires and a helicopter force of 45 Royal Marine Commando. While the infantry held selected bases, "B" and "C" Squadrons of the Royal Horse Guards patrolled whatever was the area under surveillance, alternately, on a 24-hour basis. The number of political detainees on the island had grown to over 600 and it was in that season too that "B" Squadron was given the task not only of escorting the whole body of them from one camp (Pyla) to another (Camp K) but also of providing drivers for the buses and Black Marias in which the prisoners, many of whom behaved in a most truculent manner, travelled.

The next major regimental drama was the appalling wounding of the eponymous Auberon Waugh, then a National Service officer in "C" Squadron. Here is Cornet Waugh relating his experience:

"My troop was sent to take up a position between the Turkish village of Guenyeli and the Greek village of Autokoi on the Nicosia-Kyrenia road, to discourage reprisal raids and generally keep them apart. On patrol, we always travelled with a belt in the machine guns of the armoured cars, but without a bullet in the breech. The medium machine guns we had trained on, called Besa, needed two cocking actions to put a bullet in the breech. The Browning .300, which we had in Cyprus, needed only one. It is most probable that I cocked the gun in a moment of absent-mindedness, but that did not explain subsequent events which were the result of excessive heat and a faulty mechanism. I had noticed an impediment in the elevation of the machine gun on my armoured car, and used the opportunity of our taking up positions to dismount, seize the barrel from in front and give it a good wiggle. A split second later I realized that it had started firing. No sooner had I noticed this, than I observed with dismay that it was firing into my chest. Moving aside pretty sharpish, I walked to the back of the armoured car and lay down, but not before I had received six bullets – four through the chest and shoulder, one through the arm, one through the left hand.

"My troop corporal of horse, who had been on patrol between the two villages, arrived back at that moment and swore horribly at my driver, whom he imagined to be responsible. In fact nobody had been in the armoured car, as I explained from my prone position. I was rather

Field Marshal Sir John Harding, Governor and C-in-C (*right*) addressing Corporal of Horse Lippe, commanding the quarter guard at Camp Elizabeth, Nicosia. Corporal Tucker is next in line behind CoH Lippe

worried and thought I was probably going to die, as every time I moved the blood pouring out of holes in my back where the bullets had exited, made a horrible gurgling noise. To those who suffer from anxieties about being shot I can give the reassuring news that it is almost completely painless. Although the bullets caused considerable devastation on the way out, the only sensation at the time was of mild tapping on the front of the chest. I also felt suddenly winded as they went through a lung. But there was virtually no pain for about three quarters of an hour, and then only a dull ache before the morphine began to take effect.

"The machine gun had shot nearly the whole belt – about 250 rounds – into the Kyrenia road, digging an enormous hole in the process, before being stopped by Corporal Skinner, who showed great presence of mind by climbing into the armoured car's turret from behind. In the silence which followed, Corporal of Horse Chudleigh came back to me, saluted in a rather melodramatic way as I lay on the ground and said words to the effect that this was a sorry turn of events. He was a tough Bristolian parachutist and pentathlete. On this occasion he looked so solemn that I could not resist the temptation of saying: 'Kiss me, Chudleigh'.

"Chudleigh did not spot the historical reference, and treated me with some caution thereafter. At least I *think* I said, 'Kiss me, Chudleigh'. This story is denied by Chudleigh. I have told the story so often now that I honestly can't remember whether it started life as a lie . . ."[11]

Early in July there was a particularly unpleasant incident in the eastern sector of the island for which "A" Squadron (under command 51 Brigade) had the armoured reconnaissance responsibility from June, 1957, until March, 1959, when the Regiment sailed home. The saga began when the members of one of the troops distributed leaflets explaining the benefits of the Macmillan proposals in a large village called Avgorou, southwest of Famagusta. They were summarily stoned by a large and vociferous crowd. A week later, after another troop proceeded through Avgorou on a routine patrol, the troop leader (Cornet A. H. G. Broughton) reported that he had recognized, from his "wanted man" booklet, a terrorist called Andreas Karios. "A" Squadron's terrorist dossier was kept by their intelligence NCO, Corporal of Horse Godfrey-Cass, a man with a remarkable detective ability. Two days later a third troop was dispatched to the village to seek out this criminal. The troop leader (Lieutenant

H. D. Blake) started by ordering a youth to remove an EOKA notice from a wall, and attempting to arrest a provocateur. Being then surrounded and attacked by a force of over 200 villagers he radioed for assistance and was joined by the stand-by troop (Cornet I. A. D. Pilkington).

By this time Lieutenant Blake, finding ferocious Cypriots swarming over his vehicles and himself threatened by a youth hurling bricks, fired his turret Browning machine gun and killed the youth. The crowd then dispersed and a party from the Royal Ulster Rifles arrived to impose a curfew. Although, unfortunately, a ricochet from the troop leader's gun killed a woman in the crowd, he received unqualified support from his superiors. On 10 July the Secretary of State for the Colonies read out Sir Hugh Foot's statement on the incident in the House of Commons: "The village of Avgorou has a bad reputation and a long history of EOKA association. The patrol commander was clearly carrying out his duties, first in ordering the EOKA slogan to be removed and later in endeavouring to arrest the man whom he considered to be the ringleader of the attacks ... Throughout the incident he acted with great calmness and restraint, and the moment of opening fire was delayed as long as possible, and was then only done by himself personally to save the lives of his men and to protect his vehicles." The Editor of *The Times of Cyprus* described the Avgorou fight as "the fiercest village battle of the emergency."[12]

A tragic sequel ensued. Among the wreaths at the Cypriot funeral were two from Grivas with the message "I shall avenge your blood – Dighenis". Sure enough three days later two Blues National Servicemen, Cornet Hon C. S. Fox-Strangeways and Trooper Procter, were shot in the back and killed while shopping for mess supplies in Hermes Street, Famagusta. One small compensation for all this was that, shortly afterwards, the squadron arrested some EOKA couriers, who, under interrogation, disclosed the hiding place of Andreas Karios, of Avgorou, and eight other terrorists, four of whom were killed (including Karios) and five captured, in a gun fight with the Royal Ulster Rifles, the celebrated Battle of Liopetri, and a huge cache of arms was taken.

Back at Camp Elizabeth the regimental correspondent to *The Household Brigade Magazine* was writing:

"the strain imposed on all ranks by these concentrated operations in the dust and heat of a typical Middle East summer can be better understood when it is realized that the best that a trooper can expect is one night in bed out of two. Curfews, restrictions and areas out of bounds have further added to the general unpleasantness. In spite of all this the Regiment's morale has remained extremely high ... Early in September the alertness of one of our Regimental policemen saved us from what could have been a costly tragedy. A NAAFI cook was found to have a time bomb in his suitcase at the gate, obviously intended for the canteen. We are glad to report that the gentleman in question is now at the beginning of a ten years' prison sentence."[13]

Grivas and his allies in Athens were becoming increasingly alarmed at the high profile given, on the international stage, to the Turkish Cypriots. As a result of the threat this posed to the Enosis cause, EOKA's intimidation of the Turkish villages and of Turks in mixed villages was stepped up. There then followed the saddest and most barbaric chapter in the annals of the Cyprus emergency. It was marked by widespread assassination, burnings, looting and torture by Greeks against the Turkish minority – and homelessness. The first and worst inter-racial clash involving the Regiment took place close to Guenyeli, a Turkish village near Nicosia. Major R. M. F. Redgrave,[14] commanding "B" Squadron recorded the crescendo of the drama as follows:

"It had been building up, with busloads of these Greeks descending on Turkish villages, when a young RAF officer driving through a village suddenly spotted thirty-five Greeks in a bus about to duff up the Turkish community ... He alerted the nearest armoured car troop that he saw and we arrested these people and took them to the police station eight miles away in Nicosia. But as we approached the ramparts of Nicosia a frantic message came over the radio from the police station saying, 'For God's sake don't bring those people here. We have a Turkish riot going on at the moment and if those Greeks come here they'll eat them!' We wondered what the hell to do, so I said to the convoy, 'Take the next turning off and get away from Nicosia'. We drove through two Turkish villages – the Greeks hung their blue-and-white flags up and the Turks their red flags, so you knew which was a

Greek and which was a Turkish village as you drove through – and when we were clear of the village of Guenyeli the Greeks could see their little village in the Kyrenia range. I said, 'Stop the bus. Make them get out and as a punishment make them walk back to their village across the fields'. There was a platoon of Grenadiers on duty in the area and they escorted this group of Greeks across about five hundred to eight hundred yards. Then it looked okay and they let them go. But they'd hardly disappeared out of sight when suddenly the sky was filled with black smoke. A cornfield had been set on fire either by the Greeks or by the Turks to produce an incident. By the time our armoured cars had got back – and it was a bumpy ride – to where these Greeks were, four of them were dead. Guenyeli is a village of professional butchers, and the Turks had really got stuck into them. Then we had the most tremendous cops-and-robbers afternoon with Turks on motorbikes gripping knives in their teeth being chased by scout cars or by light Auster planes."[15]

With the heightening of tension between the communities "A" Squadron had two troops detached daily to escort Turkish workers' buses from the villages of the Karpas peninsula into Famagusta, with an 0300 hours start, and often not finishing the day until well after dark. Greeks were now everywhere ejecting Turks from mixed villages, the homeless Turks having no option but to seek refuge in all-Turkish villages and, as Blues patrols witnessed every week at this time, old vendettas were settled and the most appalling atrocities committed on the pretext that "all's fair in civil war". But the army's main thrust was still against EOKA, and the Royal Horse Guards made many attempts to spring surprise by varying their patrolling methods. That autumn "A" Squadron employed both donkeys, hired from the Turks, and bicycles, donkeys being particularly effective in trackless forest areas and for the reason that they did not give the soldiers' approach away by setting the village dogs barking. Several EOKA couriers were intercepted in this way.

The terrorists had now learned the art of making quite effective mines – pressure and electrically detonated – the explosive being often a crude compound of potassium chlorate and sugar. Cornet J. A. F. Wilson's scout car was thus blown from a narrow loop in a track in the eastern Kyrenia mountains. His driver, Trooper Birch, was hurled to his death with the Ferret into the valley

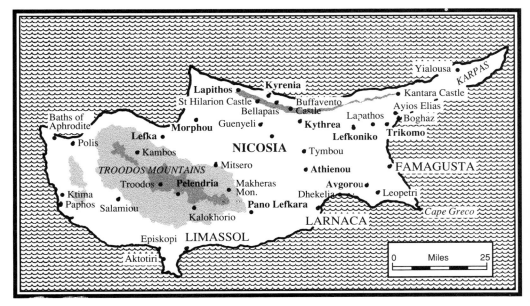

The island of Cyprus

below, but the troop leader won a miraculous escape by gripping a precarious ledge on the mountainside. Both were National Servicemen. The officer commanding the Regiment's extremely hard-working REME Light Aid Detachment devised a mine-clearing instrument to be fitted to the front of one vehicle per troop; but, as the regimental diarist lightly recorded, "whether or not our Regimental funds will benefit from a War Office inventor's prize remains to be seen!"[16] EOKA ambushes were also on the increase prompting the Regiment to fit scout cars with 2-inch mortars firing illuminating flares, "which technique," says the same writer, "being very successful, was widely adopted by various other units on the island".

The Blues won a variety of decorations during the Cyprus Campaign, the most notable of which was Corporal Marklew's George Medal. On 8 December, 1958, he and Trooper Baxter, both "C" Squadron men, rescued a pilot from a burning Auster aircraft.

The end of the emergency came in February, 1959, with the

115

signing of the London-Zurich agreement. Grivas moved from his Limassol hideout to a new lair in Nicosia, and EOKA was disbanded. "But not before a series of parades and celebration church services had been held," noted The Blues diarist, "which necessitated confining everyone to camp in order to avoid clashes between soldiers and the Greeks. The whole effect was rather ludicrous, with a great many youths, who had been hiding in holes in the ground for the past three years swaggering around in uniforms which they would never have dared to wear in the emergency, and which were all too obviously brand new".[17] On 1 March Makarios flew in from Athens to start the job of fashioning the new Cyprus in a manner that proved to be far removed from the fulfilment of his Enosis dream. A little over two months later the Royal Horse Guards, having handed over their camps and vehicles to the 12th Lancers, sailed home. Major Redgrave wrote:

"There were hundreds of little boats to greet us on the Solent and everybody was honking their hooters and sirens. It was an amazing experience. Then when we got to Windsor our old friends the Irish

Sandown, 1958. Captain Sir Nicholas Nuttall Bt, who was adjutant in Cyprus, receiving the Grand Military Gold Cup from Her Majesty the Queen after his win with Stalbridge Park. Sir Nicholas won the race with the same horse again in 1961. *The Association Press Limited*

Guards met us with their band and we marched through the town to our barracks with the place absolutely packed. We really felt great heroes and terribly pleased with ourselves".[18]

NOTES AND REFERENCES

1. *The Household Brigade Magazine*, Summer, 1956
2. Ethniki Organosis Kypriou Agoniston (The National Organization of Cypriot Fighters)
3. In May, 1957, Field Marshal Harding was appointed Colonel of The Life Guards and Gold Stick. As a Household Cavalryman he was thereafter addressed by The Blues as "Colonel".
4. Major General Sir James Eyre, KCVO, CB. Joined The Blues, 1955. IO RHG Cyprus 1957–59 (despatches); comd The Blues and Royals, 1970–73; Silver Stick, 1975–78; GOC London District and Major-Gen comd Household Division, 1983–86. (With hindsight General Eyre doubts the authenticity of this *Household Brigade Magazine* quote!)
5. *The Household Brigade Magazine*, Summer, 1956
6. Ibid, Winter, 1956–57
7. "A" Squadron journal
8. *The Household Brigade Magazine*, Autumn, 1958
9. Ibid.
10. Colonel Hon Julian Berry OBE. Joined The Blues 1939; 1HCR 1939–45 (Bronze Star medal (USA), Chevalier Order of Crossed Swords (Sweden); comd RHG, 1958–60; comd Household Cavalry and Silver Stick, 1960–64
11. Auberon Waugh. *Will this Do?* pp 104–5
12. Charles Foley, *Island in Revolt*, p 202; compare with *The Memoirs of General Grivas* (Longmans, 1964) pp 148–49
13. *The Household Brigade Magazine*, Autumn and Winter, 1958–59.
14. Major General Sir Roy Redgrave, KBE, MC. Joined The Blues 1943; 1HCR 1944–45; comd B Sqn RHG, 1958–59 (despatches); comd Household Cavalry Mounted Regiment, 1963–64; comd RHG, 1965–67; British Comdt Berlin, 1975–78; comd British Forces Hong Kong and Major-Gen Brigade of Ghurkas, 1978–80.
15. Charles Allen, *The Savage Wars of Peace*, pp 154–55
16. *The Household Brigade Magazine*, Winter, 1958–59
17. Ibid, Spring, 1959
18. *The Savage Wars of Peace*, p 156

RHG

January 1958

Commanding Officer: Lieutenant Colonel Marquess Douro, MVO, OBE, MC
2 i/c: Major Hon J. Berry
Adjutant: Captain Sir Nicholas Nuttall Bt.
RSO/IO: Lieutenant J. A. C. G. Eyre
RCM: WOI Neill
Chief Clerk: WOII Harrison

A Squadron
Sqn Ldr: Major J. N. P. Watson
2 i/c: Captain Lord Patrick Beresford
SCM: WOII Ford

B Squadron
Sqn Ldr: Major R. M. F. Redgrave MC
2 i/c: Captain Hon B. C. Wilson
SCM: WOII Woods

C Squadron
Sqn Ldr: Major C. V. C. Booth-Jones
2 i/c: Captain T. G. Coombs
SCM: WOII Whennell

HQ Squadron
Sqn Ldr: Major M. K. Tatham
Quartermaster: Captain (QM) C. E. Firth
Tech Quartermaster: Captain (QM) Coles
TQMC: WOII Rixon
SCM: WOII Mantell

Mounted Squadron
Sqn Ldr: Major M. A. Q. Darley
2 i/c: Captain D. J. Daly
SCM: WOII Evans

Band
Director of Music: Captain J. E. Thirtle
Trumpet Major: WOII Andrews

Chapter VI

"JUDGE US BY OUR DEEDS!"[1]

(1954–1959)

While the Royal Horse Guards were at Combermere Barracks, Windsor, in 1954–56, the Royal Dragoons were ensconced 80 miles south of Hamburg and 15 east of Celle, in Combermere Barracks, Wesendorf; and during The Blues' involvement in the anti-terrorist campaign in Cyprus the Royals were at Harewood Barracks, Herford, a station to which The Blues were to proceed in 1962. This is to say that the Royals had a five-year stretch with the British Army of the Rhine during the second half of the 1950s. Which of the two Regiments had the most difficult task to perform during the years 1956 to 1959? Without any doubt the Royals. For a regiment on active service, on counter-insurgency operations, such as The Blues were then, it is for the most part a matter of reacting to a series of dangerous and urgent problems, rather than having to create and contrive a stimulating life of its own, while its members are aware of the considerable glamour attached to their work, and that they are very much in the limelight.

On the other hand a regiment in the Cold War situation, which was the lot of everyone with Rhine Army from the late 1940s onwards, particularly until the late 1980s, would have found itself in rather a negative role with a monotonous life style, without the inspiring leadership at all levels necessary to counteract that condition. However much the generals may have regarded the Soviet military threat as real and imminent, and however proud they and their staffs may have been to belong to the NATO shield, for the average soldier in Rhine Army the concept of atomic, or nuclear, war against the Russian empire, against Russian armies and air forces which, in numerical terms, were

119

The old Guidon being marched off parade on the occasion of the Guidon presentation by Field Marshal Sir John Harding at Tidworth on April 27, 1954. (*Left to right*) Sergeant Lynd, RQMS Jones and Sergeant Stirling

vastly superior to their own, was a fantastic and somewhat nebulous concept, apparently belonging more to science fiction than to the real world. And it was something which, if it did come to pass, could only result, they imagined, in Armageddon. All the same, commanding officers were at pains to keep their units continuously at battle readiness – to fight if necessary, in the case of an armoured reconnaissance regiment such as the Royals, across the north German plain, through the Harz Mountains up to the Elbe and back again.

So the soldiers were kept very busy. In the British Army's entire history there can rarely have been a peacetime theatre that was ever so active as BAOR. There had to be a constant effort to keep both fighting and administrative vehicles roadworthy and battleworthy, along with a relentless cycle of seasonal training which, roughly speaking, consisted of individual and troop training in the winter months, squadron training in the spring, and regimental and formation training in the summer and autumn. The generals ensured there was a steady annual programme of brigade, divisional and corps manoeuvres; and indeed most soldiers in Germany were never happier than when they were in the field, practising their skills as crewmen and their battle drills and fieldcraft, and spending nights in bivouacs, in squadron harbours or leaguer areas. National Service was still in full swing, and throughout those five years which the Royals spent in Rhine Army they were receiving about twenty drafts of recruits a year from the armoured car training regiment at Carlisle, or, occasionally, from the Royal Armoured Corps Boys Squadron at Bovington: recruits who, on arrival, must be put through the regimental drill course and undergo further trade training, in driving, wireless or gunnery to render them useful crewmen. The apparently endless turnover of trainees having to be prepared for pass-out parades and trade tests must have seemed to the instructors at times like bad dreams.

And life in Rhine Army would have often appeared rather bizarre to the National Servicemen themselves. Here is a memoir from ex-Trooper Hogg:

"During 1956 I was training to be a chartered surveyor, when despite deferments to sit examinations, I was called up for National Service in the Army during the Suez crisis. After training at Carlisle and Catterick, I joined the 1st Royal Dragoons at Wesendorf, West Germany, in "C" Squadron, as company clerk to Capt R. C. T. Sivewright, squadron commander. Wesendorf was a large isolated camp close to the East German border. The situation in East/West affairs was tense and after a few weeks I was given my first guard duty.

"After being handed a pickaxe handle, small torch and whistle I was informed that, at any sign of movement from the East, I was immediately to blow the whistle and help would arrive. About midnight my stint came and I was delivered by truck to the distant perimeter fence facing the might of the Iron Curtain. After patrolling my section, the lights of the camp being at least a mile away, it occurred to me that blowing a whistle would not alert anyone at that distance. I decided to try out the whistle with a modest blow first, then a really good shrill one, interrupting the silence on Luneberg Heath.

"Unbelievably, within a few seconds, I saw a vehicle, headlights blazing, in the distance heading towards me. As the vehicle got closer it started to zig-zag and I heard rifle shots. I did not know what I was going to say, certainly not 'I accidently blew it' or 'I thought I heard something from over there', or even worse, 'I blew it because I didn't believe you would hear it, Sergeant'.

"The vehicle was now close, and it occurred to me I was going to tell the truth. I switched on the torch and started to wave it about. The vehicle (about fifty yards away) stopped and after a short delay I saw a young second lieutenant in full dress uniform emerge, carrying a rifle. Just as I was about to confess (I think) he sheepishly said, 'We've just had a good evening in the officer's mess, so we decided to do a spot of rabbit shooting in the headlights; shouldn't really; best if we don't say anything, OK?'

'Yes, Sir, suits me,' I confirmed."[2]

No commanding officer anywhere, least of all in Rhine Army, could hope to maintain morale simply through providing programmes of hard work, leaving leisure time to individual initiative. As a start, for one reason and another, there was never a very strong dialogue between British troops and local Germans. Consequently leisure activity had mostly to be found within the garrisons. The most fruitful method of keeping Rhine Army

Brigadier A. H. Pepys, Colonel of the Regiment, presenting the Makins Shield to Captain J. W. E. Hanmer. *Army PR*

soldiers physically, mentally and emotionally happy has proved to be to sharpen their competitive ardour. And if they could perceive that their officers are as keen for them to shine as well at sport as at work that device reaped great dividends for morale.

The Royals may well have displayed the finest example of how healthy rivalry is best achieved with the eagerness and impetus which they put behind the various competitions for the Regiment's Makins shield.[3] This greatly coveted prize went to the squadron which aggregated the highest number of points in trials of proficiency and agility over a number of subjects, which included skill-at-arms, vehicle maintenance and driving, drill, assault troop work, football, hockey, cricket, athletics, swimming and boxing. In 1954 Colonel Wilson FitzGerald, visiting the Regiment for the last occasion as Colonel before handing over to Brigadier Pepys, presented the Shield to "C" Squadron. In 1955 it went to HQ Squadron. ("Let no other squadron congratulate HQ in their notes," said their *Eagle* correspondent; "we must congratulate ourselves on winning the Makins Shield, and . . . let there be no more jibes about HQ being chairborne.") And they won it again in 1956, the great prize being handed back to them, as was the custom, on Waterloo Day. In 1957 "C" Squadron carried it off, "having been declared 100–1 outsiders by know-alls in other squadrons", noted their reporter. In 1958 it went to "B" Squadron and in 1959 to HQ again. ("The efforts of the football, boxing and basketball teams were chiefly responsible for our victory.")

Another hotly contested prize was the Ashton Memorial, given in memory of Lieutenant Arthur George Ritchie Ashton, who died in 1956, by his parents, the memorial being in two parts, a trophy and a sword. The trophy, a silver model of a Daimler armoured car, was awarded annually, with a present of £10, to the outstanding junior regular soldier of the year (corporal and below), while the sword was worn by the orderly officer.

"The Regiment has taken part in six exercises at formation level," the editor of *The Eagle* recorded in 1956, "and has been honoured by visits from at least six important personalities ranging from the ADMS up to the Army Commander, who came to inspect us early this year. Not the least of our series of visits was that of the BRA, who came to attend our administrative inspection. These were the big events. But there was (and is) always an undercurrent of audit boards, trade tests, quarterly arms inspections, clothing exchanges, battle efficiency tests, range courses, promotion cadres and education courses."

Nor was that litany exhaustive in a Rhine Army year. The Royals, being close to the Russian zonal border between 1954 and 1956, were responsible for keeping a stretch of the sinister Iron Curtain under observation, with particular reference to any troop movement there may have been behind it, as Trooper Hogg has shown us. There were tactical drills to be practised and perfected; there were rifle and machine gun meetings; there were tests at the Hohne ranges in the speed of loading and the accuracy of firing the armoured car weapons; there were demonstrations of armoured car tactics to be laid on for visitors, such as students from the Staff College or the Imperial Defence College; there was stocktaking and command vehicle inspections; there were the annual parades for Waterloo Day and Alamein Day, and all the rehearsals those implied; there were visits to, and return visits from, the Royals' affiliated Regiment, also stationed in Germany, the Royal Canadian Dragoons; there were Christmas and New Year festivities, always celebrated with the Royals' traditional élan, one of the highlights of those being the frivolous officers-versus-sergeants soccer match. And there were dances and concerts and "smokers", those get-togethers in squadron cellars or attics, at which the comedians put on their acts and choral groups their songs, and where a good deal of beer was drunk.

The gradual changes in military technology brought further work. For example NCOs who had qualified, say, as wireless or gunnery instructors in the 1940s would require refresher courses in the 1950s. Then again new vehicles and new armaments came on the scene in the guise of the replacement armoured personnel carrier and command vehicle, the Saracen, and the six-wheeled Saladin armoured car, with its 76 mm gun, to which the old Daimler gave way. And there were weapons a great deal more devastating than those in the arsenals. The changing vision of the defence of Europe had its inevitable repercussions on the tactical outlook of an armoured car regiment.

Regiments employ much imagination and spend a good deal of

devoted effort in improving their accommodation when they move into a barracks, in shaping and decorating their quarters to suit their character. On the whole orders to move are not welcome. Towards the close of 1957 the Royals were transferred from Wesendorf (the popular "Dorf"), 100 miles west to a little town between Osnabruck and Bielefeld, to Harewood Barracks, Herford, "which are very cramped by comparison," complained HQ Squadron.

"Our days of living in luxury have now passed," sighed the Quartermaster, "and we must continue in our efforts to get our camp up to the high standard to which we are accustomed. Great credit must be given to the rear party for all their hard work which ensured that a first-class handover was affected ... The farewell party given to the civil labour turned out to be a great success and many tears were shed at our departure." Writing of the orderly room's move the Chief Clerk, Sergeant Leech, stated that "delving into the stationery cellars [at Wesendorf] was quite an eye-opener on how much rubbish one can accumulate in three years. With gay abandon the staff, dressed in denims, put the lot

Troop brew. (*Left to right*) Sergeant Mackey, Troopers Jordan and Harvey (on the Saladin), 2nd Lieutenant Arnison-Newgass, and Troopers Fraser, Smith, Graham and McAll. *Army PR*

to fire. This now has made a famous answer: 'Sorry, Sarge, I can't find it, it must be burnt!' Anyhow we have now formed our 'Kremlin' in Harewood barracks and are firmly established to repel all intruders."

Major Geoffrey Armitage,[4] who had been Colonel Massey's Second-in-Command, relieved him in command towards the end of the Regiment's Wesendorf days. Awarded the Sword of Honour at Woolwich in 1937 and commissioned into the Royal Artillery, Major Armitage transferred to the Royals in 1951, then taking over HQ Squadron in Egypt. He was one who welcomed the move to Herford. Looking back from 1992 he writes:

"Wesendorf was very much situated on its own. All ranks and families got to know each other and the country round about, but contact with other parts of the army was somewhat limited. Being close to the border, behind which waited the Russian menace, obviously affected our outlook. All this changed when the Royals moved to Herford, out of the country into the town. Outlook broadened . . . the barracks were more compact and suited us well enough."[5]

"The outstanding event of the year [1958] and also the saddest," the sergeants' mess representative said, "was the departure of RSM 'Skip' Edwards . . . who was dined out by the mess at full strength." Edwards, a great sportsman, footballer, boxer and equestrian, joined the Royals at Shorncliffe in 1936, and following three distinguished wartime years in the Middle East, sailed with the Regiment to North-West Europe, where he was wounded in France, won the Belgian Croix de Guerre and a C-in-C's certificate for outstanding work. He returned to carry the Royals' Guidon at the Victory Parade. His successor as RSM was Mr Vowles.

The Royals, as usual, went all out to triumph in practically every sport and game in the book. Their skiers, who were always successful in these Rhine Army years, won the 7th Armoured Division inter-regimentals in the 1955–56 season. But their footballers could never quite secure the prize for which they yearned, that most prestigious of trophies, the Cavalry Cup, despite the organizing and coaching ability of their time-honoured manager, Major "Spud" Lewis, the Quartermaster, staunchly supported by RSM Edwards. We have seen how, after they emerged as the Rhine Army leaders in 1954, they were beaten in the final by The Blues. The following year they lost the BAOR semi-final to "the Skins", who emerged as the overall victors. In 1956 the Royals reached the BAOR finals again, but went down against the Greys; in 1957 it was the 4th Hussars who vanquished them and, in 1958, the Carabiniers. But they may well have consoled themselves with the thought that they fielded the most consistently good side of the late 1950s!

The Royals were on a level with The Blues as a racing regiment. In 1955 Major Philip Fielden (who was to succeed Colonel Armitage as Commanding Officer early in 1959) won the Grand Military Gold Cup for the second occasion, this time with his brown gelding Skatealong. The Regiment triumphed again in the Grand Military in 1959 when Captain Simon Bradish-Ellames won it with Golden Drop, Lieutenant N. Upton, 9th Lancers, being jockey.

Despite Major Fielden's absence from the Regiment on staff appointments at this time, the Royals – with their head lad, the egregious Corporal Beeforth, "continuing to produce the horses in peak condition" – could boast, in 1959, that, with a total of 13 winners, they "were the most successful stable in BAOR for the third year running." They continued, too, to find very useful showjumping and polo teams. This report in the 1957 *Eagle* reflects the basis of most of their equestrian endeavours in Germany:

"At one stage during the summer, we were maintaining a stable of just under 30 ponies and horses; our numbers have never yet fallen below a total of 20, even in the winter. We have built three paddocks on the airfield, and these have helped us to economize on forage in the summer. Over three-quarters of the officers in the Regiment are supporting the stables financially, and there are also a number of keen casual supporters, including members of the band, the P.T. staff, the padre, the doctor and the W.V.S. ladies, not to mention the school teachers! Without such support, it would not be possible to maintain such a large stable. Three rides have been organized during the past year. The Commanding Officer's polo ride has been attended by all those who have played polo here at Wesendorf. The more experienced players have taken the young

127

ponies on this ride to school them. The young officers, before graduating to the Colonel's ride, the complete beginners, and the showjumping team, have been under the supervision of Mrs Sivewright and Cpl. Cooke, the NCO in charge of the stables.[6]

Mention of Mrs Sivewright recalls that a commanding officer is also responsible for the welfare and good conduct of the regimental families. The Regiment was reminded of it, too, for example, by such "regimental routine order" notices as this one: "It has been generally observed that certain individuals are using NAAFI food trolleys as perambulators for their children. This practice is thoughtless, unhygienic and detrimental to NAAFI property, and will therefore cease". (One wonders whether there followed a brisk market in prams.) The Royals organized, as did most regiments in Germany, a wives' club. Apparently its members did not much mind the transfer from Wesendorf to Herford. "The move went very quickly and smoothly," their honorary secretary recalled,

Royals recruiting team at Crawley New Town, Sussex, 1959. *Soldier Magazine*

"with few ticks, and the wives' club is once more in circulation after an interval of nearly three months. We have the use of the dining room above the sergeants' mess, which has proved to be ideal. At the moment the club is being run in squadron rotation, but this is only experimental. The school here is on a much bigger scale than at Wesendorf, having in the region of ten teachers. On the whole the children have settled down well. The self-service NAAFI here has proved to be a much quicker way of shopping, but generally thought not to be money saving! At this point we would like to say "hail" to all families who have recently joined the Regiment, and "farewell" to those who have left. A special goodbye to Major and Mrs Greaves who have left us for civvy street. "A" Squadron wives gave Mrs Greaves a farewell party in one of "A" Squadron cellars which is now commonly known as "Danny's Dive". Mrs Greaves was presented with a wall clock."[7]

Towards the end of 1958 Colonel Armitage was pointing out, in forceful terms, that the Regiment then included 289 conscripts, meaning that 62 per cent of their total strength was thus composed. The last call-up was to be in the winter of 1959–60, and by 1962 the army would have no more conscripts. Colonel Armitage's message rang out loud and clear: "The National Service soldier has got to be replaced by the regular. But where is the regular coming from? To all of you, Royal Dragoons and Old Comrades, I can say with confidence that we shall stand or fall by our own efforts to get these regulars. It is up to us!"[8] In May, 1959, the new Commanding Officer, Lieutenant Colonel Fielden, sent an armoured car troop around the Royals' new recruiting area, Sussex, Surrey and Greater London. "Directly we gained nineteen recruits", the troop leader summed up,

"and registered twenty more. This is surprising when one considers that applicants were prepared to sign for six or nine years after a fifteen-minute look round. A number of these failed the medical and intelligence tests; some have gone elsewhere. Indirectly, the name and function of the Regiment was advertised widely over the recruiting area. A large number of boys saw the equipment and something may come of this. The recruiting staffs throughout the area now know the Regiment. Certainly it was worth while and should be repeated regularly. It is unfortunate that at this vital time the Regiment is abroad".[9]

The Commanding Officer with some of his Warrant Officers. *Back row*: (*left to right*) WOII Clark, WOII Phillips, WOII Ayrton, WOII Bradley, WOII Brennan, WOII Baker (RAEC). (*Front row*) WOI (ASM) Churcher (REME), RSM Vowles, Lieutenant Colonel G. T. A. Armitage, MBE, Bandmaster Evans and the adjutant, Captain W. R. Wilson FitzGerald. *Foto-Kortzitze*

The winter of 1958–59 was a momentous season in the Royals history. Besides coming under a new Commanding Officer a little after the end of their first Herford year, being re-equipped earlier that winter with the Saladin, winning the BAOR cross-country championships, and beginning to consider how their ranks would be filled post National Service, on 1 January they finished 12 years' affiliation with the Fife and Forfar Scottish Horse – to begin a fresh partnership with the 3rd/4th City of London Yeomanry (the Sharpshooters), for whom they now provided some dozen permanent staff. Towards the end of 1958 they also received the news that they were to be posted to the Middle East within a year. Having carried out their last BAOR exercise of the 1950s (against the QDG) in July, 1959, they prepared to hand over at Herford to the advance party of The

Life Guards. And, after a few weeks spent at Tidworth, from whence nearly everyone was sent on leave, they embarked on the *Devonshire* at Southampton on 22 October and arrived in Aden on 7 November to take over from The Life Guards.

NOTES AND REFERENCES

1. The Royals motto: *Spectemur Agendo*. Used by the Regiment since 1740, it was a motto of the Churchill family. The 1st Duke of Marlborough was Colonel of the Royals, and captain of a troop, in the 1680s. The 2nd Duke was Colonel of the Regiment in 1739–40
2. In a letter from Mr D. C. Hogg
3. Presented by Brigadier General Sir Ernest Makins, KBE, CBE, DSO: Col, Royals, 1931–46
4. Major General G. T. A. Armitage CBE. Commissioned RA, 1937; Served France and Belgium, 1939–40; N. Africa, Italy, N–W Europe, 1942–45; transferred Royals 1951; comd Royals 1956–59; Director, Royal Armoured Corps, 1968–70
5. In a letter from Major General Armitage
6. *The Eagle*, June, 1957
7. Ibid, June, 1958
8. Ibid, June, 1959
9. Ibid, June, 1960

1st ROYAL DRAGOONS

January 1958

Commanding Officer: Lieutenant Colonel G. T. A. Armitage, MBE
2 i/c: Major P. B. Fielden, MC
Adjutant: Captain R. C. Bucknall
RSO: Captain D. S. A. Boyd
Intelligence Officer: Lieutenant D. M. Jacobs
RSM: WOI J. Edwards
Chief Clerk: Sergeant Leech

A Squadron
Sqn Ldr: Major J. B. Evans
2 i/c: Captain J. W. E. Hanmer
CSM: WOII Bradley

B Squadron
Sqn Ldr: Major P. D. Reid
2 i/c: Lieutenant B. J. Lockhart
CSM: WOII Vowles

C Squadron
Sqn Ldr: Major J. A. Dimond MC
2 i/c: Lieutenant P. W. F. Arkwright
CSM: WOII Fletcher

HQ Squadron
Sqn Ldr: Major R. H. D. Fabling
2 i/c: Captain N. H. Matterson
Quartermaster: Major (QM) C. W. J. Lewis MBE
Tech Quartermaster: Lieutenant (QM) E. L. Payne
RQMS: WOII Jones
TQMS: WOII Ayrton
CSM: WOII Phillips

Band
Bandmaster: WOI G. Evans

Chapter VII

ROYALS IN THE EAST

(1959–1962)

Once a regiment gets settled into a new station and has things organized according to its character and style, its members rarely like to be budged unless there is a real prospect of great adventure in view. The Royal Dragoons, having been reluctant to leave Wesendorf for Herford in 1957, were not overjoyed at being posted from Westphalia to Arabia in 1959. When they sailed to Malaya in 1960 there was a yearning for desolate Aden; and when they returned to the United Kingdom in 1962 there was a deep nostalgia for the Far East. The moral of this was that morale had been high everywhere. Even so, Aden must have looked very bleak as the *Devonshire* coasted into port with them on 7 Novem-

Aden, 1959. Visit by the C-in-C. (*Left to right*) Major J. A. Dimond, MC, Air Chief Marshal Sir Hubert Patch, Captain D. S. A. Boyd and Corporal Millett. The Royals are wearing their "hats Beau Geste", which were specially designed for the tour

133

Convoy escort on the Dhala road. *Soldier Magazine*

ber, 1959. A Royals scribe agrees with a 1930s Governor of the Protectorate who wrote in his journal: "Arrived in Aden. It looked just like a penal settlement. And the nearer one got the more unprepossessing the place became". A Royals observer was cynical in a different respect: "Aden is an odd place; the finest cameras can be bought, probably cheaper than anywhere else in the world, but what is there to photograph? Similarly, wirelesses can be bought for next to nothing, but there is virtually nothing to listen to". Another contributor to *The Eagle* wore at once a stiff upper lip and a sardonic smile: "In 1952, partly as a result of the closure of the Abadan Refineries,

a British-American enterprise initiated operations in Little Aden by building 100 huts for the labour force destined to complete the construction of the Refinery in the record time of 22 months. Yes, the reader has guessed correctly – a third of these huts are now shared by the Regiment and the infantry battalion also stationed here. A far cry from the splendid barracks ... which the Third Reich designed for her military forces: a far cry indeed and a challenge such as the British cavalry soldier has never failed to meet ... For those interested in bringing the family to sunny Little Aden, we can only boast a limited number of quarters/hirings, some 20 miles away: in contrast to BP who produced for *their* employees, within the space of 20 months, married accommodation for 169 Europeans and 550 craftsmen and other workers."[1]

Very few Royals families were given the opportunity of taking the plunge. Lieutenant Colonel Fielden, being aware from the outset that his Regiment's Aden tour would be only for a year – and that, anyhow, two squadrons would be stationed in non-family locations – restricted families to HQ Squadron, which would be stationed permanently in Little Aden. Quite a number of postings were arranged to reduce hardship.[2]

Apart from being such a forbidding and inhospitable place, both in visual and climatic terms, this was then one of the world's trouble spots. Annexed by Britain in 1839 as a conveniently located port and refuelling station – still more so when the Suez Canal was opened – Aden had been under the governorship of Bombay until 1932 when its administration became the direct responsibility of the British *raj* in Delhi. From 1937 it was an independent protectorate, with a British Commissioner, and self-government in non-federal matters. At the time of the Royals' tour of duty the British also had protective treaties with (and subsidized) the neighbouring Arab states eastwards from the mouth of the Red Sea, along the Arabian coast and through Muscat and Oman into the land lying against the south-east of the Persian Gulf.

Before its Turkish occupation Aden had been Yemen's principal port, and successive Imams of Yemen laid claim to the place. The troubles at the north-eastern end of Britain's Arabian responsibility, over 1,000 miles from Aden, arose largely from tribal leaders rebelling against the Sultan of Muscat and Oman; also from Saudi Arabia claiming oil sites on the Omani side of the Saudi border. All these threats, being anti-British, were vociferously backed by both Russia and Egypt, and there was also an undercurrent of revolt in parts of the hinterland. Since the 1920s Southern Arabia had been an RAF command. The Royals'

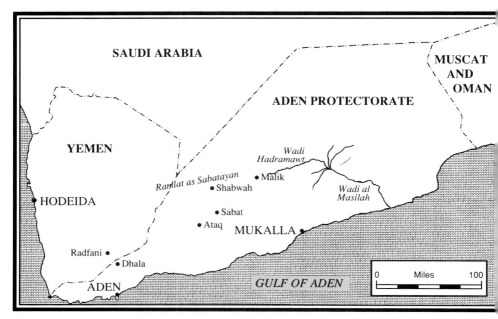

The Aden Protectorate

Commander-in-Chief was Air Chief Marshal Sir Hubert Patch, but they took their orders mostly from the Land Forces commander, Major General Bray. One subaltern remembers being

"stationed in Little Aden, a second promontory to the west of Aden Colony, where we inhabited a hutted camp, built for the workers who had constructed the BP oil refinery. I am sure we all have an enduring memory of the smell and sound of the ceaseless burn-off flame, in the shadow of which we were to live for a year. The camp was tatty, but air-conditioned – a priceless commodity. We took over from The Life Guards, whose officers had created, outside the mess hut, a tiny, but lovingly preserved garden. This was almost unique in the Colony and the ferocious games of "cross-country" croquet that took place around its minute pond were equalled in intensity only by our defence of the precious foliage against a swarm of locusts that arrived one Sunday afternoon. We defeated the enemy by mobilizing each and every racquet, bat or like implement that could be found."[3]

136

No sooner had "A" Squadron disembarked than they were emplaned on two Hastings aircraft and a Beverley and whisked 1,200 miles away to Sharjah on the Persian Gulf coast. ("The distance from Sharjah to RHQ was further than from London to Gibraltar" noted a regimental diarist.) There they were under command of the Trucial Oman Scouts for general purposes; and for special purposes, such as training marches in Muscat, of HQ Land Forces Persian Gulf. Three months later the Squadron was reporting that "we have already seen most of the Trucial States and a lot of Oman". The rebels were in the habit of laying mines haphazardly on the tracks in Muscat and it was on an "A" Squadron patrol that the Regiment suffered a serious casualty. Their Commanding Officer wrote:

"Patrick Keightley [a troop leader] ran over a mine in his scout car . . . one of his feet was badly injured and his Squadron Leader, Chris Banham, realised that, if Patrick was to get the early treatment in hospital that was clearly vital, he must call up Sharjah airfield for the immediate dispatch of a light aircraft. Fortunately the wireless link to Sharjah, planned for such emergencies, worked. A landing strip was quickly cleared and marked, an RAF Twin Pioneer flew in, and Patrick was in Bahrain hospital that afternoon and was operated on that evening . . . It was Chris's efficiency throughout the drama that redeemed an ugly situation".[4]

Anyhow "A" Squadron declared that, despite "some very unpleasant moments, these were offset by many amusing incidents . . . We all remember some 400 Arabs dragging a Saracen and a Scammel out of the mud at Sohar; the Dawson Trucking Company, always on time, having travelled for miles over the desert without maps; and Christmas with its donkey polo, though that will only be remembered by the very few abstainees."

The remainder of the Regiment took up residence in Little Aden, "C" Squadron supplying part of the internal security force in the town and port of Aden and producing convoy and VIP escorts. "B" had the up-country commitment, that was to say supporting the Aden Protectorate Levies with troop detachments at Ataq, Dhala and Lodar, and furnishing escorts for regular convoys to Dhala and Lodar. They enjoyed these roles. An *Eagle* correspondent said that, "The most value in Arabia is gained by troops operating in the Protectorates:

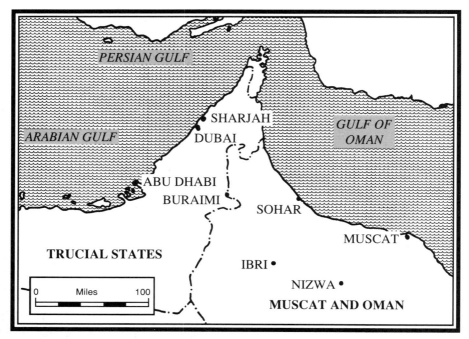

The Persian Gulf

"the Regiment has a troop at Ataq, on the border of the Eastern Protectorate – a station which has the supreme advantage that it cannot be reached by road. Here, at 5,000 feet above sea level, the air is crisp and the nights cool, and the sharp and wonderful colouring of desert and wadi reminds the be-medalled of Palestine and Trans-Jordan. At Dhala, too, the mountain air injects pure *joie de vivre*, uncontaminated by air-conditioning, into the minds and bodies of the garrison serving there, which consists usually of a battalion of Aden Protectorate Levies, a company of British Infantry, a section of gunners, a couple of armoured car troops – not forgetting an admixture of Federal National Guards and Tribal Guards...

"Up-country stations are commanded by Aden Protectorate Levy battalion commanders and it is into their hands that the welfare and training of the armoured car troops up-country is entrusted; but with no regrets, our troops have been splendidly looked after on both scores".[5]

The rest of "B" Squadron was held in reserve for operations in one or other of the Protectorates. There was also a requirement

138

for "desert treks", which were carried out jointly by "B" and "C". From March to November the heat in the coastal and desert lowland regions was at times insufferable. The up-country troops regarded themselves as the lucky ones, not least, as one troop leader put it smugly, "because squadron leaders had to ask permission to visit". At the other end of the regimental scale of activity the motor transport section were saying that "the road from Aden to Little Aden is now horribly familiar to us all".

The Royals were hardly established and going about their military business with their customary high spirits when they set about winning the MacEwan Cup, what they called "the *ne plus ultra* of football in Arabia". The regimental magazine was

Royals Ferret Scout Car being boarded on a Beverley at Nairobi en route to Aden

fulsome in the credit given both to the team and to the Quartermaster:

"This triumph was particularly gratifying to our football manager, Major Lewis, who retires on completion of 37 years' service in December, 1960. Despite theatre-wide renown, the regimental team have never succeeded in winning the Army Cup, but the famed 'MacEwan' ... [a] splendid trophy remains in our possession for a year. This feat compared favourably with the other two recent outstanding Regimental sporting achievements, the winning of the Grand Military Gold Cup at Sandown and the B.A.O.R. Cross-Country Championships at Iserlohn (a remarkable 1959 double)".[6]

There was also both polo and racing at the Union Club, Khormaksar, the racetrack encircling the polo ground. "An assorted band of devotees, including the Chief Justice of Aden and a number of APL and RAF officers", Lieutenant Colonel Fielden recalls, "used to foregather at the club ... to play polo on the 'prepared sand' twice a week during all but the hottest months; and they welcomed our arrival. The ponies were a mixed bunch and had come originally from Kenya, Iraq or Somalia."[7]

Cavalrymen love swanning, wandering beyond their immediate localities in search of pastures new. To name one such Royals enterprise, on 23 December, 1959, Major Banham (formerly "A" Squadron, now regimental Second-in-Command), Captain S. E. M. Bradish-Ellames, Lieutenants J. G. Hamilton-Russell and A. E. Woodward, Staff Sergeant Pitcher, Lance Corporals Yates and Smith and Trooper Collingwood set off on a 1,250-mile odyssey, the excuse for which was to discover whether armoured cars could drive from Aden into the Eastern Protectorate and up to the Rub al Khali, the sand sea that forms the undefined border between Saudi Arabia and the Protectorate. The unofficial mission was to see the fertile Hadhramaut Valley, a great natural rift in the arid mountains, long inhabited and of great scenic and cultural interest. Christmas Eve found them way up in the "stony hilly desert, where to their astonishment,

"over a small rise there appeared a shining white house that would have looked in place at Cap d'Antibes. Smart gates led into a green garden, the front door stood open and from inside came the notes of Holy Night

Brigadier Pepys (*right*) in the Corporals' Mess, Malaya

filtering out of the damp evening air. This was a mirage indeed ... And eight dusty Royals presented themselves. Inside were two wonderful people, Karl and Giesla Schlatholz, the only Europeans living in an area about the size of Wales. Herr Schlatholz turned out to be an irrigation engineer ... We sat down to a true German Christmas."

Having stayed the night there, they proceeded higher into the mountains and "as evening fell we were climbing a 6,000-ft pass on a narrow track hung onto the cliff edges. We stopped to put on woolly sweaters and leather jerkins and to listen to the Queen's broadcast with Mukalla and the sea 4,000 ft below us ... The Queen's voice came through loud and clear." Their 11-day journey included a good deal of hospitality and much scenic enjoyment. "We had all had an unforgettable journey, had seen many wonderful places, made many good friends, and had learned much about the Arabs and their way of life."[8]

141

Redeployment in May, 1960, saw "A" Squadron back on IS duties in Aden, "B" replacing them at Sharjah, and "C" taking on the up-country commitment. In June "A"'s new Squadron Leader, Major W. R. Wilson FitzGerald, took a couple of troops to Kenya for exercises with the Coldstream Guards and the King's Regiment who were stationed there. "It was not all sight-seeing and some valuable training was accomplished, together with a thorough testing of the scout cars in altitudes up to 10,000 feet around Gilgil and the continual hammering over some 1,800 miles of rough country and dirt-track roads." Back in Aden in August the Squadron was thwarted of some expected excitement when the Legislative Council passed a bill illegalizing strikes.

Being put on 24 hours notice in case of riots, they were on their toes and their vehicles well supplied with ammunition. However, "for those of us who were prepared for howling masses of stone-throwing Arabs

the come-down could hardly have been sharper. A band of sixty wandered aimlessly up and down Marine Drive and that was literally all. At 2000 hrs we were stood down and went back to camp. It was a great disappointment all round, especially after the long hours of standing by on the 'big set' in Aden – mainly by the Squadron Leader, sunray minor and Sergeant Bayne."

The Royals made good friends with the ever-helpful General Manager and staff of the BP company and with a squadron of the Queen's Own Hussars, "whose unenviable task was to open up a new camp at Bir Fuqum, and whose NAAFI club became known, somewhat appropriately, by the affectionate name of Fuqum Hall." The sergeants had the BP community hall for their annual Waterloo Ball, at which they "gave the Aden messes a taste of the cavalry method in which this great day should be celebrated. Well over 300 guests from Aden, 30 miles away, and from all three Services, enjoyed a ball to be long talked about. One must give credit to RSM Vowles for his personal touch."9

When it was the Dragoons' turn to say goodbye to Aden and head further east Lieutenant Colonel Fielden received a warm telegram from the Commander Land Forces Persian Gulf, saying, "My staff and I join in wishing the Regiment *bon voyage* and an enjoyable tour in Malaya and wish to record our thanks and appreciation of the excellent record of efficiency and helpful cooperation gained from both "A" and "B" Squadrons ... It has been both a privilege and a pleasure to have them under command." The Royals, gaining a great reputation in Aden, too, with the RAF, the Aden Protectorate Levies and the various echelons of government within the Protectorate, not to mention the civilian population, were sure to be a difficult act to follow. The saddest farewell was from the Quartermaster's group, who had "the very unpleasant task of saying goodbye to 'the gaffer', Major Lewis, who had been the boss since September, 1942. We wish him the best of luck in his new appointment as station staff officer at Verden ... We must also wish his successor, Lieutenant (QM) Ayrton all the best."

On 17 November the *Nevasa* arrived at Aden with the Royals band, who played the relieving regiment, the 11th Hussars, ashore. Two hours later they played on to the ship their comrade dragoons who, said the bandmaster, "came aboard looking very swarthy after their stay in Aden. Members of the band were reluctant to sunbathe on board ship with such contrast of body colour all around them". The band had been fulfilling a busy programme from Shorncliffe during the Aden tour. It was most significant that they should be back with the Regiment now.

Not only the band, but, of infinitely greater importance for morale, all the families could now rejoin their husbands. With the communist terrorists crushed, the Malayan Emergency, which had endured for twelve gruelling years, was finally declared at an end in the summer of 1960. Even so Britain was pledged to underpin the security of the new Federation of Malaysia, which had won independence within the Commonwealth three years before that. And the British presence remained very strong. The Royals inherited the dispositions of the 13th/18th Hussars, "A" Squadron going to Singapore island, with the internal security duties under command 99 (Gurkha) Brigade, and the remainder of the regiment north-east, to Ipoh in Perak, where "B" Squadron were with 28 (Commonwealth) Brigade and "C" (the training and reserve internal security squadron), RHQ and HQ Squadron with 17 (Gurkha) Division.

There was sport of every kind, racing, polo and many other team games and a great diversity of recreational activities. But, as things turned out, said Lieutenant Colonel Fielden, "most of us, after a few months, missed the urgency of life on the Arabian Peninsula".[10] The internal security duties transpired to be almost entirely preventive and protective – convoy and VIP escorts, manning check points, signals communications and generally "showing the flag". But, arriving in a country of contrasting terrain and vegetation from that of Aden, and with a quite different military situation, there were new tactics with which the Royals must become acquainted. There was an airportability role to be rehearsed, there were numerous different internal security deployments and drills and traffic control duties to be practised, and the men were sent on jungle warfare courses. "Once dug in at Singapore," said "A" Squadron, "we proceeded to go on never-ceasing IS exercises," while "B" reported that "when such tactics as snake patrols and ambushes had been practiced we were able to relax in the warmth of the South China sea, bordering our leaguer area." "C" Squadron had variety too; "To familiarize ourselves with moving and living in primitive jungle we instituted a number of weekly marches. The mountains of Upper Perak are covered with thick jungle, rising steeply from the Perak River plain to over 2,000 feet in the Cameron Highlands, so training could start right on our doorstep. It is hardly surprising that some of our uniform is not now fitting us."

There were a host of inspections to be contended with, from among others, Generals Hull (before he departed to become Chief of the Imperial General Staff), Poett (Commander-in-Chief Far East Land Forces), Hopkinson (Director of the Royal Armoured Corps) and Goodbody (the Adjutant-General), down to the brigade commanders and their technical staffs. More welcome than these were visits from Major General Desmond Fitzpatrick, the senior serving Royal, who was then Assistant Chief of the Defence Staff, and, most appropriately, in the Regiment's tercentenary year, their Colonel, Brigadier Tony Pepys, who had recently been instrumental in securing for them the Freedom of the City of London.

"On October 21st, 1661, a troop of horses, one hundred strong

The Malayan peninsula
and Singapore

with three officers, was raised by proclamation of Charles II to form part of the garrison of Tangier", Major D. J. S. Wilkinson, the *Eagle's* editor, reminded his readers:

"The horsemen were gathered together for formal mustering at what was then known as St George's Fields in the borough of Southwark. With the troop mustered on that day, the Royal Dragoons today can trace an unbroken continuity of connection, and this fact established the Regiment as the oldest cavalry regiment of the line in the British Army."[11]

Major K. F. Timbrell, who had been DAA and QMG to the Sultan of Muscat's Armed Forces in Oman and Arabia since November, 1959, took over command from Lieutenant Colonel Fielden in July, 1961. Interestingly, in the context of this history, Kenneth Timbrell, having enlisted as a trooper in The Blues a few months before the outbreak of the Second World War, saw service with 1HCR before being commissioned into the Royals in 1942. In Malaya, in August, one of his first jobs as Commanding

Officer was to supervise the changeover of "A" and "B" Squadrons. They met on the road and leaguered together "for a short time to exchange news and views over a brew". And, commented "B" Squadron, "Singapore was a welcome sight after the long drive and monotonous panorama of rubber plantations". "C" assumed "B"'s operational tasks while "A" took on the airportable role. Early December found "A" Squadron "in the cool of the Cameron Highlands", they recorded. "Here, on a diet mainly of curry and glutinous porridge from our 24-hour packs, we sampled our first taste of jungle-bashing, culminating in a memorable climb up Gunong Brinchang and delved into the mysteries of the new voice procedure under the able guidance of Sergeant Hatch."[12]

One former "B" Squadron officer writes: "Shortly after the Squadron arrived in Singapore, under 99 Ghurka Brigade, there was a general feeling that we might find ourselves at the vanguard of a British force joining a Commonwealth Division with the Australians and New Zealanders in Vietnam. As a result we did many jungle exercises. We also provided the on-shore enemy for the Far East fleet and its commando brigade far up the east coast

Troop leaguer, Malaya. (*Left to right*) Sergeant Mackay, 2nd Lieutenant Williams-Wynn, Troopers Barber, Gillmartin, Searle and Lynch

of Malaya. Indeed we were the first armoured car unit to get to Kuala Trengganu, two-thirds of the way up the east coast, having crossed several large rivers by local ferry."[13]

The Royals' last National Serviceman left in June, 1962, "some 5,200 of them having passed through our hands between 1947 and 1962, forming at times up to three-quarters of our total strength ... However great the advantages of the all-regular Regiment that we now enjoy, we owe the National Serviceman a great debt of gratitude ... "A" and "C" Squadrons finished the Malayan tour well under strength (priority going to "B" in Singapore), but that did not prevent the Regiment from entering fully into all activities or from producing a first-class handover to the Queen's Royal Irish Hussars ... We had a wonderful summer cruise on board the *Oxfordshire*, " said the "B" Squadron correspondent nostalgically, "until we were rudely awakened by a storm in the Bay of Biscay, since when the sun has simply been a memory".[14] And so home to Tidworth, and conversion, for the first time in the Regiment's history, to tanks.

NOTES AND REFERENCES

1. *The Eagle*, June, 1960
2. In a letter from Colonel Fielden
3. In a letter from Mr M. P. T. de Lisle Bush
4. Philip Fielden, *Swings and Roundabouts*, p 113
5. *The Eagle*, June, 1960
6. Ibid
7. *Swings and Roundabouts*, p 116
8. Anonymous article, *A Journey to Hadharamaut*, in *The Eagle*, June, 1960
9. *The Eagle*, June, 1961. RSM Bradley then took over from Mr Vowles who went to the Sharpshooters.
10. *Swings and Roundabouts*, p 120
11. *The Eagle*, June, 1961
12. Ibid, June, 1962
13. In a letter from Major General P. D. Reid
14. *The Eagle*, June, 1962

1st ROYAL DRAGOONS

January 1962

Commanding Officer: Lieutenant Colonel K. F. Timbrell MC
2 i/c: Major B. J. Hodgson
Adjutant: Captain D. M. Jacobs
RSO: Lieutenant J. G. Hamilton-Russell
Intelligence Officer: Lieutenant A. P. G. Stanley-Smith
RSM: WOI J. Bradley
Chief Clerk: Staff Sergeant Leech

A Squadron
Sqn Ldr: Major T. A. K. Watson
2 i/c: Captain B. J. Lockhart
SSM: WOII Crabb

B Squadron
Sqn Ldr: Major P. D. Reid
2 i/c: Captain C. B. Amery
SSM: WOII Titmarsh

C Squadron
Sqn Ldr: Major W. R. Wilson FitzGerald
2 i/c: Captain P. T. Keightley
SSM: WOII Ranson

HQ Squadron
Sqn Ldr: Major M. B. Noble
2 i/c: Captain D. Miller
Tech Quartermaster: Lieutenant (QM) E. L. Payne
Quartermaster: Lieutenant (QM) A. S. Ayrton
TQMS: WOII Fletcher
RQMS: WOII Clark
SSM: WOII Beachaller

Band
Bandmaster: WOI G. E. Evans

Chapter VIII

AIRPORTABILITY AT WINDSOR

(1959–1962)

The Royal Horse Guards came home to Windsor from their three years' active service in Cyprus, under the command of Lieutenant Colonel the Hon Julian Berry, in 1959, to witness, with mixed feelings over the next two years, the builders pulling down their cherished old Victorian barracks and raising stark new blocks and offices and messes in their place. "B" Squadron, who were quartered in accommodation at the old Imperial Service College, returned from block leave to embark on the airportability role they inherited from The Life Guards. There was much for them to learn. Major R. M. F. Redgrave, the Squadron Leader, takes up their story:

"We were given an establishment of Ferret scout cars, Saracens, three-ton trucks and Land Rovers, only half of which could be transported by air, the rest were to come by sea weeks later ... I proposed that the Squadron should be entirely airportable with twenty-two Ferret scout cars and eleven Land Rovers-and-trailers, which only required a tiny sea-tail of four three-ton trucks. The total strength was to be 96 men including the LAD REME. The organization we proposed was four troops of four scout cars able to provide eight patrols, a liaison and reinforcement troop of four scout cars, a headquarters of two scout cars and two Land Rovers and an airportable echelon of nine Land Rovers with trailers. This provided a long-range net of twenty-nine radios which was equal to that of the infantry brigade ...

"I explained that we could provide surveillance right across any brigade frontage, or give flank protection, but that we must always work as a squadron direct to force headquarters. In addition to landing with full tanks, we carried a further five hundred miles of fuel, ammunition and seven days' rations ... We began to learn the complicated drills of stowing vehicles, driving onto transport aircraft and lashing down ...

"Our role, however, was very frustrating after the freedom of movement we had enjoyed in Cyprus. An infantry airportable brigade could scarcely think beyond a frontage of 2–3 miles. They had to be prevented from considering each car just as a fire-support vehicle ...

"It became apparent that our main weakness, apart from fatigue due to only having two-man crews, was a lack of anti-tank weapons ... However, we developed a contact with the Vickers Company at Weybridge who were testing a wire-guided anti-tank rocket called Vickers Vigilant ... When we were deployed by air to a disused airstrip north of Salisbury Plain to take part in a divisional exercise, one car in each troop carried two dummy Vickers Vigilants on their turrets. They looked most impressive and sowed the seeds for developments in that field which materialized years later. The umpires, however, were much put out and accused us of upsetting the balance of power on which they had planned exercises."[1]

15 July saw "B" Squadron drawn up on the square at Combermere, with their vehicles and specialist equipment, for inspection by the Commander Royal Armoured Corps, Third Division, the strategic reserve formation; and, a few days later, they paraded alongside the airportability brigade (1 Guards Independent Brigade Group) at Aldershot. In the autumn they and the other squadrons were busy manoeuvering with the Guards Brigade on Salisbury Plain, and, early in 1960, "B" Squadron began preparing for Exercise Starlight, the Brigade's airportability scheme in Libya. "The main problem for the Squadron," thought one of the officers, "will be desert navigation; car commanders have already been introduced to the mysteries of the sun compass; and it is interesting to note that there are very few members of the Regiment left who wear the Africa Star, the tradesman's badge of desert warfare."[2]

"Starlight" was described by the Brigade Major as:

"The most ambitious joint Army/RAF exercise ever carried out in peace, thanks to the courtesy of the Government of the Kingdom of Libya ... The units of the Household Brigade that took part in the exercise were "B" Squadron, Royal Horse Guards (The Blues); 1st Bn Grenadier Guards; 2nd Bn Scots Guards; and three companies of the 1st Bn Welsh Guards to augment the three infantry battalions. [The Brigade's third battalion was from the Duke of Edinburgh's Royal

Officers of the Mounted Regiment 1959: *Top row*: (*left to right*) Lieutenant S. C. Cooper (LG), Lieutenant A. A. L. Wills (LG), Lieutenant J. H. G. Cotterell (RHG), Major (QM) D. Robarts (RHG) on Siegfried, Lieutenant S. T. Clarke (RHG). Lieutenant Lord Chetwode (RHG), Veterinary-Major P. W. Dean (RHG). (*Front Row*) Lieutenant D. S. Carey (RHG), Captain D. J. Daly (RHG), Major A. N. K. Chieseman (LG), Lieutenant Colonel C. G. M. Gordon (RHG), Captain Hon. E. N. C. Beaumont (LG), Captain W. R. Edgedale (LG) and Major M. A. Q. Darley (RHG)

Regiment] . . . During the whole exercise the Brigade Group was supplied entirely by air, including every pint of water consumed . . . Exercises of this nature may be far more expensive than the normal dreary gallops across Salisbury Plain, but their value to commanders, staffs and all units far outweigh their disadvantages . . . It is to be hoped that the financiers will be bludgeoned into spending the money to enable each formation of the strategic reserve to have at least one major exercise overseas."[3]

Meanwhile "A" and "C" Squadrons of The Blues, who had also been involved in more than one of that Brigade Major's "dreary gallops across the Plain", in 1959 were preoccupied with other vital roles. "C" Squadron for example manned a camp for 1,500 army cadets at Pirbright, while "A" set off on recruiting drives. We have seen how, at this juncture, the Royals, faced with the end of conscription, were giving recruiting priority. It was perhaps a matter of greater urgency for the Household Cavalry, considering the ceremonial commitment. Captain R. F. Abel Smith led a fruitful recruiting tour in 1959 and Captain G. F. Lane Fox another, with "two Saladin armoured cars, a Ferret scout car and four troopers, mounted and in full dress", in 1960. One of the last measures Lord Douro took in 1959, before relinquishing the post of Silver Stick to command the 22nd Armoured Brigade (TA), was to send out a clarion call for recruits. "Towards the end of this year," he wrote in a letter for the Comrades Association

"the last National Serviceman will have been called up and the Army will depend on the regular soldiers that it can enlist . . . Since it was decided that the Army would become all-regular by 1962, other regiments and corps have stepped up their recruiting efforts to a degree unknown before. We in the Household Cavalry have also made every effort to publicise the advantages of a career for young men of intelligence, good bearing, and a wish to take advantage of one of the most varied of lives the Army can offer.

"As you know, our standards, both physical and intellectual, are high. This fact, combined with very considerable competition from the Line Cavalry and the Foot Guards, have reduced the number of recruits who joined in 1959 to half that of 1958. The position is already serious, and unless we can attract more recruits in the near future there is a danger that we will have insufficient men to meet our commitments. The result of this might be that we would have to lower our standards or even effect some further reduction in our establishment that might well involve amalgamation of the two Regiments ... We can offer a young man a life of variety, with horses, or modern armoured vehicles, at home and overseas. Conditions of service are improving all the time. Our barracks are being rebuilt, pay and pensions are being increased. In fact a career in the Household Cavalry has never offered so much. I would ask you all to do what you can to explain this to your young relations and friends."[4]

It is not, and was not, always appreciated how much harder-worked the mounted dutyman usually is than the average member of a Household Cavalry service regiment. In fact it has been said, with some truth, that the Knightsbridge trooper can most frequently claim to be the busiest man in the army. Hardly ever can he have been more strongly entitled to that claim than in 1960, when Colonel Julian Berry, who had succeeded as Silver Stick, watched over an *annus mirabilis* on the ceremonial side of his command. "On reassembling after Christmas and New Year," said a representative of the Mounted Regiment, "we went through a period of stocktaking, [during which] troop drills have been the order of the day – this is in order to harden those horses that have been out to grass during the winter, and secondly to acquaint those members of the Regiment, who have not taken part in an escort, with the vagaries of that duty."[5]

The 1960s high-pressure programme started in earnest with the whole of the Household Cavalry Mounted Regiment being represented, along with nearly all the other ceremonial elements of the Household Brigade, on Horse Guards, for a review on 7 April by President de Gaulle, which was the largest parade that had ever taken place on that square.[6]

Not content with this novel undertaking, the Regiment was required to produce no fewer than three Sovereign's escorts over the period of the visit by the French President and Mme de Gaulle. Within hours of returning to barracks from the review the Commanding Officer was informed by Colonel Berry that he was to find both a Sovereign's and a Captain's Escort for the wedding of HRH Princess Margaret to Mr Antony Armstrong-Jones on 6 May. "The weather could not, that day, have been

Inspection of the Quarter Guard, Combermere Barracks, by the Major General Commanding the Household Brigade, Major General Johnson, 1959. *David Barry*

kinder," notes the same writer; "like humans, horses respond far more easily when the weather is fine." He has, too, a complimentary word for the humans. "The Regiment received congratulations from all quarters ... Much of the credit for this success is due to the efforts made by the ordinary dutyman ... The majority of men taking part have only a couple of years' service behind them and these were, for many, their first State duties."

The Queen's Birthday Parade and the Garter Ceremony followed as usual, on top of the daily guard duties and the musical ride commitments; and, fast on the heels of all that, came the regimental obligations for a State visit by the King and Queen of Thailand. On that occasion the climate was not so generous.

When the escort proceeded with the Siamese King and Queen from Victoria station to Buckingham Palace,

"the heavens opened . . . and before they [the escort] managed to arrive back in barracks they were soaked to the skin. At four o'clock that afternoon it seemed doubtful if the Regiment would be able to turn out next day to escort their Majesties to the Guildhall. Everyone, however, rose to the occasion, and the last tunic was pressed just before 6.0 am. Most of the breeches were still very damp, but the turn-out was up to standard and the escort went off very well."[7]

As though the soldiers at Hyde Park Barracks did not have enough to contend with that year they suffered a particularly wet Pirbright, and there were quite serious outbreaks of equine 'flu and strangles, notwithstanding which they produced two first-class escorts for the State visit of the King and Queen of Nepal, which were promptly followed by fulfilling their customary duties for the State Opening of Parliament in November, not to mention a troop for the Lord Mayor's procession and a detachment at the Cenotaph for Remembrance Sunday. At the same time the Mounted Regiment had been playing an increasingly prominent part in competitive horse activities.

It must have been quite a relief when the demands of 1960 were at an end. "The winter months have passed quietly," we read. "With the absence of Her Majesty the Queen on her State visit to India, Pakistan, Nepal and Persia, short guards have been mounted at Whitehall and pressure of public duties has become reduced."[8] 1960 was not quite a typical Knightsbridge year, but it was not far above that mark. It is worth nothing here that The Blues squadron leader, Major M. A. Q. Darley, went on the French army's long equitation course at Saumur in 1961, and, not content with winning a three-day event in that country, proceeded to pass out top of the course.

1960 marks another landmark in the Household Cavalry's history of mounted duty. A committee was set up at the barracks "to enquire into ways of . . . making the dutyman's task an easier one". Stainless steel bits and stirrups were in general use by the end of the year, new exercise head kits and bridles were issued and trials on plastic crossbelts and sword slings, to replace the old buckskin variety, were put in motion. "We are also trying," said

The succeeding Major General, Major General Burns, inspecting Beaumont Ride during his annual inspection of the Regiment a year later. (*Left to right*) RCM Evans, Captain Lord Chetwode (adjutant), General Burns, Lieutenant Colonel D. J. St M. Tabor MC (Commanding Officer) and Major Langley, LG (Staff). *David Barry*

the committee's first report, "to procure an issue of knee boots, in lieu of puttees, to all other ranks." The first plans for the new Hyde Park Barracks appeared in the following year, the reaction being that "it is fascinating to see how the Household Cavalrymen and horses may live in the twenty-first century."[9]

The service regiment which had been under command of Lieutenant Colonel D. J. St M. Tabor[10] since the end of 1959, also enjoyed quite a dramatic 1960. In May The Blues returned from the Stanford practical training area in Norfolk to receive the startling news that they were to return to Cyprus to relieve the 12th Lancers. It was thought that by then an armoured car regiment would no longer be necessary on the island, but there was a delay in ratifying the terms of the London agreement and the 12th were due for posting elsewhere. "At present the barracks is a hive of telephonic activity," to quote the regimental diary, "as draft warning orders and suchlike are churned out by the dozen, and morning coats and hats are returned to cold storage for an Ascot meeting perhaps a few years hence." The main party, based on two airportable squadrons, arrived at Famagusta aboard the *Devonshire* on 25 June and proceeded to their old lines at Camp Elizabeth, which "had grown older", they judged, "without becoming more attractive".

During the next two and a half months they were kept busy on a series of manoeuvres. Radio communications proved a problem, and old hands were losing faith in the time-honoured 19 set. On the last exercise, "RHQ had a very heavy commitment keeping three separate sets going constantly. This, however, was made considerably easier by the loan, from 203rd Brigade Signals Squadron, of C11 and C12 wireless sets . . . together with vehicles and operators. The sets proved vastly superior." After several delays the political agreement was signed and The Blues sailed home on the *Dilwara* on 15 August.

Here, with a flashback to the late spring, when the Commanding Officer was ordered to stand the Regiment by for the Cyprus posting, is Colonel Tabor's amusing memory of the whole episode:

"Not long after I had taken over command, I had a telephone call from the MA to the CIGS summoning me to a meeting in the Chief's office next morning at half past ten; no reason for the summons was given but I naturally assumed that I was to be sacked. Nevertheless, although I racked my brains, I could think of no pretext for dismissal so soon after taking command.

"Next morning, rather apprehensively, I presented myself at the CIGS's office at the stipulated time; somewhat to my surprise I received a very friendly welcome. General Frankie Festing had a reputation for unconventional dress; on this occasion he was wearing service dress, breeches and puttees. After some polite preliminaries he said, 'I have some bad news for you; you have got to take your Regiment back to Cyprus in order to provide an additional military presence whilst the final negotiations leading to independence are completed.' I was sworn to complete secrecy but was equally told to be ready to move the Regiment at very short notice – two totally conflicting requirements.

"I decided that I must obtain more details of when, how, and where, otherwise there was a risk of the move turning into a shambles. After a little research, I discovered that the key man at working level, who was also in regular communication with Cyrpus, was the GSO1 in SD1 at the War office – Lieutenant Colonel Alun Gwynne Jones (who later became Lord Chalfont). His assistance to me was invaluable, and, in the end, the move back to Camp Elizabeth at Nicosia, which I had helped to build as Second-in-Command in 1956, was carried out without undue difficulty. My brief was to make our presence felt, so I carried out a series of exercises throughout the island with the dual aim of showing the flag and keeping the Regiment happy. In point of fact, both Greeks and Turks seemed so relieved at the prospect of independence that the internal security situation gave virtually no cause for anxiety.

"Among the exercises we carried out was one in the area of Polis – of about a fortnight's duration and in conjunction with HMS *Ark Royal* which was operating in the area. After some ten very hot days on the side of a mountain, my RHQ was visited by the C-in-C Middle East, General Basil Eugster, an old friend and ally of the Regiment. After a social call he asked if I had any problems. I said, jocularly that I had run out of ice for the gin-and-tonics! He laughed, but about an hour later we were notified of the arrival of a Wessex helicopter which landed half a ton of ice slung in a net under the fuselage.

"The finale came a few weeks later when the Regiment was ordered to embark at Famagusta harbour on Independence Day: lighters carrying the majority passed the incoming Greek battalion. Luckily only cheerful waving was the order of the day.

159

"That evening I stayed at the Ledra Palace Hotel preparatory to my flight to England the next day. The order had gone out that uniform was not to be worn in case it provoked an incident with the celebrating Greeks. I am afraid that I disobeyed the order and walked from the Ledra Palace to my favourite restaurant through cheering crowds. I received nothing but politeness and welcome."[11]

Back at Windsor the Regiment was now officially called "the Airportable and Training Regiment Household Cavalry" (two airportable sabre squadrons, a conventional headquarters squadron and a training and depot squadron). The higher chain of

RCM J. Neill (*centre*) with two former Blues Regimental Corporal Majors, Mr C. D. Maxted, MM and (*right*) Mr T. Poupart

command was intricate. "Responsibility seems to be more or less equally divided between London District and 3 Division. All in all this makes us answerable to seven commands or formations. We only hope we can play this complicated set-up to our advantage."[12] Anyhow, by mid-October "A" and "B" Squadrons were back at Stanford which they had left just five months before.

We have seen that the Royals celebrated their tercentenary in Malaya, in October, 1961. The Royal Horse Guards preceded them, it being on 16 February, 1661, that Charles II's Royal Regiment of Horse was raised on Tothill Fields, Westminster; and, on 16 February, 1961, a tercentenary dinner was held in the new officers mess at Combermere, over sixty celebrators past and present, attending. While the port was circulating some enterprising young officers fetched Colonel Tabor's charger, Clancy, from the stables and paraded her round the dining room table.

A week later the regimental rugby team which possessed such a long heritage of triumph won the Household Brigade Prince of Wales Challenge Cup again. The contest was particularly noteworthy in that, led by their veteran captain, Regimental Corporal Major Evans, the fifteen met their comrades in the Mounted Regiment in the final, beating them by six points to three. At soccer the Regiment did well in 1962 to reach the semi-final of the United Kingdom section of the Cavalry Cup, losing to the 9th/12th Lancers who were to reach the main final.

The years 1961 and 1962 were remarkable for the wealth of Blues sporting achievements. In 1961 the young officers polo quartet won the Captains and Subalterns Cup, beating the 3rd Royal Horse Artillery 5–3 in the final. (It was the first time this trophy had come to their mess since 1905.) As for the regimental team they were content that year to gain the Champion United Services Cup at Smith's Lawn, where they defeated the Queen's Own Hussars from Rhine Army 6–5. In 1962 not only did the Captains and Subalterns retain their prize with a 3–1 victory against The Life Guards, but the Royal Horse Guards also carried off the inter-regimental at Tidworth, their finalist opponents being the Rhine Army victors, the Queen's Dragoon Guards. (The Blues had last won it in 1912.) The pivot player on all these occasions was the formidable Captain Lord Patrick Beresford. In

1962 the fencers, having won the Eastern Command Championships, came second in the Army contest. The ski team gained
some very creditable placings at Army level, with Captain D. S.
Carey winning the inter-services slalom. Cornet A. H. Parker
Bowles,[13] who represented the Army in the Inter-Services athletics championships, was then awarded his Army colours. His
specialities were the 100 yards and the 220. (He went on to receive
his Army colours for polo and for the Cresta.)

There was more triumph in the equestrian field. Major Darley
was unfortunate to be "vetted out" when lying third at Badminton, but Lieutenant J. D. Smith-Bingham was second in the
Army three-day event at Tidworth securing the Shaftesbury Cup
for "the best placed soldier". Again in 1962, Captain Sir Nicholas
Nuttall, who had won the Grand Military Gold Cup on his
indomitable Stalbridge Park in 1958 and in 1961, was now second
on the same horse. Three other Blues officers rode in the famous

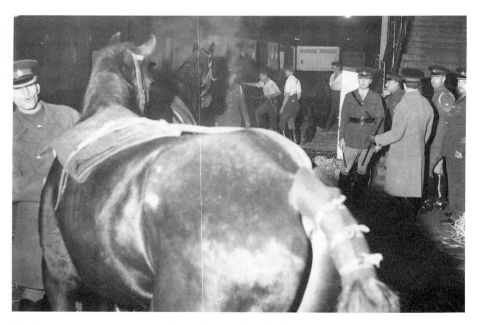

Boxing up at King's Cross for Edinburgh. The horse in the foreground,
Kingpin, is being calmed (*left*) by Corporal of Horse Hunter. The officer
facing Kingpin is Lieutenant the Hon. P. T. Conolly-Carew

Sandown race that day: Cornet Lord Fermoy (fourth on Blunt's Cross), the adjutant, Captain Lord Chetwode (fifth on Gentleman Jinks), and Captain Lord Patrick Beresford on Cornet. "On the second day," says the diarist wryly, "Lord Patrick recouped some of the Regiment's losses by coming second on Superflash." (The writer refers to the two-mile chase, the Past and Present, which Beresford had won with Superflash in 1961.)

Corporal of Horse Chudleigh (who had been one of the pioneer Blues to volunteer for the Guards Parachute Company in 1955) was selected to be a member of the British Joint Services Alaska Expedition, which, in June-July, 1962, made the first-ever British team assault on 20,320 feet-high Mount McKinley. For a graphic account of sheer courage, endurance and fortitude in sub-zero temperatures, readers are recommended to look up Corporal of Horse Chudleigh's article. *Mountaineering in Alaska*, in the Autumn, 1962, issue of the *Household Brigade Magazine*.

"At the time of writing," the magazine's representative was saying, concurrently with these exploits, "the Regiment is in the middle of a concentrated training period." Lieutenant Colonel H. S. Hopkinson[14] was now at the helm, Lieutenant Colonel Tabor having gone to SHAPE, and away went The Blues, with the 19th Infantry Brigade, on exercise "Swansong" and, with 3 Division, on exercises "Crossover" and "Panthers Leap" ("which had its exciting moments as we encountered the Gurkhas who had recently arrived in this country"). Then there was what the Regiment called its "self-inspired" scheme of the season, "Spey Cast", for which they harboured with some old Blues, including (in Yorkshire) Colonel Lane Fox at Bramham Park, and (in Dumfriesshire) Sir John Buchanan-Jardine[15] at Castle Milk. Then they carried out withdrawal manoeuvres all the way to Windsor ("just in time to have a bath and get up to London in time for the Comrades dinner which was, as usual, a great success"). And, when exercise "Berengaria" and exercise "Crossbelt" were concluded, it was time to prepare to leave Combermere, after ten years' absence from Rhine Army, to head for Lower Saxony, to Herford, where The Life Guards, having taken over from the Royals, had been since 1959. The rebuilding at Combermere was by no means concluded. "We are still surrounded by an indescribable pile of rubble. Hot steam, emerging from underground pipes, makes part of the barracks look like mud baths.[16] There are dust and unmade roads and contractors' vehicles everywhere. At last, however, the new Warrant Officers' mess looks as if it will be comfortable. It is modern, spacious, well planned, and the accommodation is excellent. Let us hope when we return to Windsor in three years' time The Life Guards will be able to hand over to us a wholly modernized barracks. We feel apologetic for having to let The Life Guards come home to a half-finished development."[17]

Squadron harbour, Bramham Park, Yorkshire, 1963

NOTES AND REFERENCES

1. In a letter from Major General Sir Roy Redgrave
2. *The Household Brigade Magazine*, Spring, 1960
3. From article *Exercise Starlight*, by Lieutenant Colonel R. J. D. E. Buckland, Coldstream Guards, *Household Brigade Magazine*, Summer, 1960
4. Comrades Association Annual Report, 1960
5. *The Household Brigade Magazine*, Spring, 1960
6. The Regimental Standard was carried, on this occasion, by Regimental Corporal Major J. Neill. Although Mr Neill, who had been RCM throughout the Regiment's 1950s Cyprus sojourn, where he was mentioned in despatches, had more than 20 years service behind him, he had never been on State duties before 1959. A third generation Blue, his grandfather joined in 1864, and his father (as a band boy) in 1886. Two uncles and a brother of Mr Neill's also served in the Regiment.
7. *The Household Brigade Magazine*, Summer, 1960
8. Ibid, Spring 1961
9. Ibid, Autumn, 1961
10. Major General D. J. St M. Tabor, CB, MC. Joined The Blues, 1942; 2HCR, 1944–45; comd RHG, 1960–62; Silver Stick, 1964–67; comd Berlin Inf Bde, 1967–68; MA Washington, 1968–71; Defence Attaché, Paris, 1972–74; GOC Eastern District, 1974–77
11. In a letter from Major General Tabor
12. *The Household Brigade Magazine*, Autumn, 1960
13. Brigadier A. H. Parker Bowles, OBE. Joined the Blues, 1960; adjutant RHG 1967–69; adjutant Blues and Royals, 1969–70; Senior Military Liaison Officer, Rhodesia, 1979–80 (Queen's Commendation); comd Mounted Regiment, 1981–83; Silver Stick, 1987–90; Director RAVC, 1991–
14. Brigadier H. S. Hopkinson, MBE. Joined the Blues 1943; 2HCR 1944–45; comd RHG 1962–64; Silver Stick, 1967–69; Brigadier 1974–78
15. Both Sir John Buchanan-Jardine and his son (Major Rupert, of 2HCR fame) frequently played hosts to the Household Cavalry during northern manoeuvres, as Major Sir Rupert Buchanan-Jardine has generously done since to The Blues and Royals.
16. The steam was caused by urine from the stables corroding, and causing punctures, in the pipes.
17. *The Household Brigade Magazine*, Winter, 1962–63

RHG

January 1961

Commanding Officer: Lieutenant Colonel D. J. St M. Tabor, MC
2 i/c: Major A. F. L. Hutchison
Adjutant: Captain Lord Chetwode
RSO: Captain Lord Patrick Beresford
RCM: WOI L. Evans
ORQMC: WOII Slade

A Squadron
Sqn Ldr: Major R. D. Black
2 i/c: Captain J. H. Pitman
SCM: WOII Mantell

B Squadron
Sqn Ldr: Major Sir Nicholas Nuttall Bt
2 i/c: Captain R. G. Angus
SCM: WOII Price

Depot Squadron
Sqn Ldr: Major G. F. Lane Fox
2 i/c: Captain T. N. P. W. Burbury
SCM: WOII Lippe

HQ Squadron
Sqn Ldr: Major E. J. R. M. P. de Lisle
2 i/c: Captain Hon B. C. Wilson
Medical Officer: Surgeon-Captain D. H. Matthews
Quartermaster: Major (QM) C. E. Firth
Tech Quartermaster: Captain (QM) C. J. Coles
RQMC: WOII Cummings
SCM: WOII Kidman

Mounted Squadron
Sqn Ldr: Major H. S. Hopkinson MBE
2 i/c: Captain G. T. Coombs
SCM: WOII Stringer

Band
Director of Music: Captain J. E. Thirtle
Trumpet-Major: WOII Andrews

Chapter IX

THE ROYALS GO TRACKED

(1962–1967)

After the Royals sailed back, under Lieutenant Colonel Timbrell's command, from Malaya in October, 1962, a combination of the sharp contrast in climate and a strong tinge of nostalgia was what seemed to affect them most as they faced the prospect of a bleak Tidworth winter and conversion, for the first occasion, from armoured cars to Centurion tanks. "It is sometimes hard to conjure up the past," said a "B" Squadron scribe,

"and to imagine Singapore and Malaya now we are at Tidworth... Do you remember the smell of the kampongs; the lush greenery everywhere, the heat and the damp; Johnny Wee trying to sell you a car 'very cheap'; working on your armoured cars in the sun, stripped to the waist; Mohammed Ishaq providing you with ice-cold drinks at any time of the day or night?...

"After leave we all assembled at Tidworth. We looked at each other, the weather, the barracks and the tanks; used a few of the more common military expletives, spat on our hands and had a go... We manned the tanks with whoever was available, and out we went come snow, come rain... At the beginning of March we drew up some more tanks; and, at the same time, developed a healthy respect for them; though opinions differed after we slipped off our tracks in the snow once or twice."[1]

Opinions differed, too, as to whether the Army's decision to make tank and armoured car regiments interchangeable was a wise one. There is no doubt that, at the time, members of the armoured car regiments, being masters of the art of reconnaissance and having enjoyed the freedom of wheels, and, since the war, the interesting peacekeeping and counter-insurgency postings that came with those benefits, felt the change as a severe blow and deprivation. They therefore imagined the traditional tank regiments would be celebrating their conversion to armoured

Brigadier-General Sir Ernest
Makins. Colonel, The Royals,
1931 to 1946. He commanded
the Regiment between 1910 and
1914. *Portrait: Oswald Birley*

'Reflections'. *Artist unknown*

Officer and Sergeant of The Royals *c* 1909. *Artist: T. Ivester
Lloyd*

'Son of the Empire'. *Artist: W. Frank Calderon*

2nd Lieutenant John Spencer Dunville, VC, Ist the Royal Dragoons.
The *London Gazette* announced his posthumous award of the Victoria
Cross as being "for most conspicuous bravery. When in charge of
a party consisting of scouts and Royal Engineers engaged in the
demolition of the enemy's wire this officer displayed great gallantry
and disregard for all danger". *Portrait: William Carter*

cars with the greatest glee. But that was not necessarily so. Brigadier Arthur Douglas-Nugent, formerly of the 17th/21st Lancers, which was until the 1960s a dyed-in-the-wool tank regiment, looks back to those days with some regret:

"In the 15 years following the Second World War the Royal Armoured Corps was divided between armoured and armoured car regiments. Each had developed their own special skills in battle and these had been passed on to a younger generation who benefited from the command and guidance of those who had been through it all. The tank soldier was more stolid, less flamboyant, more used to company around him than his armoured car opposite number, who had agility and flexibility of mind; was often used to operating over long distances out of radio contact with his immediate superior; but who had the ability and determination to get through when it really mattered. There was more to all this than sheer professional skill. Each knew his job as well as the other and each had a different mental approach to it.

"All this residual skill and experience was squandered almost over-

The Royals' first Centurions at Tidworth. *Army PR*

night by the Royal Armoured Corps when it was decided, at the end of the 1950s, to rerole. Vast sums and effort were wasted in retraining on different radio equipments (HF and VHF); different guns (76 mm and 105 mm); different vehicles (Centurion, Chieftain or Conqueror to Saladin, Saracen, etc); and different tactics. After the initial training was completed, many officers and NCOs (who provided the key to all this) left, and often returned from extra-regimental employment without residual knowledge. (I, for example, was forced to put a sergeant as troop leader of a Scorpion reconnaissance troop, a man who had only served in tanks. Needless to say he was hopeless.) Just when the Regiment had gained knowledge of the role, it was all change again. All this was done for the sake of giving regiments a chance to serve out of BAOR, which they did for 10 years subsequent to 1980 without any bad effects. Quite the contrary . . ."[2]

Lieutenant Colonel R. E. (now General Sir Richard) Worsley[3] who, in 1963, took over from Lieutenant Colonel Timbrell as Commanding Officer of the Royals, does not agree. He argues, as perhaps the majority of senior officers have done since, that it would have been wrong for the Royal Armoured Corps to have remained divided into two camps, each as specialist arms, and particularly unfortunate for armoured car personnel to be denied the experience of operating in a brigade (all arms) battle group, the army's prime fighting force.

Lieutenant Colonel Worsley's elevation to command of the Regiment came about like this. Lieutenant Colonel Timbrell's tenure was shortened by his being required in the post of Head of the British Mission in Saudi Arabia, and there was no officer within the Royals eligible to succeed him. Looking outside the Regiment, Brigadier Pepys, as Colonel, selected Lieutenant Colonel Worsley, a top calibre Rifle Brigade man, who was then the senior staff officer (GSOI) on the headquarters of 3 Division, the Strategic Reserve formation containing the Royals. The first inkling Colonel Worsley had of this change of direction was when Colonel Timbrell visited him in his office at Bulford saying "our Colonel would like to have a talk with you". From the moment he took command Colonel Worsley entirely and irrevocably rejected his old regimental identity and has remained a faithful Royal ever since. Colonel John Evans, who was one of his squadron leaders and subsequently his Second-in-Command, writes:

"The appointment of Dick Worsley heralded a successful period in the history of the Regiment, as Dick was extremely able and tough, but also charming . . . It was not an easy job to come to command a proud cavalry regiment with little experience of armour or reconnaissance tasks. He did it all with the greatest skill and tact, notwithstanding several major interruptions to what should have been a quiet period dedicated to conversion to tanks. We were immediately made aware that his loyalty to his new Regiment was absolute and that it was his aim to see us become an armoured regiment of the highest standard before we had to go to BAOR. His handling of his squadron leaders at this delicate time was sure: he let them have their heads but was always there with the right message and advice when needed. In exchange he readily admitted his lack of experience of armoured affairs and of our regimental history and traditions and relied on us to guide him when necessary. In the matter of the administration and organization of the Regiment he needed no advice . . . Officer and NCO career planning, recruiting and training programmes were overhauled and put into action very rapidly. One characteristic of Dick Worsley, which was of enormous benefit to us, was that he seemed to know almost every general in the army and we never lacked for help during the whole two years I served with him. One of his first tasks was to see us through the Tercentenary events, in particular taking up our Right as Freemen of the City of London. He masterminded the dismounted parade and the ball in the Mansion House that followed."[4]

It was on 22 October, 1963, that the Regiment exercised their privilege of marching through the City, with 270 officers and men. Having been inspected by Brigadier Pepys at Armoury House, they were led, with "Guidon flying, drums beating and bayonets fixed" and with their squadrons in files of six, by Lieutenant Colonel Worsley and the adjutant, Major D. S. A. Boyd (both mounted), to the City boundary. There they were challenged by the City Marshal (also mounted), who escorted them past the Mansion House, where the Lord Mayor took their salute at noon. ("Like everyone else," a "B" Squadron officer commented, "we enjoyed our march through the City and felt very proud of ourselves. And, to be honest, the practice parades were quite fun; but thank goodness there is a Brigade of

Guards!"[5]) The officers' Tercentenary ball was staged that evening, with Queen Elizabeth the Queen Mother as the principal guest. Albeit delayed two years by dint of their Asian service, it took place, most appropriately, around the time of the Royals' El Alamein celebrations. The sergeants put on their Tercentenary ball at Tidworth a couple of months later.

Returning to the spring of that year and the Regiment's *raison d'être*, the Royals had sufficient tank crews trained in one trade to allow the whole Regiment to shoot at Lulworth before Easter, and by mid-June nearly all the crews possessed two trades. In June and July "B" and "C" Squadrons trained closely with their affiliated infantry battalions, and, said *The Eagle* editorial, "despite the initial disappointments of the change in role, the Regiment has thrown itself wholeheartedly into conversion and is enjoying the change greatly"[6].

Showing the Flag, Cyprus OP, 1964. (*Left to right*) Corporal Best, Lance Corporal Kennedy and Trooper Bloomfield. *Army PR*

January, 1964, found the Royals training on the Plain, when, out of the blue, General Carver's 3 Division was required to reinforce the army in Cyprus; "C" Squadron (Major Evans), along with the Regiment's reconnaissance troop and other elements, arrived at Akrotiri on February 4. They were there to fulfil much the same task as The Blues had undertaken in 1960. The situation, however, had deteriorated sharply. It was clear that the two-nation state, as established under the London-Zurich agreement, was not functioning as envisaged. The Turkish minority feared that its position was being undermined, while the Greeks asserted that the substantial Turkish participation in the administration was unworkable. When Makarios threatened to abrogate the 1959 agreement violent fighting broke out between the two communities. "C" Squadron, having just converted to tanks, found themselves with Ferrets again.

They adopted the vehicles of, among others, the Guards Parachute Company, producing "five recce troops, each of two Ferrets and two Land Rovers. It may take a year to convert to tanks," they added wryly, "but it only took two days in Cyprus to re-convert to our old friends".[7] They provided routine patrols and road bocks and they removed Cypriot road blocks and fortifications. "We have practised first aid on all and sundry. We have been spat at, and have returned the compliment accurately: (well done, Trooper Wilson!) ... We have organized removal of the injured and burial of the dead. But, most difficult of all, we have had to sit and watch the fighting, sometimes at very close quarters, unable to do anything but report; there is no point in starting a three-cornered fight throughout the island."[8]

"A" Squadron (Major Bradish-Ellames) was hard on the heels of "C" in the third week of the month, moving into Slim Barracks, Dhekelia, and after a few days spent patrolling in the Larnaca area, joining them in the Western zone, at Ktima, where they built themselves Waterloo Camp. "It was not long before we had our first blooding," they recorded. "On 3 March the Squadron Leader and half of fifth Troop under Sergeant Matthew

were rushed to stop fighting between two villages up-country. This was quickly accomplished, but for the next four days two troops and a section of Gunners had to remain in the area to keep the peace by occupying the hill between them. On 6 March Sgts Wood and Cameron, who had temporarily relieved Lt Roberts an hour before, were successful in stopping fighting at a village near Polis. They earned a special commendation for their skilful and quick action from the CO of 26 RA.

"On 7 March heavy fighting broke out in Ktima with a Turkish spoiling attack. First and Third troops and an ad hoc Troop of Squadron Leader, SSM, SQMS and Sgt Cameron, were quickly in the town manoeuvring between both sides, and later when a cease-fire came, assisted in the evacuation of casualties and trapped civilians in the town centre. An uneasy truce followed, until the Sunday evening, with constant patrolling in the town by three troops. With the announcement of a hostage exchange that evening tension eased . . . Monday morning saw the start of a major Greek attack at first light, using rocket launchers, mortars, grenades, as well as armoured bulldozers. Third and Fifth troops, who were so rudely interrupted at breakfast in the town, were quickly joined by First Troop, but by 0630 hours no further movements into or out of the town were possible owing to road blocks, and this state of affairs continued until Thursday evening. 2Lt Casey was fired at, breaking through a road block at 0630, and had two tyres punctured. The three troops in the town had a thoroughly unpleasant day motoring between both sides with buildings disintegrating . . . For the first hour they were allowed to slow up the tempo of the fighting by getting in the way and in particular by blocking the armoured bulldozers. This they did extremely successfully, and at 0720 hours L/Cpl Kennedy was forced to fire at a bulldozer that refused to stop and came very close to him, firing over his head. It retreated hastily".[9]

In March the Cyprus problem became essentially one for the United Nations, which meant the sky-blue beret for the Royals. The following month "A" handed over to a squadron of The Life Guards and "C" to a Swedish battalion. "Not a man in either squadron would have missed those three months . . . Instances of provocation, frustration, horror, danger and excitement were felt by most of them . . . It is a period of soldiering," said *The Eagle* editorial, "they will not forget".[10] They returned from the island in April, allowing some seven months for the completion of their conversion to tanks, before "C" went to be demonstration squadron at the School of Infantry. The Regiment spent almost the whole of August on Salisbury Plain. Although National

174

Service had ended, soldiers were mostly serving on short engagements and there was still a steady turnover of recruits. So, particularly during the winter, there was much trade training to be done.

Major Evans, commanding "C", writes, "We had the good fortune to be sent as the demonstration squadron to Warminster for three months. This was the perfect way to end conversion and bring ourselves up to operational effectiveness before we went to join 20th Armoured Brigade at Detmold in the spring of 1965".[11]

The Royals took over from the Queen's Own Hussars in Germany in February. Major Evans, now Second-in-Command, recalls that

"Brigadier Dick Ward was a very hard taskmaster at 20 Brigade and put us on probation for the first month or two until he was sure we were up to the standard he insisted upon. No one was under greater pressure than Colonel Dick Worsley, because of his lack of armoured experience; but the Regiment responded by giving of their best. I remember the day that Brigadier Ward relaxed his tight rein for the first time, coming to see the Regiment undergoing squadron training at Soltau when we were testing every troop round a course of problems in turn. From that moment we were made to know we were part of the brigade."[12]

The Royals' annual Rhine Army programme for the next four years would be, fundamentally, one of troop training at Soltau and firing their tank weapons at Hohne, followed by regimental training and autumn formation exercises. At this peak time of the cold war the Army was resolute in its determination to be ready for battle at any given moment. Regiments were, of course, dependent on a steady flow of recruits and General Worsley recalls that none was in a better position than the Royals.

Being always well up to strength he was able to have sporting teams in training, sometimes for months on end, while formation commanders and staff officers frequently expressed astonishment at finding, almost wherever they went, members of the Royals on extra-regimental employment.[13] This was owing to the laudable efforts of the former Quartermaster, Major "Spud" Lewis, and his recruiting team, who, said *The Eagle*, "once again placed the Regiment top of the recruiting league in the Royal Armoured

Lieutenant Colonel R. E. Worsley dispensing beer in the troopers'
dining hall on Christmas Day 1964

The WOs' and Sergeants' Mess, Tidworth, 1964. Dining out RSM and Mrs Bradley.
The camera shows former Quartermaster Major C. W. J. Lewis to the left of Mrs
Bradley

Corps in 1964. With a cap badge strength of 588 all ranks, the Regiment is in a most enviable position . . . This achievement is a most remarkable one, stemming from August, 1961, when the Regiment was able to organize recruiting properly and to form a home headquarters . . . To Spud and his organization, therefore, we send our sincere thanks."[14] The young officer situation was also most favourable. General Worsley remembers the last batch of National Service subalterns all "signing on", either on short service commissions or as regulars. And Brigadier Pepys was celebrated for his very conscientious and successful officer recruiting. In October, 1964, Colonel Tony retired as Colonel of the Royals after ten illustrious years in the post, his successor being the present Colonel of The Blues and Royals, (then) Major-General Desmond Fitzpatrick, Chief of Staff, BAOR.

One highlight of the summer of 1965 was the Rhine Army parade for the Queen on 26 May, the largest-ever of its kind, the Royals being strongly represented in 20th Armoured Brigade among the 900 men and their armoured vehicles drawn up for inspection in the second (mounted) parade on Sennelager training area, the first parade having been for the infantry. But that caused a serious interruption: "The Queen's parade had eaten into our training time; and, as a result, we had to load [on to transporters] and move to Soltau the same evening".[15] The other principal red-letter days were those for the celebrations of the 150th anniversary of the Battle of Waterloo. The Royals were duly represented at the dinner given by the Army Board at the Banqueting Hall and the ceremony following it on Horse Guards Parade; the officers mess replica of the Waterloo Eagle was loaned for the Embassy exhibition in Brussels, and the Regiment found a detachment of fifty-five for the memorial service at Hougoumont farm. A group of officers attended, too, the party given by the British military attaché in Brussels. But, noted one of them, "the French attaché excused himself on the grounds that he could not understand why we were celebrating Waterloo. And he regretted he would be away rehearsing for 1966, the 900th anniversary of the Battle of Hastings."[16]

Lieutenant Colonel Worsley handed over to Lieutenant Colonel P. D. Reid[17] at the end of the year. And so the Royals

Lord Mayor's Show, 14 November 1964. Having received the Freedom of the City of London in 1963, the Royals were invited to take part, on this occasion, with two officers and 50 other ranks. They were from "A" Squadron. *The Central Press Photos*

Sergeant (later Corporal Major) Cox and (*right*) Lieutenant (later Captain) J. F. Mackie after their troop won the regimental inter-troop battle run at Hohne in 1966

trained on into 1966 and 1967 at the same tempo of activity. Major General Reid looks back nostalgically on mid-summer, 1966:

"Training took place at Larzac in the Aveyron region of the south of France. The whole Regiment moved south over a period of a week, the tanks and other 'A' vehicles going by rail flat and the wheels by road convoy to a French army training camp on the high plateau. We had a company of the 1st Bn Grenadier Guards with us and, on occasion, a company of the 1st Parachute Regiment of France. Training in the sunshine of the South of France was a paradise compared with the endless Soltau and Hohne training areas we had known before, and no doubt the good local red wine helped things along! Unfortunately our three and a half weeks were over all too soon and we had to pack up and wend our way home. Altogether we had been away from Detmold for six sunny and successful weeks."[18]

Meanwhile the Chieftain tank replaced the Centurion. "Jam today!" "C" Squadron rejoiced at the end of 1967. "The Regiment's first three Chieftains have arrived and are stabled in "C" Squadron's fitters' hangar. No sooner had UEI [the Unit Equipment Inspection] finished than we sent three drivers and three gunners under Corporal Dixon down to the 17th/21st Lancers to learn about the new beast."[19]

Here is Major General Reid on the subject:

"We were the third regiment to be converted, and conversion to the new tank was a slow deliberate business with officers and NCOs being sent on courses well ahead of the conversion date and then beginning the conversion one squadron at a time. We first received a few training tanks, and then tanks arrived at two-monthly intervals in squadron batches; a big administrative and training effort was needed from all concerned. Apart from having a diesel engine, probably the greatest change was in the turret, a new 120 mm gun, new fire control and gun control systems and, an innovation, a ranging machine-gun. Also the ergonomics of the tank were a great improvement on the Centurion. Operationally the most significant difference, other than the lethality of the gun, was the much shortened tactical redeployment time over a few miles compared with the Centurion."[20]

The Royals ski-ed, raced, boxed and played football and polo with honour and were more certain than ever that they were second to none and would remain so. However, "1967 is seeing some pretty drastic surgery on the body of the British Army," said *The Eagle* editorial rather uneasily,

"from which neither BAOR nor the Royal Armoured Corps has escaped intact. The blade-work is being effected under all sorts of headings: phased withdrawals (a one-way ticket to Blighty?): restructuring (a chance to join industry's assaults on the markets of the world?), and cost-effectiveness studies. But whatever the heading, limbs of the khaki corporation have been dropping off all around us, sadly not excluding regimental friends of very long standing.

"Happily the Regiment has come through so far unscathed, the 1st Dragoons as always: long may we remain. Regrettably there exists no long-term all-risks insurance policy against involvement in reductions, but surely the best policy, to which we must subscribe, is professional eminence? What of Tangier, Balaclava and Waterloo, or Ypres and the Somme, or Alamein, Sicily and Normandy? None of these past successes puts any weight in today's balance; battle honours just aren't negotiable currency".[21]

That was an ominous comment. On 3 November the officers were greeted at the regimental dinner by Colonel Desmond with the momentous news of the forthcoming amalgamation.

NOTES AND REFERENCES

1. *The Eagle*, November, 1963
2. In a letter from Brigadier Douglas-Nugent
3. General Sir Richard Worsley, GCB, KCB, OBE 2 Lieut, Rifle Bde, 1942; Comd Royals 1962–65; Comd 7 Armd Bde, 1965–67; GOC 1 (Br) Corps, 1976–78; Quartermaster General, 1979–82
4. In a letter from Colonel Evans
5. *The Eagle*, July, 1964
6. Ibid, November, 1963
7. Ibid, July, 1964
8. Ibid
9. Ibid
10. Ibid, December, 1965
11. In a letter from Colonel Evans
12. Ibid
13. General Sir R. Worsley in an interview
14. *The Eagle*, December, 1965
15. Ibid
16. Ibid
17. Major General P. D. Reid, CB. Lieut, Coldstream Guards, 1945; transferred Royals, 1947; comd Royals, 1965–68; Director Royal Armoured Corps, 1975–78; Director armoured warfare studies, 1981
18. In a letter from Major General Reid
19. *The Eagle*, September, 1967
20. In a letter from Major General Reid
21. *The Eagle*, September, 1967

1st ROYAL DRAGOONS

January 1965

Commanding Officer: Lieutenant Colonel R. E. Worsley OBE
2 i/c: Major J. B. Evans
Adjutant: Captain P. W. F. Arkwright
Signals Officer: Captain J. M. Loyd
Intelligence Officer: Lieutenant D. H. Spencer
RSM: WOI J. Clark
Chief Clerk: Staff Sergeant Muir

A Squadron
Sqn Ldr: Major W. R. Wilson FitzGerald
2 i/c: Lieutenant D. G. Hanmer
SSM: WOII Crabb

B Squadron
Sqn Ldr: Major M. B. Noble
2 i/c: Captain A. E. Woodward
SSM: WOII Warren

C Squadron
Sqn Ldr: Major D. J. S. Wilkinson
2 i/c: Captain J. G. Hamilton-Russell
SSM: WOII Simpson

HQ Squadron
Sqn Ldr: Major S. E. M. Bradish-Ellames
2 i/c: Captain T. P. Hart-Dyke
Tech Quartermaster: Captain (QM) W. G. Baker
Quartermaster: Captain (QM) A. S. Ayrton
TQMS: WOII Titmarsh
RQMS: WOII Leech
SSM: WOII Paul

Band
Bandmaster: WOI G. E. Evans

Chapter X

THE BLUES AT HERFORD

(1962–1967)

More than a decade had elapsed since the Royal Horse Guards were last in Germany when, in the autumn of 1962, it was their turn to serve there again. Airportability was to be left behind for three years. They were to be once more a conventional armoured reconnaissance regiment. So, while the 1st Dragoons were sailing home from Malaya The Blues advance party flew to Gütersloh airport, and thence to a one-time home of the Royals, Harewood Barracks, in the old Wehrmacht garrison town of Herford, Westphalia, where they set about taking over from The Life Guards at the start of what would prove to be the second coldest winter since the war. As for the autumn it was one of the bitterest in the history of the Cold War. It was the moment in which President Kennedy set up his naval blockade of Cuba, in reply to the Soviet missile sites on the island; and the atmosphere in Rhine Army was extremely tense until Khrushchev announced that the bases would be dismantled and returned to Russia. History does not relate how close the Royal Horse Guards were to being dispatched to their battle stations.

The Blues were one of three armoured car regiments – the others being the Queen's Dragoon Guards and the 15th/19th Hussars – under command of CRAC (Commander Royal Armoured Corps), who was at that time the former Silver Stick, Household Cavalry, Brigadier Marquess Douro. Their role, in the event of physical Russian aggression in Europe, would be to provide a covering force from the moment the Soviet armies crossed the inter-zonal frontier until those forces reached the main defensive positions of 1 (British) Corps along the River Weser. Since the threat of a Russian invasion seemed quite a

The Blues on the retreat from Mons. *Artist: Lady Butler (by kind permission of the Royal Hospital, Chelsea)*

The Royal Horse Guards (The Blues), 1661–1945. *Artist: Ernest Ibbetson*

Blues Musical Ride, Olympia, 1933. *Artist: Gilbert Holiday*

reality in those early 1960s, the NATO armies were in a state of fair readiness, as the preceding chapter has indicated. On receipt of the codeword "Quick Train" The Blues had just two hours' grace, at any time of the day or night, to man their vehicles, load up and "bomb up" as for war, and to be out of the barrack gate on the way to their battle locations.

The Regiment also had the task of patrolling the interzonal border. But that demarcation line showed a very different image from the one older Blues had known ten years and more before. The former single barbed-wire fence had, owing to the increasing numbers of East Germans who were endeavouring to escape to the West, been replaced by an almost impassable barrier, festooned with anti-personnel mines and booby traps, a barrier regularly punctuated with watchtowers holding armed guards with searchlights who were ready to gun down any compatriot making a bid for freedom, while sentries leading Alsatians were vigilant in the intervening stretches of the Iron Curtain. This *cordon sanitaire* was so broad that a great many East German villages were deserted.

The task of those regular Blues patrols was to observe and to

Major-General Sir Richard Howard-Vyse, KCMG, DSO, Colonel of The Blues and Gold Stick, 1951–63. *Lafayette*

report anything suspicious or of military significance. On a great many occasions, between 1963 and 1966, the Regiment was given other frequent reminders of the sinister East-West situation; that was in providing escorts and guards for nuclear weapons and launching sites. Notwithstanding this fragile state of peace General Yakuborskii, the Commander-in-Chief of the Eastern Zone, visited BAOR in the early summer of 1964 when a guard of honour from the Regiment was found to greet him, under the command of Captain Lord Patrick Beresford.

Despite the pressures of cold war soldiering, like all good cavaliers they took their fun where they found it. Adventure training was high on the Rhine Army agenda and, soon after arrival, The Blues sent parties to the Italian Alps and to Holland, with inter-squadron climbing, map reading, treasure hunting and endurance tests. A high proportion of the Regiment went skiing most weekends in the Harz Mountains; elsewhere, where the

Lieutenant J. D. Smith-Bingham, Royal Horse Guards, competing at Badminton, 1962. His horse, By Golly, which was in training for the Olympics in 1960 and 1964, came second in the Burghley Horse Trials in 1961 and second at Badminton in 1964. Horse and rider were three times winners at the Army Horse Trials at Tidworth

The Russian C-in-C, General Yakuborskii, inspecting a Blues guard of honour at Bielefeld, 1963. The guard commander (*left*) is Captain Lord Patrick Beresford. *Army PR*

snow lay thick, Captains Carey and Lord Chetwode became ski champions again, this time in the 4 Division contests. Cornet Van Cutsem started a craze for go-karting in the barracks; the Regiment won the 1963 Rhine Army pentathlon; and, although they were only second in that five-pronged event in 1964 they found the individual champion once more – Trooper Drummond. To mention just one other of their many games successes, in the winter of 1964 Lieutenant Smith-Bingham carried off the BAOR squash plate. Nor was evening entertainment neglected in the barracks. Weekly smokers and sing-songs took place in the attics and cellars of squadron blocks which had been converted into canteens and bars.

On arrival at Herford the Regiment took over 14 Household Cavalry horses from The Life Guards; and The Blues' riding team, with Corporal of Horse Johnson as manager, excelled wherever they went. These horses also enabled members of the Regiment to follow one or two of the local drag hunts, whose activity entails galloping across 40 or 50 hunt jumps in pursuit of a scarlet-coated man with a fox's brush fixed to his shoulder, and is carried out in an atmosphere of intense horn-blowing, garlanding, schnapps drinking and excited sportsmanship. Meanwhile, in 1963, Lieutenant Lord Fermoy flew home to ride his new horse, Baxier, in the Grand Military and won it by one-and-a-half lengths,[1] with Captain Lord Patrick Beresford third on Captain Parker Bowles's Shavings.

The Blues Gold Stick, Major General Sir Richard Howard-Vyse, who had been their beloved Colonel "Wombat" since 1951, died at the end of 1962. "We mourn the passing of a really true and great Blue who will be remembered with much affection and respect by us all for many years to come",[2] wrote his

Carol singing at Herford. The NCO in charge (*right*) is Corporal of Horse Cowdery. *Army PR*

regimental obituarist. It is significant that Colonel Wombat's seven successive predecessors were Field Marshals, and fitting, too, that his own successor should be greatest of all post-war soldiers, and one who would prove to be a most capable, dedicated and equally cherished Colonel, Field Marshal Sir Gerald Templer, famous nationally as "the Tiger of Malaya". Sir Gerald (soon to be a Knight of the Garter and Constable of the Tower of London) paid his initial visit to the Regiment in Germany in July, 1963.

That was the year, too, of the first issue of the new regimental magazine *The Blue*, published under the editorship of the signals officer, Captain W. N. H. Legge-Bourke. Writing the foreword Sir Gerald stated that "as my famous predecessor so often said, the Regiment has always been known for its friendliness and for its family feeling. Long may these qualities continue."

His first task as Gold Stick was to be in attendance on the Queen, with Field Marshal Lord Harding, Colonel of The Life Guards, at the 1963 presentation of new Standards to the Household Cavalry on Horse Guards Parade, the ceremony which occurs regularly once every ten years. "We present our humble duty to Your Majesty as our Sovereign and Colonel-in-Chief," said the Silver Stick, Colonel the Hon Julian Berry, commanding the parade, "and we are indeed proud to carry these Standards, which are the symbols of the trust which Your Majesty has placed in us." Then the Squadrons returned to their barracks, the Mounted Squadrons to Hyde Park and the representative Blues armoured car squadron to Herford, Westphalia.

The Regimental Standard, at home in the office of the Commanding Officer at Harewood barracks, was to be carried at some epic Continental ceremonies in 1965. The first of those was when the Queen inspected the massive Rhine Army parades (mentioned in the context of the Royals in the last chapter). The Blues provided Her Majesty with an escort of two troops, this being the first occasion, outside the British Isles, of an armoured car Sovereign's escort. It was commanded by Major T. N. P. W. Burbury, with the Standard carried in the Saladin command car by Squadron Quartermaster Corporal Swann. The other Continental event, also, as we have seen, shared with the Royals, took place on 18 June at Hougomont Farm in Belgium. It was the drumhead service for the 150th Waterloo anniversary. The Standard was then carried by Squadron Corporal Major Kitney. He had been a pioneer Household Cavalry volunteer for the Guards Parachute Company ten years before, and was a veteran of the Cyprus and Suez campaigns. A further item of Belgian ceremonial for the service Regiment was the provision, in 1966, of a staircase party, under command of Cornet Viscount Somerton, at the British Embassy, on the occasion of the Queen's State Visit.

A diverting interlude in those stirring Rhine Army days of the 1960s was the week spent in Denmark with the Jutland Dragoons. Typical of autumn training excursions, was the one, in 1964, devoted to manoeuvres with the other two armoured car regiments in the American zone with the 14th US Armoured Cavalry as enemy, in exercise "Lundy's Lane" (named after the bloody battleground near Niagara during the Anglo-American war in 1812–14.) The CRAC relieving Lord Douro was Brigadier Mat Abraham, whom the Regiment had known in Cyprus when he commanded the 12th Lancers, on taking over from The Blues there in 1959. Early in 1965 he set the new Commanding Officer, Lieutenant Colonel Roy Redgrave, the task of staging a one-day tactics study period, the gymnasium floor at Harewood barracks being converted to represent 30 square miles of Germany. The TEWT was attended by key personnel, down to troop sergeant level, from the 4th/7th Dragoon Guards and the Queen's Royal Irish Hussars, as well as The Blues. Regular reappraisal of the situation of that kind rendered tactics training constantly refreshing for all ranks.

In April, 1966, the Regiment sent three troops home to Windsor, under command of Major J. A. C. G. Eyre with Corporal-Major Tolometti as the SCM. This detachment, which was to proceed to Malaysia with The Life Guards, was subsequently increased to a full squadron, all keen volunteers; and, like the Royals three or four years before, they were to be based, initially, in Singapore (in their case, in Nee Soon Barracks) as part of the internal security and counter-insurgency contingency. Early in 1967 they were reporting that "We have trained in vehicles and on foot in the very congested area of Singapore island, in the relatively straightforward country in Malaya covered by rubber

The new Colonel of The
Blues, Field Marshal Sir
Gerald Templer, riding on
his first Queen's Birthday
Parade as Gold Stick, in
1963, alongside his fellow
Blue, the Duke of Beaufort,
Master of the Horse

On manoeuvres in Westphalia, 1965. The adjutant, Captain A. H. G.
Broughton, in dialogue with (right) the Commanding Officer,
Lieutenant Colonel R. M. F. Redgrave MC

plantations and paddy fields and in jungle. A substantial proportion of the Squadron has become fully trained in airportability and a similar part will have experience of amphibious warfare, including beach landing. Finally we have worked more closely with helicopters than we have been able to in the past, and have learned what an invaluable asset they are".[3]

Back in Germany, in the summer of 1966, the remainder of the Regiment prepared to return to Windsor. The Household Cavalry's long association with their affiliated Yeomanry, the Inns of Court, was about to end, pending that Regiment's disbandment in the reorganization of the Territorial Army. And, in June, The Blues, completing their final zonal border patrol, were joined by some eighteen yeoman enjoying their last fortnight's attachment. The following month the advance party of the 4th Royal Tank Regiment arrived at Herford to take over. It was commanded by an officer soon to be well known to The Blues and Royals, Major Richard Vickers.

The Royal Horse Guards, as such, said farewell to Rhine Army for the last time in August, to return, as they put it, "to a very different Combermere from the one we had left behind. The new barracks is very well designed and a wonderful change from the grimness of Herford's Harewood Barracks. The Life Guards had left the Guards Parachute Company as sole occupants; and the latter, commanded by Major Sir Nicholas Nuttall [Royal Horse Guards] could not have been more welcoming and helpful."[4] Anyhow they were back to being an airportable regiment within the Strategic Reserve, and it was not long before they returned to the Plain. Meanwhile the Household Cavalry Depot had, earlier in 1966, moved to Pirbright as the Household Cavalry Training Squadron, an integral part of the Guards Depot.

1964 and 1965 were highlight years in the annals of the Mounted Squadron. It was in 1964 that sanction was given for a new home on the old site. Living conditions in the Victorian Hyde Park buildings were insanitary, uncomfortable and bleak. To name just three of the old accommodation's drawbacks: the barracks had been built without a troopers' mess hall; the draughty troop rooms were more dependent for warmth upon the stables below them than upon their tiny coal grates; and the married quarters were so primitive that, since they were abandoned, most families had to be quartered far from central London, which often obliged married men having to leave home at 4.30 in the morning to be on parade at 6 o'clock.

A sympathetic House of Commons lobby resulted, that year, in a visit by the Secretary of State for War, Mr John Profumo. He was accompanied by a redoubtable member of the Labour Opposition, Miss Jenny Lee, who, having seen the evidence from end to end, made the historic comment that "the inmates of Wormwood Scrubs are better accommodated". Approval for a new barracks was duly "rubber-stamped". And early in September, 1965, the Household Cavalry Mounted Regiment rode out of Hyde Park Barracks with a long *au revoir*; and so to Birdcage Walk, beyond which temporary stables and a riding school had been erected for them on the side of the square at Wellington Barracks, whose ancient, but rather more amenable, accommodation would be their home for the next three years and more.

On patrol in Malaya, 1966. Lance Corporal White with (*right*) Trooper Oakley

In the first half of 1965 the Mounted Squadron fulfilled its role, among other ceremonial commitments, for the funeral of Sir Winston Churchill. Then, on 8 May, the Mayor, Aldermen and Burgesses of New Windsor conferred on the Household Cavalry the Freedom of the Borough, "in recognition of the long and close association between the Royal Borough and the Regiments, and of the Regiments' distinguished achievements in the cause of the Nation and the Commonwealth".[5] Unfortunately, owing to an outbreak of equine 'flu, there were no horses on parade. But a crowd of some 15,000 local enthusiasts revelled in the ceremony, which included impressive drill displays by the crews of two squadrons of Ferret scout cars, besides a detachment from Hyde Park Barracks in dismounted review order.

Erection of permanent horse-lines and other work being in progress at Stoney Castle Camp, Pirbright, in 1965, The Blues

The Mounted Squadron with a farewell gesture for their hosts, Lord and Lady Egremont and their daughter, Caroline, at the close of camp, Petworth Park, Sussex, 1966

Mounted Squadron carried out their annual weapon classification at Aldershot that summer, then rode south to Petworth Park, Sussex, at the Tillington village end of which they pitched camp and set up rope-and-post horse-lines, as the guests for five days of Lord and Lady Egremont. This camp was so popular that they applied to repeat it in 1966, on that occasion for ten days. For one exercise, involving horsemanship, mapreading and ingenuity, each troop produced four teams to ride to the beach at Clymping where competitors changed into bathing trunks and rode their horses out to sea. Bing Crosby, who was staying at Petworth House at the time, entertained the Squadron with a concert of such ditties as *Pennies from Heaven, White Christmas* and *Road to Morocco*, accompanied by Corporal of Horse Tribe on the mouth organ. The Tillington pub, which was much frequented by the cavaliers during both sojourns, was then renamed "The Horse Guards".

"1967 was a very eventful year." Thus Captain Legge-Bourke opened his 1968 editorial of *The Blue*. "A" Squadron went to Cyprus for six months; most of "B" squadron returned from Malaysia; and "C" went to Wales

"... stopping with the adjutant [Capt Legge-Bourke] at Crickhowell (his farm accounts now show a serious loss of milk and trout, thanks to their gluttony); and then carried out live firing and battle runs on Castlemartin ranges ... This left the barracks very empty, and, as usual this was the time when everyone wanted lots done. In the recruiting world we visited Middlesex, Dagenham, Liverpool and Guildford, and we lent our vehicles to practically every cavalry regiment for their recruiting teams to use ... They all came back plastered with weird slogans ... In July we practised packing ourselves into our vehicles in preparation for a quick move by air. Now that, at last, the RAF have enough aircraft to move us all there is nowhere to go ... After weeks of rumour, on 23 November the Colonel came down to announce our amalgamation ... to our old friends, the Royals ... Everyone realized we were very lucky to be having such splendid comrades. Both our-selves and the Household Brigade will be strengthened by this infusion ... Most of us are also reconciled to a change from armoured cars to tanks for a spell [in Germany, in 1969], particularly as we will have Chieftains. While one cannot use them to visit all the places one would wish, at least one travels in comfort, with unlimited kit, or so they say."

NOTES AND REFERENCES

1. This brought the Royals' and Blues' tally of wins in that race since the First World War to nine, the names being Lee Bridge, 1924 (Lieutenant R. Shaw RHG); Slieve Green, 1931 (Captain R. B. Moseley, Royals); Castletown, 1932 (Lieutenant Sir P. Grant-Lawson, Bt. RHG); Atom Bomb, 1953 (Major P. Fielden, Royals); Skatealong, 1955, (Major P. Fielden, Royals); Stalbridge Park, 1958 (Captain Sir N. Nuttall, Bt, RHG); Golden Drop, 1959 (Captain S. Bradish-Ellames, Royals, with Lieutenant N. Upton, 9th Lancers, as jockey); Stalbridge Park, 1961 (Captain Sir N. Nuttall, Bt, RHG); Baxier, 1963 (Lieutenant Lord Fermoy, RHG)
2. *The Household Brigade Magazine*, 1962–63
3. *The Blue*, 1967
4. Ibid
5. Ibid, 1966

RHG

January 1965

Commanding Officer: Lieutenant Colonel R. M. F. Redgrave, MC
2 i/c: Major J. N. P. Watson
Adjutant: Captain A. H. G. Broughton
RSO: Captain W. N. H. Legge-Bourke
IO: Captain J. D. Smith-Bingham
RCM: WOI W. Stringer
Chief Clerk: WOII Slade

A Squadron
Sqn Ldr: Major C. V. C. Booth-Jones
2 i/c: Captain D. V. Smiley
SCM: WOII Giles

B Squadron
Sqn Ldr: Major P. A. Lendrum
2 i/c: Captain J. W. N. Mitchell
SCM: WOII Godfrey-Cass

C Squadron
Sqn Ldr: Major T. N. P. W. Burbury
2 i/c: Captain Hon P. T. Conolly-Carew
SCM: WOII Ladds

HQ Squadron
Sqn Ldr: Major D. J. Daly
Medical Officer: Surgeon Major D. H. Matthews
Technical Quartermaster: Major (QM) C. J. Coles, MBE
Quartermaster: Captain (QM) F. Whennell
RQMC: WOII Cummings
TQMC: WOII Beadle
SCM: WOII Martin

Mounted Squadron
Sqn Ldr: Major Hon B. C. Wilson
2 i/c: Captain J. S. Crisp
SCM: WOII Kidman

Band
Director of Music: Captain E. W. Jeanes
Trumpet-Major: WOII Andrews

Chapter XI

AMALGAMATION

(1967–1969)

When the Government's intention of further defence cuts was announced in the mid-1960s – and they made clear that reductions in the number of tank and armoured car regiments would again be severe – three senior cavalry regiments, which had never previously suffered amalgamation, contemplated the future with considerable uneasiness. Those were one from the Household Cavalry, the Royal Horse Guards (The Blues), and two from the Royal Armoured Corps, the 1st the Royal Dragoons and the Royal Scots Greys (2nd Dragoons). All three were made quickly aware that they could not remain untouched. By early autumn General Sir Desmond Fitzpatrick, then Vice Chief of the General Staff, was informing the Royal's Commanding Officer, Lieutenant Colonel Peter Reid, that it was no longer a question of "if we are to be amalgamated, but when?" More urgently, the problem was "with whom?"

The Royals' first instinct was for a union with their sister regiment, the Second Dragoons, the Royal Scots Greys, with whom they shared a place in the old Union Brigade, and with whom indeed they had enjoyed the closest associations since the 18th century. But the Greys were substantially a Scottish regiment with a totally Scottish character, recruiting solely from Scotland, while the Royals, who were essentially English, envisaged their identity vanishing almost without trace in such a merger.[1] Nor at first did they look upon the prospect of absorption into the Household Cavalry with any great relish. They had not joined the army to serve time on mounted duty in London. On the other hand The Blues and the Royals had always been on the most friendly terms, and their Warrant Officers and NCOs had honorary membership of one anothers' messes. There was a

The Park entrance to the old Hyde Park Barracks. The Household Cavalry
Mounted Regiment was accommodated in Wellington Barracks from 1965 to
1970 when the new barracks was completed for their return to Knightsbridge

feeling of kindred spirit from top to bottom in the two Regiments. From the viewpoint of most of The Blues, the Royals was the next best regiment in the army; and, if they were to integrate with a cavalry regiment of the Line it seemed logical that it should be the oldest of them.

So The Blues had their eyes on the Royals almost from the first moment of being made aware that they must seek a "marriage partner". Considering it would not have been right, however, for a regiment of the Household Cavalry to solicit, The Blues' Gold Stick, Field Marshal Sir Gerald Templer, a master of diplomacy, began by suggesting to Major General Basil Eugster (commanding the Household Brigade) that he should sound out Colonel Desmond circumspectly. How would the Royals take it if they were told they were to become Household troops? "General

200

Eugster spoke in obscure terms," says Colonel Desmond; "I didn't know quite what he was getting at. But it was clear he was casting a fly".[2]

Be that as it may there was no doubt in Colonel Desmond's mind, by this time, that amalgamation with The Blues would be the right solution for his Regiment. He therefore sought an interview with Colonel Gerald, who greeted him at RHQ Household Cavalry with the words to the effect of "we have been expecting you". Colonel Desmond went back to his office where he told the Chief of the General staff that his Regiment was to be one with The Blues. "My superior looked up for a moment, simply said, 'Oh, good', then returned to his work," recalls Colonel Desmond. Higher command was concerned with more pressing matters!

It remained to decide upon such particulars as the name of the new Regiment, what "flags and banners" it should carry, how it should be dressed and accoutred, how the ranks should be named, and what music it should have. These points were hammered out during the ensuing months between the two Colonels, the Silver Stick, Colonel Harry Hopkinson, the commanding officer of The Blues, Lieutenant Colonel Mark Darley, and Lieutenant Colonel Peter Reid, commanding the Royals. Many favoured the title "The Horse Guards (The Blues and Royals)". But that suggestion was overturned in favour of "The Blues and Royals (Royal Horse Guards and 1st Dragoons)".[3] And the Queen duly approved.

Clearly the uniforms had to be, intrinsically, those of the Household Cavalry – of The Blues – but a host of compromises were made, among them that the Royals' "Eagle" was to be worn on every order of tunic, and placed in the regimental crest. Mess kit was to be, in essence, that of the Royals;[4] the Royals' Guidon was to be added to The Blues' Standards, and all battle honours to be incorporated; officers' chargers were to wear the Royals' black beards on their bridles; and the Royals' black cloth, (carried in memory of Second Lieutenant John Spencer Dunville VC) was to be worn beneath officers' badges of rank. Warrant Officers' and NCOs' styles of rank were to be those of The Blues. Colonel Gerald would be Colonel of the new regiment, with Colonel

Desmond as Deputy Colonel. Amalgamation would take place in Germany in the spring of 1969.[5] "Gerald Templer was absolutely marvellous throughout," adds Colonel Desmond.

Major General Eugster paid the Royals a visit at Detmold in December, 1967, to find out for himself whether the proposed absorption of this particular Line regiment into the Household Division would present any problems, and returned entirely satisfied.[6]

Before these historic events had even germinated Colonel Reid's successor in command of the Royals had been named. Once again the Regiment had not been able to find an eligible candidate. From a shortlist of four outstandingly able officers of the Royal Armoured Corps, who were blocked for promotion within their own regiments, Colonel Desmond selected Lieutenant Colonel Richard Vickers, Royal Tank Regiment, who was then an instructor at the Staff College.[7] Colonel Vickers assumed command of the Royals at Detmold in July, 1968. Soon after news of the amalgamation was broadcast it was decided that he should go on, too, to command the new Regiment.

The choice was in every way auspicious. For no one in the

Royals Centurions with guns dipped for their drive past on the occasion of the Queen's review at Sennelager, 1965. *Soldier Magazine*

army knew better than this officer how to weld together a newly formed Chieftain regiment. Moreover, as an Equerry to the Queen for three years during the 1950s, Colonel Vickers had seen a good deal of the Household Brigade and he already knew The Blues from commanding the 4th Royal Tank Regiment's advance party when they took over at Herford in 1966, not to mention having had a good deal of contact with their sporting teams. But, perhaps the first reason why Colonel Vickers was the ideal choice was because, having belonged to neither Regiment prior to 1968, he could be relied upon to be impartial, to bring the strands together without favour. He accepted the additional challenge with wholehearted enthusiasm, and a bare nine months were to pass before he changed his cap badge for a second time.

His Second-in-Command, Major Bradish-Ellames, by way of bowing the Royals, as such, out of the Army, organized an historical pageant, in which the band took centre stage, and old regimental photographs were projected onto a screen, and, at the end of which show the "Last Post" was played. "It was," says Colonel Vickers, "an extremely moving occasion". The Royals, owing to their exceptional recruiting efforts, being overstrength were obliged to bid farewell to a large number of old friends. The Blues, on the other hand, having manned only two small sabre squadrons in the airportability role, were below strength. However, the plan was that each Regiment should provide precisely equal numbers to the new Regiment, and that those should be integrated, on equal terms, not just to troop level, but down to tank crews, storemen and office personnel.

Meanwhile The Blues, who had known virtually no other fighting vehicles than the armoured car and the scout car, had to learn about the Chieftain tank. Having received a farewell visit from the Queen they proceeded to Perham Down, near Tidworth, for conversion training, early in October, 1968. They staged a last parade for Colonel Darley in February, 1969, and in the same month their advance party left for Detmold, the main body flying out in March.

Among the key appointments to be then filled by The Blues in the new Regiment was that of adjutant which went to Captain A.

H. Parker Bowles; Quartermaster to Captain W. A. Stringer; and Regimental Corporal Major to Mr Godfrey-Cass.

The new Regiment was formed on 29 March. The loyal address from Colonel Gerald to the Queen ran as follows: "On this day, which marks the formation of The Blues and Royals, a new regiment in Your Majesty's Household Cavalry, formed by the amalgamation of the Royal Horse Guards (The Blues) and The Royal Dragoons (1st Dragoons), we, the officers, warrant officers, non-commissioned officers and troopers of The Blues and Royals, offer our loyal greetings to your Majesty, our Colonel-in-Chief, assuring your Majesty that we shall continue to bear true allegiance and strive faithfully to uphold the honour and high example of the two ancient Regiments from which we are formed." The Queen replied: "I send my sincere thanks to all officers, warrant officers, non-commissioned officers and troopers of The Blues and Royals for their message of loyal greetings. In welcoming you all as members of the new Regiment, formed today by the amalgamation of the Royal Horse Guards and the Royal Dragoons, I know that you will be faithful to the history and traditions of these two famous regiments. United may you go forward with confidence for the future." Two days later [31 March] Colonel Gerald, accompanied by Colonel Desmond (who was now Commander-in-Chief Rhine Army), took the vesting parade. Having inspected the Regiment, Colonel Gerald greeted them with these words:

"Up till the day before yesterday, we were two proud and individual Regiments, each with three centuries of loyal and distinguished service to our Sovereign and to our country.

"We now enter in to another phase of our being ... The late Blues are immensely proud to wear the Eagle and the Dettingen black of the Royals. And I know the late Royals are equally proud to wear the embellishment of The Blues.

"It is indeed a privilege for us all to form part of the Household Troops, and that honour carries with it corresponding responsibilities, as you all well realize.

"I hope you noticed how I addressed you as 'Gentlemen – of the Blues and Royals'. That is an old fashioned form of address in the British

Army, which the officers and men of both our Regiments have always observed. Long may it continue.

"For me it is a great honour to have been appointed your Colonel and it is an especial satisfaction to me that, with the approval of Her Majesty, General Sir Desmond Fitzpatrick is the Deputy Colonel. Between us, I can assure you all, we will do our best for the well-being of the Regiment – as, I am quite aware, will all of you.

"I think it is significant that the day after tomorrow, at the Horse Guards in Whitehall, Her Majesty The Queen will inspect The Queen's Life Guard – the first time this has ever happened in the lifetime of any Sovereign – and that on that day the guard provided by the Regiment will consist both of former Blues and former Royals. I think you will agree – a great portent for the future.

Gunnery class, 1968. Her Majesty the Colonel-in-Chief talking to Lance Corporal Heathcote during a visit to The Blues at Combermere Barracks. The NCO on the end of the line is Corporal of Horse Hawley and the Gunnery Officer (*right*) is Lieutenant H. W. Davies. *Household Cavalry Museum, Windsor*

"I have not the slightest doubt that our new Regiment will not only maintain the traditions of the past, but will set the highest standard of loyalty and military efficiency in the future.

"Gentlemen of The Blues and Royals – it is up to us to achieve that, and I have no doubt that you, the serving members, will ensure it".[8]

Britain is, perhaps, the most tribal of Western nations. And there can be nothing more humanly tribal in the world than her regimental system. Regiments deliberately, if unconsciously, forge their own distinctive characters, their special personas by which their members are recognizable to others within the system; not only by their colours and insignia but often, too, by their very attitudes, mannerisms and bearing. This is a cult at the root of which is a determination to be the best, although the strivings are pursued and the goals achieved in a seemingly carefree manner, for buoyancy is an important outward and visible sign of high morale.

The older and prouder a regiment is the more jealous it is likely to be of its unique identity. And that is why, apart from the dual-role factor of the Household Cavalry, many doubted that the amalgamation of The Blues and the Royals would work well. But such were the underlying mutual strengths that the sceptics were quickly and decisively proved wrong.

This seems to be an appropriate moment in our story, therefore, to take stock, not only of the remarkable circumstances in which veteran Blues and veteran Royals now found themselves; but also of the transformation of both Regiments in the thirty years that had elapsed since the start of the Second World War signalled the demise of the warhorse. The secret and unique merit of the regimental system lies in pride and meaningful tradition and healthy rivalry. The character of a regiment is founded on officer unity. The cohesion formed, from the commanding officer down to the newest-joined subaltern, permeates and harmonizes the whole regiment.

Proud cavalry regiments form fraternities of officers enjoying similar backgrounds, ideals and interests. In the old pre-war cavalry the horse was perhaps the foremost unifying factor. Cavalry officers shared their leisure hours, for the most part, on the racecourse, in the hunting-field and on the polo ground. Many

Her Majesty inspecting the Queen's Life Guard (the first Blues and Royals Guard) the day following the amalgamation vesting parade, 1969. She is accompanied by the Officer of the Guard, Lieutenant the Earl of Normanton, and is followed by the Silver Stick, Colonel H. S. Hopkinson MBE and (*right*) the Gold Stick, Field Marshal Sir Gerald Templer

shared a love, too, of field sports other than hunting, and, for example, of sailing, skiing, flying and cricket. And while there was a great deal of "free time", a participation in all forms of sport was enthusiastically encouraged. It was important that young officers should suffer no financial embarrassment by the money their friends spent on their sport and their social lives. The pre-war days were still the days of low taxation and death duties. Until 1939 a Household Cavalry officer was required to show that, in addition to a capital sum to cover the cost of all his uniforms and a substantial civilian wardrobe, he could command a private income of at least £2,000 a year. That, in the 1930s, was a very large sum. And it should not be forgotten that The Blues served exclusively either in London or at Windsor.

Nor were officers of the Royal Dragoons provided with free uniforms, nor expected to live on their pay, far from it, notwithstanding the fact that they were at least as often abroad as at home. A high proportion of Blues officers, and many in the Royals too, often the sons of substantial landowners, joined the Regiment with no intention of serving for more than a few pleasant years, during which, having made lifelong friends, they returned to look after their family estates. Soldiering for them was, compared with today's tempo, a leisurely affair interspersed with much sport and other distractions, in a social life that was full of rigid convention and shibboleth.

The Second World War changed all that irrevocably. A pre-war horsed regiment had a complement of no more than twenty officers. An armoured car regiment required more than twice that number, and they had to be recruited very quickly. Many were, of course, from rather different backgrounds, and a number of those, in both Regiments, signed on as regulars. Then the war emergency commission became the National Service commission. Colonels were naturally anxious to obtain the type of young officers that they rubbed shoulders with when they were young officers, and, particularly considering the large scale of officer recruiting during the late 1940s and the 1950s, they succeeded remarkably well, calling, in the first place, on those with family connections. When conscription ended, at the end of the 1950s, both the Royals and The Blues strove to fill their

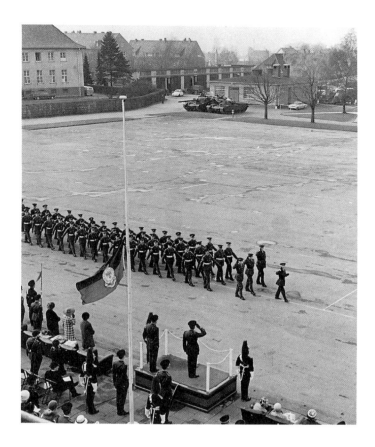

Detmold, 31 March 1969. Field Marshal Sir Gerald Templer takes the Salute. *Soldier Magazine*

regimental places with the stamp of officer found in the old days.

By that time, however, cavalry officers had become more professional in the broader military (less essentially regimental) context; many were looking beyond the Regiment for a full career; large private incomes had become the exception rather than the rule, while the pay was now an incentive in itself; and the NCOs and men they commanded were of a higher educational standard than the previous generations, with obvious implications for the officers. Consequently, both The Blues and the Royals were casting their officer recruiting nets over a rather wide area to find the very best for modern times. Yet, judging by the large numbers of old regimental names that have continued to crop up on the rolls since the 1970s, it looks remarkably like a case of *plus ça change* ... that is to say that the officers of The Blues and Royals are, in essence, cast in the old mould.

Be all this as it may, in 1969 the new Regiment, which, like the dazzling young phoenix of Egyptian and Greek legend, rose triumphant from the noble ashes of its parent, could afford quite freely to pick and choose its members from top to bottom. And in no other regiment in the British Army, in 1969, could there ever have been a stronger feeling among all its members that theirs was the finest that had ever existed.

It is now time to witness the sequel to the genesis, to see how the promise was fulfilled.

NOTES AND REFERENCES

1. The Greys' amalgamation, which was delayed until July, 1971, was with the 3rd Carabiniers (Prince of Wales's Dragoon Guards), to form the Royal Scots Dragoon Guards (Greys and Carabiniers)
2. From a talk with General Sir D. Fitzpatrick
3. The title's abbreviation suffered a rather bizarre career. B/R was ruled out for its railway connotation. RHG1stD was therefore chosen. However, prior to amalgamation, that abbreviation, being misread by an orderly room clerk, the Regiment became known, quite illogically, as RHG/D. But the inscription on the regimental buttons followed the original instruction, RHG1stD.
4. The decision on mess kit was perhaps the most controversial compromise. The Blues thought it absurd that the tunic should be anything but their traditional "Oxford Blue"; but the Royals insistence on "the Queen's scarlet" won the day. The Warrant Officers and Corporals of Horse, led by Regimental Corporal Major Godfrey-Cass, favoured a scarlet jacket and blue waistcoat from the start.
5. The previously affiliated territorial units of both Regiments were also to come under the aegis of The Blues and Royals. Those were: the Royal Canadian Dragoons, The Canadian Governor-General's Horse Guards and "C" Squadron (Sharpshooters) the Royal Yeomanry Regt.
6. In a letter from Major General Reid
7. Lieutenant General Sir Richard Vickers, KCB, LVO, OBE. 2 Lt RTR, 1948: Equerry to HM The Queen, 1956–59; transferred Royals 1968; Comd Royals, 1968–69; Comd Blues and Royals, 1969; Dir-Gen Army Training, 1982–83; Comdt, RMA Sandhurst 1979–82.
8. From *The Blue and Royal*, 1970

RHG

1968

Commanding Officer: Lieutenant Colonel M. A. Q. Darley
2 i/c: Major Sir N. Nuttall Bt
Adjutant: Captain A. H. Parker Bowles
RSO: Captain Hon G. Lambert
RCM: WOI G. Martin
Chief Clerk: WOII Craig

A Squadron
Sqn Ldr: Major R. C. Rayner*
2 i/c: Captain D. V. Smiley
SCM: WOII Cowdrey

C Squadron
Sqn Ldr: Major B. H. F. Wright*
2 i/c: Captain J. R. W. Palmer
SCM: WOII Beynon

HQ Squadron
Sqn Ldr: Major T. C. Morris*
2 i/c: Captain C. J. Simpson-Gee
Medical Officer: Surgeon Major J. P. A. Page
Technical Quartermaster: Captain (QM) O. M. Price
Quartermaster: Captain (QM) W. Stringer
RQMC: WOII Swann
TQMC: WOII Beadle
SCM: WOII Clark

Mounted Squadron
Sqn Ldr: Captain H. O. Hugh Smith
2 i/c: Captain Sir R. Mackeson Bt
SCM: WOII Giles

Band
Director of Music: Captain E. W. Jeanes
Trumpet-Major: Corporal of Horse Watson

*These three squadron leaders had all transferred from regiments of the Cavalry of the Line.

1st ROYAL DRAGOONS

1968

Commanding Officer: Lieutenant Colonel P. D. Reid
2 i/c: Major S. E. M. Bradish-Ellames
Adjutant: Captain J. G. Hamilton-Russell
RSO: Lieutenant J. W. S. Lewis
Intelligence Officer: Lieutenant J. C. Leech
RSM: WOI Clark
Chief Clerk: WOII Weaver

A Squadron
Sqn Ldr: Major J. J. F. Scott
2 i/c: Captain D. H. Spencer
SSM: WOII Lloyd

B Squadron
Sqn Ldr: Major W. S. H. Boucher
2 i/c: Captain C. M. Barne
SSM: WOII Leese

C Squadron
Sqn Ldr: Major D. S. A. Boyd
2 i/c: Captain J. Aylen
SSM: WOII Tucker

HQ Squadron
Sqn Ldr: Major C. B. Amery
Tech Quartermaster: Captain (QM) T. J. Williams
Quartermaster: Captain (QM) A. S. Ayrton
TQMS: WOII Titmarsh
RQMS: WOII Watorski
SSM: WOII Wood

Band
Bandmaster: WOI Mackay

ROYALS FAREWELL PARADE

February 1969

Commanding Officer: Lieutenant Colonel R. M. H. Vickers, MVO, MBE
2 i/c: Major S. E. M. Bradish-Ellames
Adjutant: Captain J. G. Hamilton-Russell
RSM: WO1 W. Watorski
Chief Clerk: WOII Weaver, BEM

A Squadron
Sqn Ldr: Captain D. H. Spencer
2 i/c: Lieutenant A. N. D. Bols
SSM: WOII Mackay

B Squadron
Sqn Ldr: Major W. S. H. Boucher
2 i/c: Captain N. M. B. Roberts
SSM: WOII Hearn

C Squadron
Sqn Ldr: Major J. A. Aylen
2 i/c: Captain C. E. T. Eddison
SSM: WOII Tucker

HQ Squadron
Sqn Ldr: Major C. B. Amery
2 i/c: Captain R. S. Bell (RCD)
Quartermaster: Captain (QM) A. S. Ayrton
Quartermaster (Tech): Captain (QM) T. J. Williams
RQMS: WOII Crabb
RQMS (Tech): WOII Titmarsh
SSM: WOII Hayes

Band
Bandmaster: WOI D. H. Mackay

BLUES AND ROYALS
AMALGAMATION PARADE
Detmold

March 31, 1969

Commanding Officer: Lieutenant Colonel R. M. H. Vickers, MVO, OBE
2 i/c: Major S. E. M. Bradish-Ellames
Adjutant: Captain A. H. Parker Bowles
RSO/IO: Captain R. C. Wilkinson
RCM: WO1 D. Godfrey-Cass
Chief Clerk: WOII Wennell

A Squadron
Sqn Ldr: Major W. S. H. Boucher
2 i/c: Captain N. M. B. Roberts
SCM: WOII Lane

B Squadron
Sqn Ldr: Major J. H. Pitman
2 i/c: Captain J. G. Hamilton-Russell
SCM: WOII Mackay

C Squadron
Sqn Ldr: Major J. A. Aylen
2 i/c: Captain R. S. Bell (RCD)
SSM: WOII Clark

Command Squadron
Sqn Ldr: Major J. S. Crisp
2 i/c: Captain A. N. D. Bols
SCM: WOII Tucker

HQ Squadron
Sqn Ldr: Captain T. W. P. Connell
2 i/c: Lieutenant (QM) W. R. Marsh
Medical Officer: Surgeon Major J. P. A. Page
Quartermaster: Captain (QM) W. A. Stringer
RQMC: WOII Crabb
TQMC: WOII Handley
SCM: WOII Heath

Part Three

TWO JOINED TRIUMPHANTLY IN ONE

(1969–1992)

A façade that has not changed in two centuries: the Horse Guards,
Whitehall

Queen's Birthday Parade, 1969. Her Majesty, leading the way to Horse Guards Parade, is accompanied by (*left*) the Duke of Edinburgh and (*right*) Admiral of the Fleet Earl Mountbatten of Burma, Colonel of The Life Guards and Gold Stick-in-Waiting. The Field Officer of the Sovereign's Escort, Major the Hon. A. H. G. Broughton, rides behind Prince Philip, and the escort commander, Captain J. F. Mackie, behind Lord Mountbatten. (Captain Mackie was the first former Royals Officer to serve with The Blues and Royals Mounted Squadron). Major Broughton's trumpeter is Lance Corporal Brown, who was to become Captain (QM) M. R. Brown

Chapter I

WELDING THE NEW TEAM

(1969–1971)

One hears so many stories of regimental amalgamations starting out in a brittle and unharmonious way, of mess members of the old regiments keeping one another at an icy distance, and of such mistrust and unfriendliness affecting morale, that it is wonderfully refreshing to find, here and there, one or two of the newly merged with whom the situation has been quite the reverse. The Blues and Royals must, from the very first of those historic spring days of 1969,[1] go on record as being famous for their happy and amicable blending and compatibility. So much so that it seemed almost as though the Dettingen black and the Waterloo Eagle had always been destined to be absorbed into the panoply of The Blues. "Amalgamation is so established," wrote one of the officers a few months later, "that nobody within the Regiment thinks about it, let alone talks about it. It is a word from the past."[2]

This memoir from a former Royals troop leader well reflects the mood:

"From the start, life in the new mess was great fun. I can remember offering one or two Blues officers drinks, thinking for a moment that they were visitors rather than brother-officers. The Blues produced a mass of orderlies which was something quite rare in the Royals, and of which I immediately approved. They also produced some nice pictures and silver which combined well with ours. Because the Household Cavalry had a minimum height restriction, the difference in height between soldiers of the two Regiments was quite noticeable, and inevitably made The Blues appear more impressive on first encounter. The Blues troopers that I was given were adequate but not too keen on tanks, at any rate to start with. One real success story stemmed from the fact that about 6 NCOs from The Blues were sent out a few months early

219

and worked in Royals squadrons. I do not know who chose them but they were a particularly good lot and I would say made a major contribution to allaying the fears of Royals about the Blues. Three I remember were Corporal-of-Horse (later Major) Jack Peck, Corporal-of-Horse (later WO2) Chapman and Lance-Corporal (now Major) Lou Villers. Peck and Villers particularly were very smart old-fashioned type Blues, but also had great senses of humour and mixed extremely well with their Royals opposite numbers. Making the change from Line to Household Cavalry would have been more daunting had not these early ambassadors from The Blues been such high-grade people."

Here the same writer looks back with a laugh:

"I remember after a few days at our first Hohne, Colonel Richard Vickers wanted to speak to the Regiment so we were all summoned in pouring rain to a large marquee. We tank crews were pretty shabby in our wet coveralls, while the officers, RCM, etc from Regimental Headquarters looked extremely clean, dry and well rested. The tent got very crowded and Mr Godfrey-Cass, the RCM, started snapping round peoples' heels trying to squeeze in all the saturated bodies off the firing-point. After Colonel Richard's preamble he asked the rhetorical question 'What are we going to do next?' to which some wag in the back row replied 'get f . . . . wet'. You can imagine the difficulty the likes of myself had restraining our mirth as Mr Godfrey-Cass flew into the middle of the crowd trying furiously to identify the mystery voice, while at the same time taking the names of those he could catch laughing."[3]

While old Royals had obviously been superior on tank tactics, gunnery and armoured administrative matters, old Blues could often teach them a thing or two about discipline in the field. The Blues were a little in awe of the Royals' acute knowledge of the Chieftain tank, and the Royals, to start with, a little in awe of the The Blues Warrant Officers and Corporals of Horse, who, not to put too fine a point on it, found a great many Royals untidy and ill-poised. The Regimental Corporal Major, Mr Godfrey-Cass, was a tower of strength at this time. "Owing to his insistence on the highest standards of discipline, turnout, bearing and promptitude," said the adjutant, "no one, from corporal-of-horse downwards, was permitted to be sloppy, scruffy or casual."[4] And he was splendidly backed by the other Warrant Officers. "The ex-Royal Dragoons among us," wrote the "A" Squadron contributor to the first edition of *The Blue and Royal*, "were horrified to see the arrival of this very large figure [Squadron Corporal Major Lane], who seemed designed to strike terror into the hearts of those of us who were more handy at fixing tanks than fixing bayonets. However, from the first drill parade, he seemed to get even the most b-minded trooper to have a go."[5] Ex-Royals learned fast that the status of Household Cavalryman demanded rather more than simply being remotely represented in London by ceremonial horsemen. It demanded a high degree of smartness and alert bearing.

Blues and Royals personnel taking part in a two-man log race at a French training centre in 1970. *Soldier Magazine*

Regiments of the Royal Armoured Corps having been re-organized technically, The Blues and Royals now deployed a "command squadron". General Vickers explains: "The innovation was to rectify the imbalance between the sabre squadrons (90 men or so each) and HQ squadron (nearly 300), which was administratively unwieldy. The command squadron had tactical sense in that it commanded the fighting elements of the reconnaissance troop, "A" Echelon and regimental headquarters (including the command vehicles (FV 432)) and a troop of tanks."[6]

Persuasive overtures were made to have the Regiment incorporated in 4th Guards Brigade (stationed around Munster) in order at once to make that brigade exclusively "blue-red-blue" and to reinforce the identity of the new Regiment as Household troops. But General Vickers resisted that. He felt his command should contend for its reputation on open terms with Rhine Army's other armoured regiments, and, remaining at Hobart barracks, Detmold, this they proceeded to do under his guidance, with the greatest honour, though they had their teething troubles. Just when The Blues' crewmen had secured their second trades and had completed their initial period of tank familiarization, disaster struck. The scene of it was Soltau, a training ground for which most armoured veterans and maestros have a certain affection. Here is a *Blue and Royal* comment:

"Soltau is part of the old Luneburg Heath, one of the great beauty spots of Germany, which can be seen north of the training area, quite unspoilt and in its natural state. However, generations of German and British tanks from the Reichswehr Wermacht and British Army of the Rhine have turned parts of it into a wilderness; a desert in summer and a morass of mud in winter. It has a long history of use as a training ground for troops, and it is fairly certain that it was used by Hanoverians and Brunswickers up until 1866 and by Prussians after that. Naturally, their limbers and horses, unlike tanks, left it unscarred. It has the great advantage of light, sandy soil which, like that of Aldershot and Potsdam, always goes with martial ardour."[7]

The excessively hot summer of 1969 rendered Soltau more like a desert than ever, and, from the heat and dust, the Chieftains suffered massive engine failure. Within three days the Regiment was reduced from forty tanks to three. It was not their fault. The question was asked: if the vehicles responded to heat like that on Luneberg Heath, how would they react to peak temperatures in an equatorial zone? The scientists were brought in and the faults corrected. "It was, however, professionally shattering for us, a most critical time and a great strain on morale," says General Vickers. "Yet the crisis helped the spirit of the Regiment in a way. It drew us together even more."[8]

As for the Chieftain crews they were more robustly bitter in their condemnation of those who had been responsible for putting the tank together. But this comment closes on a philosophical note:

"The first year had a very full programme made harder by the fact that the Royals had only taken over Chieftain the previous year. As has since been proved this was not a user-friendly vehicle. To keep it on the road required an enormous amount of work in barracks and vast ingenuity in the field. I have always resented the number of times I had to tell my troop that they would have to work late into the night or over the weekend on their vehicles. Whoever accepted Chieftain into service was thoroughly incompetent, and although he has no doubt been knighted and is sitting on a fat pension he ruined the fun of a whole generation of armoured crewmen, and thank God we never went to war. Despite all this the soldiers doggedly kept the things more or less motoring. One spin-off from a busy programme and an unreliable fleet was that the two Regiments [Blues and Royals] were really mixed up and thrown together in a common cause early on so that, by the end of 1969, a cohesive if exhausted new Regiment had emerged whose differences had been largely forgotten."[9]

"Further to the south are the Hohne ranges where the annual tank firing is enjoyed by all", wrote the previous Soltau enthusiast. "Both these training grounds figure largely in the Regiment's life, and it is said that old hands require no maps when using them." Having got over the trauma of the tank engine failure very smartly The Blues and Royals proceeded to Hohne, where they were awarded the rare "A" grading for gunnery, the epitome of a BAOR armoured regiment's prestige, and by the autumn they felt at least as ready as any other in the theatre to go to war.

Close in importance to professional proficiency comes sporting kudos, and here the new Regiment made a triumphant start. In football they won the 1969 BAOR section of the Cavalry Cup, beating the 16th/5th Lancers in the final by 5 goals to 4. The skiing, hockey, canoeing and equestrian teams excelled wherever they went, while the polo team won the BAOR inter-regimental.[10]

Another regimental masterstroke, one that was to be the envy of all other Rhine Army cavalry regiments, was the formation of the Weser Vale hunt. The Blues, as we have seen, founded a regimental pack of foxhounds in Germany in the late 1940s. The Blues and Royals were to kennel bloodhounds. At Perham Down, in the winter of 1968–69, the Royal Horse Guards were most impressed with the buoyant sight of Lady Rosemary Brudenell-Bruce hunting one of her keepers, *à la* "clean boot", through Savernake Forest with bloodhounds.

The Weser Vale Bloodhounds: In at the Finish

They decided that this would be a neat form of hunting – soldier quarry, set lines, time-economic, only a few hounds necessary – for Detmold. And, of course, they had the advantage of the black horses. The principal moving spirit behind the concept was the Quartermaster, Captain Bill Stringer, and due praise went to him for the sport he showed, and the public relations exercise he fostered among local Germans.

There is no doubt that the meets organized for the Weser Vale have been among the most morally profitable features with which the Household Cavalry has been associated in Rhine Army. Thirty-five meets were recorded in the first season, not to mention a hunt ball and hunter trials. "On the armoured brigade exercise," said one of the Masters, "hounds came into their own during the two weekend breaks by hunting over the battle area, placating as they did so all the angry and disgruntled farmers who, only the day before, were threatening all manner of reprisals for damage done by the tanks. It ended by the Germans inviting us back at the end of August next year."[11]

Of the draft of Royals who had volunteered for the Mounted Squadron at the latter end of the 1968 only Captain J. F. Mackie and one trooper passed out of riding school. The failures had not appreciated quite what a stiff challenge Knightsbridge duty presented. However, in the summer of 1969, with the bonus of some preliminary instruction on the black horses in Germany, and the presence of ex-Knightsbridge Blues to help make a second selection, some dozen more Royals, who then went to Hyde Park barracks, duly graduated as mounted dutymen.

The Mounted Squadron (Major the Hon A. H. G. Broughton) claimed 1969 to be, for them, "the busiest year since the War", and their description of it certainly supports the title. The trainee Royals whom they had taken under their wing graduated from riding school on 27 March, with parents and relations attending the pass-out parade for the first time. While the Regiment in Germany was busy with the vesting parade the Mounted Squadron staged an equivalent ceremony, with an inspection by the Major General commanding the Household Brigade (Major General the Hon Michael Fitzalan Howard).

A couple of weeks later came the Italian State Visit, for which the Squadron moved into Combermere, this being the first time since 1909 that a Head of State had been received at Windsor. The escort's three-and-a-half mile journey, which ended with a rank past in the castle quadrangle, proceeded through the town and down the Long Walk. In May they packed up again, this time heading for Edinburgh and duty at the State Opening of the General Assembly of the Church of Scotland. Half the horses were boxed up by road, the other half went by train. "Both methods of travel proved eventful," they recorded, "as children stoned the second train on the outskirts of Edinburgh and broke a window of one of the boxes which upset the horses; and five horse boxes travelling by road took over 48 hours to complete the journey owing to engine failure in one of them."[12]

No sooner had they returned from Scotland than they went straight into briefings and rehearsals for Trooping the Colour and the Garter Service. Then came the Investiture of the Prince of Wales at Caernarvon:

"Sir Michael Duff had very kindly allowed a camp to be erected on his Vaynol estate; and, thanks to a lot of hard work by the Royal Artillery and the Royal Engineers, we moved into a tented camp, luxurious as far as tented camps go. The horses were perhaps best catered for, each with its own loose box. The Squadron moved eighty-three horses from Kensington Olympia to Bangor in three train loads and the reception we received was remarkable; hundreds of people had turned out to watch us ride from the station to Vaynol Park. In fact it was typical of the welcome and hospitality bestowed on us throughout our stay. For this period the Regiment was fully stretched as it had to provide a Sovereign's Escort, a Prince of Wales' escort of two divisions of sixteen, as well as leaving sufficient men and horses in London for guard duty at Horse Guards. The Squadron Leader had the privilege of commanding the Prince of Wales Escort on this unique occasion and Squadron Corporal Major Cowdrey rode at the other wheel station. During the escort the atmosphere ... was tense, and we all heaved a sigh of relief when we delivered Prince Charles, safe and sound, to Caernarvon Castle. It was a memorable day, although a long one as the escort returned to Vaynol six-and-a-half hours after it had set out and there had only been one twenty-minute break in the middle."[13]

Following a 10-day lull on return from Wales they had another

Aspects of the new Hyde Park
Barracks:
Troop saddlery racks (*below*)
and (*left*) corner of a troop room.
Soldier Magazine

State Visit to contend with, that of the President of Finland. ("The temperature was 78° and the escort, both men and horses, returned to barracks visibly slimmer!") After camp at Stoney Castle there was the State Opening of Parliament. Time to think about sport, too. ("Unfortunately hunting prospects for soldiers with the Sandhurst and Bisley and the Drag have been curtailed because of the rabies outbreak. However, with luck we may be able to send soldiers for the odd day's sport before we start training for next year's musical ride.")

On 22 October, 1970, the Mounted Regiment returned from the temporary accommodation in Wellington Barracks, from which it had fulfilled its duties for the previous five years, on to its old Knightsbridge ground, into the new Hyde Park Barracks. Field Marshal Sir Gerald Templer, who performed the official opening, assisted by the Colonel of The Life Guards, Admiral of the Fleet Earl Mountbatten of Burma, unveiled a plaque on the barrack wall facing Hyde Park, after which the Chaplain to the Household Division said some prayers. At the reception, the architect, Sir Basil Spence, looking very pleased with himself, approached Colonel Gerald, enquiring what he thought of the buildings. Colonel Gerald, a traditionalist, saw the structures as vulgar and insubstantial. He was also economical of speech. "Bloody awful!" was his succinct reply. He went on to express considerable disapproval of the security of the place. Notwithstanding the excellent amenities his verdict on some aspects of the barrack rooms, the stables and the messes, have been roundly echoed ever since.

In the previous autumn The Blues and Royals contributor to *The Guards Magazine* in BAOR had been writing, rather cynically, that "the misaptly named 'German season' is over; the exercises are finished; the vehicles are being prepared for various complicated inspections; polo ponies are out at grass; and soldiers' thoughts are now turning, in the midst of a mild and colourful autumn, towards the dreary prospect of another bitter winter, relieved only by the thought of Christmas leave and the spring."[14]

But 1970 proved as buoyant as 1969. At the end of it Lieutenant Colonel Vickers was succeeded by Lieutenant Colonel James

Eyre. And, early in 1971, a Regimental move within Detmold was conducted, a short but most significant transfer facilitated (in the face of a good deal of opposition) with the backing of the Commander-in-Chief, General Sir Desmond Fitzpatrick, the Regiment's Deputy Colonel. The Blues and Royals evacuated Hobart, which they had shared with 20th Armoured Brigade headquarters, a regiment of horse artillery, a unit of the Army Air Corps and a field workshops, and, following the departure of the Queen's Dragoon Guards, occupied Lothian Barracks, where they were to be on their own, and where they enjoyed, among other facilities, the use of a range of stables, an indoor riding school and a manege, rendering them better placed than hitherto to provide and staff Rhine Army's centre of riding instruction.

"A" Squadron (Major H. O. Hugh-Smith) enjoyed the most rewarding 1971. Take a look at the following career for an example of armoured hyperactivity in the early '70s! The Squadron had no sooner transferred from Hobart to Lothian than they were on the move again, being detailed, temporarily, as the Force Reconnaissance Squadron to operate on the NATO flanks. They flew to Windsor where they formed a composite squadron with "C" Squadron of The Life Guards, then sailed with their scout cars for Norway and five weeks of Arctic training on exercise "Hardfall". March found them at Detmold again, handing over their tanks to another Life Guards squadron. Then

"back in England we snatched a few days leave; and, by the middle of the month, we were at RAF Aldergrove, ten miles west of Belfast, taking over from the RAC Parachute Squadron . . .[15] We had a minimum of six troops under command, the extra troops coming first from the Royal Hussars and later from the 14th/20th Hussars. Our role was to supply four troops to operate under command of the infantry battalions deployed in Belfast, and to maintain a military presence in the Police District that surrounds Belfast, with its headquarters in Antrim. We also had some responsibility for security at Aldergrove civil airport which involved squadron headquarters, the admin troop and the LAD in special patrols and in searching passengers coming off selected flights; this task was very popular. Everyone, whatever their normal job, at one time or another was involved in operational tasks.

"On 12 July the Squadron was given part of the route of the main Orange procession in Belfast to safeguard. Although the day started badly when some members of the Orange Order from Glasgow, who had landed at Larne, made trouble in a Catholic housing estate there, the processions all passed off quietly. Our part of the processional route was in a Protestant part of the town and everyone was given more cups of tea than they could ever hope to drink. While we were engaged in an area where a holiday and rather drunken atmosphere prevailed, we were reminded of the realities of the situation when we heard that a sniper had killed a soldier from the 1st Green Jackets in another part of the town."[16]

After nearly four months of Northern Irish peacekeeping they returned to Windsor to refresh themselves on conventional armoured car work, five weeks of which was spent at Stanford practical training area in Norfolk, in preparation for another dynamic overseas exercise, this time on the southern flank of NATO, on exercise "Hellenic Express" in Greece. "It was amusing to watch soldiers of seven different nations working together," they recalled in the autumn, "and the hospitality of the Greek villagers never ceased . . . We are now busily preparing for our second winter in Norway and, after that, another four months in Ulster."[17]

The remainder of the Regiment had their sojourn at Soltau in 1971 as usual, recording that

"For some this was the seventh year at Soltau, and many had exercised over this small area for three years or more. Consequently as the last Battle group exercise drew to its end at about 0330 hrs after the only really wet night, morale was amazingly high, and it was felt that a special finale was required. The entire battle group was positioned for the final thrust through an area devastated by a "nuclear explosion", and after a suspenseful countdown, was unleashed towards the objective. It is not recorded which tank reached home first – but none were far behind."[18]

By early September The Blues and Royals had done with Rhine Army for a few years. Old Blues knew as much about Chieftains as old Royals, while former Royals officers had learned long ago to click their heels to their seniors in the officers mess with the best of The Blues, and their troopers to salute without head-dress.[19] Duly welded into superb shape, the Regiment now started its first tour at Combermere barracks, though few of them were to remain settled there.

Field Marshal Sir Gerald Templer when he opened Sandes Home (Canteen) in "D" Lines, Pirbright Camp, 1971. (*Left to right*) WOII Peck (SCM Household Cavalry Squadron, Guards Depot), Major J. D. Smith-Bingham, Lieutenant Colonel Ghika, Irish Guards (Commandant Guards Depot), Colonel Gerald and RSM Holbrook, Coldstream Guards. *Household Division PR*

NOTES AND REFERENCES

1. Although the new Regiment was officially formed on 29 March and the vesting parade was on 31 March, the fusion of the two into one was virtually completed soon after The Blues arrived at Detmold on 10 March.
2. *The Guards Magazine*, Autumn, 1969
3. In a letter from Colonel P. B. Rogers
4. Related by Brigadier A. H. Parker Bowles, then adjutant
5. *The Blue and Royal*, 1970
6. In a letter from Lieutenant General Sir R. Vickers
7. *The Blue and Royal*, 1970
8. In a letter from Lieutenant General Sir R. Vickers. One wonders, however, whether the Regiment's old cavaliers saw mass sickness among the tanks in quite the same light!
9. In a letter from Colonel P. B. Rogers
10. One member of this team, Captain Parker Bowles, having finished well on "Fossa" in the 1969 Grand National, had driven out to Germany next morning to be in time for the amalgamation parade
11. *The Blue and Royal*, 1970
12. Ibid
13. Ibid
14. *The Guards Magazine*, Winter, 1969–70
15. This unit's Squadron Corporal Major was then SCM A. W. (Paddy) Kersting, Blues and Royals – now Major Kersting, curator of the Household Cavalry museum. His career as a paratrooper began with the Guards Independent Company in 1960
16. *The Blue and Royal*, 1972
17. Ibid
18. *The Guards Magazine*, 1971
19. This custom, as previously noted, originated with The Blues' Colonel, Lord Granby, saluting his Commander-in-Chief after his hat and wig flew off during the Battle of Warburg, in 1760

BLUES AND ROYALS

1971

Commanding Officer: Lieutenant Colonel J. A. C. G. Eyre
2 i/c: Major T. C. Morris
Adjutant: Captain D. P. L. Hewson
RSO: Lieutenant I. R. Knock (R. Sigs)
RCM: WOI Tucker
Intelligence Corporal Major: WOII Varga
Chief Clerk: WOII Wennell

A Squadron
Sqn Ldr: Major H. O. Hugh-Smith
2 i/c: Captain J. S. Olivier
SCM: WOII Lane

B Squadron
Sqn Ldr: Major T. N. P. W. Burbury
2 i/c: Captain C. M. Barne
SCM: WOII Clark

C Squadron
Sqn Ldr: Major B. H. F. Wright
2 i/c: Captain T. M. Hickman (Life Guards)
SCM: WOII Heath

Command Squadron
Sqn Ldr: Major J. S. Crisp
2 i/c: Captain (QM) W. R. Marsh
SCM: WOII Remfry

HQ Squadron
Sqn Ldr: Major J. C. M. L. Crawford
Medical Officer: Surgeon Major J. P. A. Page
Quartermaster: Captain (QM) W. A. Stringer
Tech Quartermaster: Captain (QM) T. J. Williams
TQMC: WOII Handley
RQMC: WOII Martin

Mounted Squadron
Sqn Ldr: Major Hon A. H. G. Broughton
2 i/c: Captain J. F. Mackie
SCM: WOII Doxey

Band
Director of Music: Major E. W. Jeanes
Trumpet-Major: WOII Wilson

Chapter II

THE NOMADIC SQUADRONS

(1971–1975)

Although the armoured car squadrons of The Blues and Royals were technically pivoted on Combermere Barracks they saw little of one another during the next four years or so. And any reader who has not been involved with the new Regiment might make an interesting comparison between life in the Household Cavalry during, say, the 1930s, and the variety of skills, along with the tempo and diversity of duty, which are mentioned in this chapter. It is quite a revelation.

"C" Squadron were scarcely home to Windsor in the autumn of 1971 than they were off to Cyprus to be the island's garrison armoured car contingent. They were quartered in Pergamos camp, five miles from Dhekelia, home of the Eastern Sovereign Base Area headquarters, and 15 miles from Famagusta. Not being allowed to exercise outside the Sovereign Base Area their tactical movement was tightly restricted. "Therefore we concentrated on trade training," they reported, "and we had recruit firing on the local Pyla range early in November ... As fast as one erects targets the locals move in to pinch them, and trying to keep the range clear of the locals and their flocks of sheep and goats is well nigh impossible."[1] However, there was plenty of less frustrating diversion, including a vast variety of sport. They ran the Dhekelia saddle club and the draghounds. And later they had a part to play in the BBC television serial *The Regiment*, the story of a Victorian infantry unit. "This sounded fun, so we agreed to provide one or two extras to help out...

One or two rapidly became virtually the whole Squadron and committed us totally for about three weeks. Unexpected complications

Northern Ireland, 1972. First crews into Londonderry "No-Go" areas during Operation Motorman. (*Left*) First into Bogside; (*right*) First into Creggan. (Names withheld for security)

appeared such as when it was realized that the modern young soldier has no idea at all how to slope arms with a Mauser or .303 rifle, and as for resting on arms reversed . . . ! But we survived, which was remarkable in the case of those representing the Boer Commando which involved them in some fairly hair-raising mounted charges, firing blanks at the gallop from horses which had never heard a rifle shot before. This of course meant that the horses tended to go in the opposite direction to that required, having first deposited their rider in the dust. Anyone who fell off had to pretend to be dead."[2]

"B" Squadron heard during their disembarkation leave from Germany that they were to relieve the Parachute Squadron RAC as the armoured car sub-unit in support of 39 Infantry Brigade in Northern Ireland. The situation there had deteriorated. After Brian Faulkner introduced the policy of internment without trial, under the provisions of the Special Powers Act, the Stormont Opposition MPs announced a campaign of civil disobedience; terrorism was stepped up; bombs began to be planted in public buildings and offices; the Orangemen formed themselves into a vanguard movement; there was growing support for the IRA in the South, while the British Army presence was increased to over 12,000. "B" Squadron were in for a tougher time than their predecessors, "A":

"Apart from endless patrolling, our ability to report and watch is invaluable to the infantry as the armoured reconnaissance patrol has the ability to assess the temperature of an area quickly. If feelings are running high the appearance of a pair of whippets (as the Ferret is known to the citizens of Belfast) can create an immediate reaction. In short, the value of the Ferrets is as follows: morale value to the infantry, a good 'thermometer' for battalion or company commanders, good radio and accurate reporting, a quick reaction force that will either draw the gunman out or deter him from his original objective; and, lastly (but never as yet employed, thankfully) a very powerful machine gun that could be employed in support of infantry . . .

"The troops have been much abused by the local people, mainly in the Roman Catholic urban areas, since arrival. This is probably due to fear and the belief that the cars will never fire unless the situation is desperate. At the start of the tour everyone was quite amused by being stoned and bottled consistently, but [the novelty] soon wore off and at times it has taken a great deal of self-control not to open fire."[3]

We left "A" Squadron preparing for their second winter in Norway, their destination being Rinnleiret, a cavalry camp North-East of Trondheim. As the provision of the reconnaissance element of AMF(L) – or Allied Command Europe Mobile Force (Land Component) – was to be a regular task of the Household Cavalry let us take a closer look at its implications. The group was formed in 1960 as a multi-national instant reaction force, approximately of brigade strength, available to the Supreme Allied Commander in Europe, ready to be flown, at 72 hours notice, to either of the NATO flanks where the military presence was less strong than in Germany. "A" Squadron formed the AMF(L) reconnaissance element for almost all the first half of the 1970s.[4]

Major J. G. Hamilton-Russell, who was to succeed Major J. D. Smith-Bingham in command of the Squadron in 1973, had this to say about exercise "Hardfall", what he called "the annual quest by the British contingent for the foulest possible conditions in which to carry out Arctic training ... Many well-established Norwegian friends are revisited and a threat of a possible visit to the Italian field hospital spurs all to an even greater understanding of the techniques of survival in the Arctic ... The efforts of the British soldier on skis have for years provided the Norwegian populace with a never-ending source of free amusement."[5]

In 1972 the Squadron's Arctic equipment included the Volvo tracked Snow Cat. "This little vehicle, with its terrific heating system, brought an incongruous note to Windsor, painted as it is in snow camouflage colours of green and white."[6]

1972 was the year of the christening of the tracked reconnaissance vehicle, a cross-country armoured car that could travel just as fast as the wheeled variety and could pack at least as hard a punch. These tracks arrived at Combermere in the guise of the

Members of the Regiment with their Ferret Scout cars during an Allied Command Europe Mobile Force exercise in Norway

Scorpion and its sister car, the Scimitar. The Scorpion CVR(T) – Combat Vehicle Reconnaissance (Tracked), to give it its full title – mounted a 76 mm gun, loading anti-tank high explosive (HESH), canister (anti-infantry scatter shot), or smoke, alongside a coaxial 7.62 mm machine gun; the Scimitar was armed with a 30 mm low-trajectory rapid-firing cannon with a co-axial machine gun. Another additional medium reconnaissance vehicle, the Mark V Ferret, carrying swingfire guided missiles, also came into regimental use at about this time.

Notwithstanding their diverse peacekeeping tasks and battle readiness, The Blues and Royals could pursue their art of ceremonial soldiering, concurrently with their military professionalism, at least as well as ever. 1972 was the year of the Guidon Parade, which took place on the cavalry exercise ground in Windsor Great Park on July 14 with two squadrons of armoured cars as well as the Mounted Squadron, the ceremony being concluded with a rank past in Windsor Castle quadrangle. There was plenty of precedent for a Guidon in the Household Cavalry. William IV presented The Blues with one in 1832, and they carried it until 1887. Charles II had given the Royals a Guidon when they were nominated as his "Regiment of Dragoons" in 1683; and, except for the period 1820–58, they carried them until the amalgamation.[7] Summing up 14 July, the adjutant, Captain E. N. Brooksbank, wrote: "By 6.30 am on the following day "B" Squadron had left for Londonderry, and most of the Mounted Squadron had returned to London to perform in the Royal Tournament. By twelve o'clock the stands, which had seated nearly 4,000 people the day before, had been dismantled, and nothing beside remained."[8]

It is not easy, in hindsight, to keep pace with "A" and "B" squadrons at this period. Their careers certainly reflect how little time there was, and is, for most members of a present-day regiment of Household Cavalry to put their feet up. Returning to the month of February, 1972, "A" squadron then came back, temporarily, from Norway to begin revising their internal security drills prior to taking over in Ulster from "B" during March. And, while the Mounted Squadron were preparing for the State Visit to Windsor of Queen Juliana of the Netherlands, "B" were getting

Skiing behind Snow Cats, Norway, 1973

ready for recruit and conversion training at Castlemartin ranges in Wales. "A" reported, at the end of their 1972 north Irish tour, that

"at times the Squadron was heavily committed in Belfast, and Ferrets were being deprived of their lights and macrilon shields at an alarming rate by the accuracy of youths armed with paving slabs ... Staff-Sergeant Davies and his LAD section did an outstanding job in keeping the vehicles battleworthy at all times.

"One of the roles was reassurance visits to country areas, leaving a

240

squadron visiting card with our telephone number and address in case of emergencies. The purpose of the visits seemed to be misunderstood in one case when Corporal of Horse Lloyd plus a section from MT rushed out in answer to a call from a 70-year-old widow in distress. The task was to move a sick cow from one loose box to another!"[9]

But they had a tragedy to report, too. Lance Corporal Chillingworth was killed when his scout car overturned on patrol. By mid-September the Squadron was back in Norway. As we have seen, "B" returned to Londonderry on July 15 in time for Operation 'Motorman', "the aim of which," recalls the Squadron Leader (Major Parker Bowles), "was to take back the 'no-go' areas of the Creggan and Bogside. Nine battalions and our Squadron were used and it was two troops of ours who led the infantry in. Every single member of the Squadron was shot at, including the cooks."[10] Nor were they without casualties:

"On 31st July Operation 'Motorman' took place. Cornet Browning's troop led the 1st Bn Royal Scots into the Creggan and Lance Corporal of Horse Stacey's armoured car was the first vehicle into the Bogside. While on foot patrol Cornet Lingeman and Troopers Perkins and Thorpe were injured by shrapnel from a mine detonated from across the border. Lieutenant Lukas and Lance Corporal Howard both received injuries to their ear drums when their Saladin was mined and blown off the road. Another Saladin accidentally went up in flames and, but for the prompt action of Corporal of Horse Sibley getting back into the blazing vehicle, his driver would have been burnt to death. There was also the usual series of injuries from broken bottles and stones thrown very accurately by small children. Even Lance Corporal of Horse Woollard's ration truck was shot at regularly."[11]

Major Parker Bowles adds another experience, one reflecting a different Ulster hazard: "On the night of 'Motorman' my headquarters were positioned, with a troop, between Londonderry and the border to prevent any gunmen escaping over it. We as near as nothing opened up and shot up a ragged section of armed men leaving 'Derry. Luckily we didn't as it was a section of the Grenadier Guards who had lost their way and sense of direction."[12] Two non-commissioned officers from the Squadron were awarded the citation of Mentioned in Despatches for their gallantry during Operation 'Motorman', Corporal of Horse

Sibley and Corporal of Horse Hughes, though they had to wait six months to hear of it.

By that time "B" Squadron had spent three months in Cyprus, having been posted there in December as part of the United Nations Force with whom, in a variety of roles, they controlled and escorted the rotation of the Turkish national contingent. By comparison "C" Squadron remained in the British Sovereign Base. "A" Squadron were home from Norway before Christmas, but back there again in February. ("We are grateful to, and proud of, our wives and families who stoically accept the burden of [our] long periods away from home ... We hope we are all the more appreciated when we visit Windsor, and we wish them to know we are not insensitive to their plight."[13])

"Many of us had not been to Norway before," said an AMF (L) tyro; "and, inspired by rumours put about by the veterans, were seen wandering around the camp like Michelin men trying to get Arctic clothing to fit, and building igloos out of ice cubes in the NAAFI in the evening."[14]

Retreating to Combermere again in the spring, they had a few weeks to perfect their drills, in the company of "C" squadron of The Life Guards, for the Presentation of new Standards by the Queen on 30 May. As they related, this was the first occasion on which Scorpions had paraded in public, and the first drive past of tracked vehicles on Horse Guards. This, they said, was

"embellished by the demonstration to our Colonel-in-Chief of the efficiency of the Scorpion handbrake by an anonymous driver who omitted to release it for the journey past the dais! It was nevertheless a memorable occasion for those who took part, and the Mounted Regiment showed commendable steadiness on parade in the face of determined backfiring from the armoured cars.

"A number of "B" Squadron personnel returned from Cyprus in time to be represented amongst the crews. Immediately following this the Squadron laid on an impressive demonstration on Salisbury Plain, for the Chief of the General Staff, of the fire power of Scorpion, Scimitar and Swingfire Ferret, before preparing for the air move to the Mediterranean."[15]

The destination was Greece and exercise 'Alexander Express', in which "at one time we were operating across a distance of 200

Captain Richard Wilkinson. Died taking part in a regimental run in Windsor Great Park, aged 37, in 1981. He was then second-in-command of The Blues and Royals

miles, which gave the signallers convulsions and the echelon no sleep . . . after which we undertook a period of troop training on Salisbury Plain culminating in a weekend exercise with the Royal Yeomanry." Then "we collected some more Scorpions and said goodbye to the last of our Ferrets before going to Warcop [Cumbria] and Otterburn [Northumberland] . . . after which we got ready for Denmark." This was for 'Absolam Express' in November.

"The climax of this exercise," Major (then Corporal Major) A. W. Kersting recalls,

"was to be a NATO march-and-shoot competition consisting of an inspection, a disciplined march over ten miles carrying weapons, ammunition etc, followed by a further inspection. The team of one officer and 24 men had to be submitted to the NATO HQ well in advance and I (with the approval of the Squadron Leader, Major Hamilton-Russell) took charge of the team. The exercise having finished, the Squadron spent the night on board ship which was due to sail late the following day. The Squadron had drawn an early start time for the competition, so an early reveille was arranged, a quick breakfast followed by a parade and roll call and the team, led by Captain Walker-Okeover, moved by 4-tonner to the start some 70 kilometres from the ship. On arrival at the stated time, there was (unusually) no sign of the Squadron Leader. But with the inspection completed, the team was on its way.

"We arrived at the finish without any real incident, carried out the firing practice and, with the second inspection completed, the team moved to the administrative area for refreshments. The Squadron Leader was there. Looking distinctly unfriendly he approached me and demanded to know why the team was there. I explained patiently that we had just taken part in the NATO Cup Competition as previously arranged. 'Did you not get my signal to the ship telling you that you were not to take part in the competition as the sailing time had been brought forward to 1200 hrs?'

" 'Everyone stop what you are doing and on to the trucks!' I ordered and then briefed Trooper Benyon that, as I was to be his Corporal-Major for the next two years, it would be in his interest to drive sufficiently fast enough not to miss the boat to the UK. On arrival at the docks we found all our personal kit had been unloaded on to the dockside and the watching troops observing from the ship (particularly the remainder of "A" Squadron) could hardly conceal their pleasure at our discomfiture. Fortunately there was a long sailing delay and we were later allowed to board with our vehicles on to the LSL. The journey by sea to Marchwood passed without incident (only remembered for the numerous boat drills, the strange films provided by the Chinese crew and Corporal of Horse Pomroy's ("the Pom's") early morning tea).

"The Squadron disembarked at Marchwood, then drove to Windsor arriving at around 2300 hrs. I was stopped in my Ferret at the barrack gate by a worried looking Corporal of Horse ('Harpo') Adams, and informed that I was to report to the Squadron Leader outside "A" Squadron Block. I approached the Squadron Leader paying the usual compliments, and was met with a stilted welcome followed by 'Why didn't you obey my signal to you on the ship, that you were not to take part in the NATO Cup competition? Do you realize how embarrassing it would have been to have to report to the Commanding Officer that one third of my Squadron had been left stranded in Denmark? I believe you received my signal and ignored it, because you wanted to take part in the competition.' I denied any knowledge of the signal and rejected any suggestion that I might have thrown it overboard. 'Anyway', the Squadron Leader replied withdrawing his hand from behind his back which held a trophy, 'You've won the b-thing; but I still think you got my signal!' "[16]

"We are setting off in the near future for Norway," "A" Squadron recorded at the end of 1973, "this time for the far north and the Arctic Circle, where, at the time of writing, the temperature is − 38°. Perhaps Belfast next June [1974] holds some attraction."[17]

"C" Squadron were last seen film-making in Cyprus. "For those in Windsor who were missing [us]," wrote one of their wags, "the remedy was easily found by switching on television sets to watch the BBC series of *The Regiment*, which featured Christopher Cazenove, Lance Corporal of Horse Challoner, Troopers Meredith, Evans and many others."[18]. Handing over their commitments to a squadron of the 16th/5th Lancers and returning to Combermere it was now their turn for Ulster, for which they were soon training in earnest. By mid-September "the support troop had already attended a 'search-and-sniffer' course at Chatham, and now the priorities lay with individual weapon handling and shooting, the setting up of vehicle check-points and improving driving skills ... VCPs could be seen springing up all round Windsor Park and support troops did a cordon-and-search 'somewhere in Buckinghamshire'."[19] They caught the boat from Liverpool on the night of 31 October, en route for Aldergrove.

During the summer the whole Regiment was concentrated at Windsor for the first time since "A" Squadron left Detmold to take up their AMF (L) role in 1970. Three whole years of dispersion. But, with "A" and "C" both departing in the autumn, that reunion was short-lived. As for "B" they were the first to serve in a regimental duty that was to be often repeated; on 4 January they were called out, together with companies of the Grenadier and Irish Guards, to assist the police in an anti-terrorist contingency role at Heathrow airport. ("On Saturday, 5 January, a Scorpion squadron descended on Heathrow airport and its surrounding areas, much to the delight of the Sunday newspapers, who, almost without exception, ran both stories and photographs of 'tanks in London'.")[20]

"Without doubt 1973 has been the busiest year for the Mounted Squadron during the last decade," claimed a representative. But could it really have been more hectic, one wonders, than that described for 1969 in the last chapter? Anyhow 1973 was certainly very active for them including as it did Princess

Security duty, Heathrow, 1973. *Army PR*

Anne's wedding, the Standards parade, and State Visits from the Presidents of Mexico and Nigeria. It was also the first year that the Mounted Regiment camped as one at Stoney Castle, instead of by squadrons, the Queen's Life Guard being mounted by the King's Troop, Royal Horse Artillery.

And so to 1974, with the pattern of hyperactivity the same as ever, starting with "A" Squadron, half trade training at Windsor, half Arctic training in Norway, where movement was curtailed by the oil crisis ("enabling us to participate in exercise 'Hardfall' only at forty per cent strength"). So the emphasis was on dismounted work, mostly on skis. When 'Hardfall' was over the Squadron concentrated at Windsor, hastened to Castlemartin to fire their guns, then prepared for their next Northern Ireland tour. "Ferrets were drawn up from the training pool, and some drivers found this the third type of vehicle they had been required to drive and maintain in four months."[21]

It was "B" Squadron whom "A" relieved. They began their year with what they called the "the Boeing patrol" at Heathrow.

246

After Northern Ireland they drew out their Scorpions and Swing-fires to reform as an armoured reconnaissance squadron, but that task was cut short by a fresh outbreak of violence in Cyprus. "The usual seven days warning was reduced at the drop of a telephone call to 48 hours. And, of course, it was a weekend. But everybody hurried about with reckless enthusiasm ... By Sunday morning we were lined up on the square at Combermere, crews front, ready for the off ... The fly-out went well enough, though our friendly local airways developed the irksome habit of putting Scorpions on one aeroplane and their crews on another ... but we motored off the aeroplane straight to the ammunition compound and then out on patrol under command of 19 Airportable Brigade."[22] They were back ten weeks later.

The first squadron for duty in Northern Ireland in 1974 was "C", their most notable incidents there, of many, "besides several finds of explosives, was a murderous attack on a patrol led by Lance Corporal Grocott ... Three high-velocity bullets passed within a few inches of his face, entering the windscreen of his Land Rover and leaving by the side window." Then the Squadron went to fire their Saladin guns at Castlemartin, after which "we became involved in a plethora of different activities, including KAPE [Keeping the Army in the Public Eye] tours ranging from Exeter to Blackpool, several minor exercises and providing large numbers to assist with the Game Fair at Stratfield Saye."[23]

August found "A" Squadron at RAF Aldergrove, "B" in Cyprus (Akrotiri) and "C" and Headquarters on Salisbury Plain, on "Salmon Leap," an ambitious and enjoyable exercise which involved all the Armoured Corps troops that could be mustered from the south of England." To end the year there were such tame, if essential, events as the Association 'At Home' day, the Major General's inspection, more shooting at Castlemartin, and some troop and squadron training in Norfolk for "A".

Rarely in the history of the British Army can a regiment have achieved such a major triple of sporting triumphs as that accomplished by The Blues and Royals in 1974. Their first and foremost glory was to carry off the Cavalry Cup. Having defeated the 4th/7th Dragoon Guards in the UK final their football XI went on to secure the great trophy on Burton Court with a 1-0

Preparing to hand over duties of the Queen's Life Guard to the King's Troop, Royal Horse Artillery, 1973. *Household Cavalry Museum, Windsor*

victory against the Queen's Royal Irish Hussars on FA Cup final day. The team was composed of SSI Smith (a regimental physical training instructor), Corporal of Horse Sibley (team captain), Corporal of Horse Birt, Sergeant Cartwright (Pay Corps), Lance Sergeant Truluck (REME), Lance Corporal of Horse Jones, Lance Corporals Healey, Ford, Guest and Porterfield, Troopers Rushton, Ironmonger and Charlton, and Musician Baines.

Then the polo team (Lieutenant Colonel Boucher, Major Pitman, Major Parker Bowles and Lieutenant Hadden-Paton) won the coveted inter-regimental cup by beating the Rhine Army victors, the 17th/21st Lancers (who, incidentally, had defeated them in the 1973 final). The third regimental triumph was accomplished by Major Parker Bowles when his horse Paki was first past the post at Sandown in March to win the Grand Military Gold Cup.

1975 continued with much the same bustling routine – Norway, Denmark, Northern Ireland, Turkey, Salisbury Plain; except that "B" Squadron (Major J. S. Olivier) spent all June in Jamaica as the guests of that island's Defence Regiment (Exercise 'Calypso Hop'), while The Blues and Royals at Combermere played hosts to "A" Company of the Jamaican Defence Regiment. "This exchange worked faultlessly," said *The Blue and Royal* editorial, "and we were all most impressed by the charm and professionalism of the Company."

The Blues and Royals, being due for Germany again in the autumn, were already turning their attention to their Rhine Army role. "B" Squadron no sooner returned from Jamaica than they embarked on Chieftain conversion. Their Colonel-in-Chief spent the day with them on August the fourth, "seeing several different aspects of regimental life and meeting a great many members of the Regiment and their wives and families. Her Majesty . . . showed particular interest in the 24-hour arctic ration pack. She was subjected, by Lance Corporal of Horse Quinn, to a detailed description of how to prepare curried chicken in a temperature of 25°C. It was the hottest day of a hot summer." Then it was recorded that "final leave was taken and everything packed up; and on 15 October our flag was struck for the last time at Combermere Barracks".[24]

The Regimental Captains and Subalterns polo team about to receive their cup
from Lord Mountbatten, having defeated the Royal Navy in the final at Tidworth
in 1975. (*Left to right*) Lord Mountbatten, Lieutenant N. Hadden-Paton,
Captain P. B. Rogers, Lieutenant M. C. O'B. Horsford and Lieutenant
T. L. S. Livingstone-Learmonth

NOTES AND REFERENCES

1. *The Blue and Royal*, 1972
2. Ibid, 1973
3. Ibid, 1972
4. "A" Squadron's first commander in this role, Major H. O. Hugh-Smith, was appointed GSO II AMF (L) in June, 1973.
5. Major J. G. Hamilton-Russell, *The Military Jet Set*, *The Guards Magazine*, Summer, 1974
6. *The Guards Magazine*, Spring, 1972. The Snow Cat was designed as an armoured troop, and stores, carrying vehicle
7. The Guidon, with which the Royals were presented in 1954, was laid up in the Household Cavalry Museum, together with the Old Blues Standard from the parade, in a further ceremony in October, 1972
8. *A Farewell to Magic, The Guards Magazine*, Autumn, 1972
9. *The Blue and Royal*, 1973
10. Ibid
11. Ibid
12. In a letter from Brigadier A. H. Parker Bowles
13. *The Blue and Royal*, 1974
14. Ibid
15. Ibid
16. In a letter from Major A. W. Kersting
17. *The Blue and Royal*, 1974
18. Ibid
19. Ibid
20. *The Guards Magazine*, Spring 1974
21. *The Blue and Royal*, 1975
22. Ibid
23. Ibid
24. Ibid, 1976

BLUES AND ROYALS

December, 1975

Commanding Officer: Lieutenant Colonel J. H. Pitman
2 i/c: Major P. T. Keightley
Adjutant: Captain P. B. Rogers
RSO: Lieutenant C. C. McColville (R. Sigs)
RCM: WOI J. Peck
Chief Clerk: WOII Desborough

A Squadron
Sqn Ldr: Major J. D. Smith-Bingham
2 i/c: Captain C. H. Boone
SCM: WOII Smart

B Squadron
Sqn Ldr: Major J. S. Olivier
2 i/c: Captain H. T. Hayward
SCM: WOII Burroughs

C Squadron
Sqn Ldr: Major G. H. Tweedie
2 i/c: Captain A. N. D. Bols
SCM: WOII Hill

HQ Squadron
Sqn Ldr: Major H. W. Davies
2 i/c: Captain (QM) R. R. Giles
Medical Officer: Surgeon Captain P. L. S. Hard
Quartermaster: Captain (QM) W. R. Marsh
Tech Quartermaster: Captain (QM) T. W. Tucker
RQMC: WOII Stephenson
TQMC: WOII MacDougall
SCM: WOII Wilkins

Mounted Squadron
Sqn Ldr: Major B. J. Lockhart
2 i/c: Captain A. S. Lukas
SCM: WOII Sellars

Band
Director of Music: Major G. E. Evans
Trumpet-Major: WOII Hayne

Chapter III

TRACKS IN CANADA, BOOTS IN ULSTER

(1975–1980)

The demands made on both the versatility and the duration of an armoured regiment in Rhine Army had increased since The Blues and Royals were last at Detmold. Now, in addition to maintaining constant battle readiness against the Russian threat, there was a regular commitment of six-months tours of active service as infantry in Northern Ireland, or, rather, two months' preparation and training for four months' duty. However, the first objective for Lieutenant Colonel Hugh Pitman, who led the Regiment back to BAOR in the autumn of 1975, was to have his squadrons fully tank-qualified once more. "B" Squadron had been Chieftain converted before leaving the United Kingdom, but "A" (straight off the AMF role) and "C" (recently in Ireland) needed to be busy, that autumn and beyond, securing crewmen's trades.

By February, 1976, all the squadrons being ready for their conversion firing and troop training at Hohne and Soltau, The Blues and Royals were again fully fledged as an effective Rhine Army force, "and no one," they said, "could fail to notice the improved performance of the tanks since we were last in Germany." Colonel Rogers recalls the scene:

"Almost more important than the major field training exercises was the annual visit to the ranges of Hohne to fire the tanks. Unfortunately, because this particular skill was one of the few with which all tank regiments could be directly compared, it was usually taken very seriously by the Commanding Officer, and became a tense period. The Regiment moved complete and took over a barracks at Hohne with each squadron having its own range. Inevitably, in order that the first round could go down the range at 0800 hrs Squadron Corporal Majors would parade their squadrons at about 0500 hrs ordering reveille for about

Household Cavalry Squadron staff, Guards Depot, 1980. Standing: (*left to right*) Corporal of Horse Whitehead RHG/D, Corporal of Horse Powell LG, Lance Corporal McAlpine LG, Trooper Gulley RHG/D, Lance Corporal of Horse Tabor RHG/D. Sitting: (*left to right*) Corporal of Horse Partridge RHG/D, SQMC Brown RHG/D, Major J. S. Olivier RHG/D, SCM Shaw LG, Corporal Forester RHG/D

0400 hours. Also, firing often seemed to happen in the spring or autumn when it could be excruciatingly cold and damp. I do not think I will ever forget the awful business of getting up after only about 4 hours' sleep and parading in the dark prior to bussing down to the firing point. First parade on the vehicles was done in the early morning mist with everything covered in frost and nowhere to keep warm. By the time firing was underway morale had usually risen, but those first few hours were miserable."[1]

In addition to the challenge of the training programme the Household Cavalry still had the responsibility of running the theatre equitation courses, while the heaviest burden of organizing horse shows also fell on their shoulders. And, of course, the prestigious Weser Vale hounds, their own inspired creation, met regularly through from the autumn to the spring. Colonel Rogers again:

"One great feature of life in Germany for me on both tours was the Weser Vale Bloodhounds. When I was adjutant and Hugh Pitman was commanding he was a strong supporter and follower of the WVH, and encouraged me to come out as well. I have many happy memories of that rolling German farmland and woods in beautiful autumn weather, where we would meet at about 12 and spin out the hunting for up to three hours. We normally unboxed in the yard of a *schloss* or *gut* (large farmhouse complex) and then hacked to the meet along minor roads in the marvellous autumn colouring. The hunting varied between really exciting moments, not far different from high Leicestershire, to some very boring pauses while hounds misbehaved, or monotonous follow-my-leader cantering along forest tracks. There was a small core of officers who took part plus a few retired officers and wives as well as an enthusiastic group of local Germans. I always found these occasions had a wonderful atmosphere and were a good way of escaping from barracks at the weekend and really seeing some beautiful country. Occasionally one might be invited for tea afterwards in a *schloss* or farmhouse."[2]

There was a new training departure since their last sojourn in Germany. The Canadian Government had lent the British army a vast area of prairie known as Suffield, by the town of Medicine Hat in Alberta, to which some six battle groups, moving out as fully integrated tactical formations, were dispatched each year. "B" Squadron was the first to sample this adventure, carrying out a 14-day live-firing exercise in company with the Royal Irish Rangers. "Having destroyed the phantasian hordes many times over, with a courage that would inspire even the most read of *War Picture Library* heroes," jested a squadron diarist, "the battle group fought its last action, capturing Lone Eagle Butte. Now the

The Mounted Squadron returning from Pirbright to Hyde Park Barracks in 1977. *Keystone*

real nerve was needed, as the battle of the washdown can bring out the worst in even the most even-tempered comrades. But ... several days on a diet of Coca-Cola and hamburgers saw a squadron of sparkling tanks ready to be handed over to the 13th/18th Hussars."[3]

By the time "B" Squadron returned, the Regiment had begun preparing for their first Northern Irish stint as infantry, putting their tanks into preservation and proceeding on two months' dismounted training. A fortnight of that was spent with the Northern Ireland Training and Advisory Team (NITAT) in what was known as "Tin City" at Sennelager. Priority was then given to physical fitness and quick, accurate shooting with the self-loading rifle (the regimental contest in marksmanship being won by Trooper Waterman with Lance Corporal Arnold second and Trooper Shaw third.)

Initially cast for a rural role in Ulster, The Blues and Royals were organized in three rifle squadrons. But, shortly before they were due to depart, they were re-roled for largely urban duty in Londonderry. So they reformed into two. Leaving behind a rear party, "to keep Lothian barracks ticking over, exchanging old tanks for new, running riding courses and guarding the interests of the families," they were now brigaded with the Second Battalions of the Coldstream and Scots Guards and were operational in Londonderry from 29 December, with special responsibility for the Shantallow estates on the north side of the city, and what was known as "The Enclave", the little portion of Ulster abutting the west bank of the Foyle there. Here are some jottings from the Commanding Officer's memories:

"The Regiment's philosophy during this period was based on the premise that we were there among the brave people of Londonderry for only a very short time; that our job was to keep the area as quiet and normal as possible (or the IRA would have won); and that our relationships with the Royal Ulster Constabulary, the Ulster Defence Regiment and all local people were of paramount importance. We therefore made every possible effort to be as competent and professional as we could be; at the same time, subject to the obvious security requirements, supporting local events to the maximum. I remember in particular: the necessary ambivalence of the Regiment on discovering that a very senior local dignitary indeed was engaged in smuggling his cattle across the Irish border in order to take advantage of the Green pound ... The police parties, where only the very clearest and purest poteen was served – the kind that does not make you go blind, such liquor having been confiscated from illegal stills ... Arresting, unnecessarily, the rather barbaric son of the editor of the local paper at dead of night at our border crossing point on not one, but two separate occasions; the second time when I was dining with his father – and happily not getting a mention in the Press ... Visiting with my patrol a large country house and finding in the drawing-room the house party – the men in red evening tail coats and the ladies in all their finery – about to leave for the local hunt ball; and joining them for a little while, for of necessity, non-alcoholic refreshment ... Enabling officers and soldiers – within the constraints of common sense and security regulations – when off duty to participate as

Ready for patrol, Andersonstown, Northern Ireland,
1978. (Names withheld for security)

Northern Ireland

much as possible in local parties and the odd day's hunting and shooting ... And the magnificent back-up and support from all those – the rear party and the wives – left behind in Detmold."[4]

Four months later, when the time came to pack up and return to Detmold, while congratulating themselves on not having suffered a single casualty, they were counting the tally of their work. They had

"arrested 154 people for questioning, and searched 32,220 cars and 103 houses. In addition every single car crossing to and from the Republic on three major roads was checked, as well as uncounted numbers of derelict buildings and acres of countryside being searched. These totals, which are typical of any regiment in Northern Ireland, are an inadequate way of describing the hundreds of hours of patrolling in vehicles and on foot, during the day and at night, in crisp clear winter weather or in sleet, snow and the inevitable spring rain which every member of the rifle squadrons endured. Nor do they hint at the endless hours spent by the men of headquarters squadron on watch in sangars and manning the main entrance to Fort George. There were undoubtedly many occasions when the monotony of the job, or the apparent lack of a solution to the problems, taxed the morale of even the most highly spirited amongst us. Conversely the reception received in many areas and the friendships struck up at all levels with Irishmen who live their lives in Londonderry, served to foster in many of us an admiration and an affection for the people and their country."[5]

We are into Silver Jubilee year and, while the Service Regiment enjoyed its well-earned leave, the Mounted Squadron was having it share of the rugged life. The Queen's visit to Glasgow involved the Household Cavalry in a first taste of duty in that city. "We lived in a lairage,"one of them recorded,

"which is the technical term for an animal market and slaughter house. This was a vast building which could have housed several regiments with room to spare, and because of its size it was bitterly cold throughout our stay. The horses loved it, each one having a large individual box with ample straw, compared with the stalls and wood-shavings of Knightsbridge. It was a Life Guard escort with the Squadron providing two Divisions founded by 2 and 3 Troops, 1 Troop having remained behind in London to provide the Queen's Life Guard. The Household Cavalry had never been in Glasgow before and there was a certain amount of

The Queen's Life Guard
(Blues and Royals)
leaving Hyde Park
Barracks for Horse
Guards. *Mike Roberts*

trepidation as to our reception there. As it turned out the Regiment was made to feel enormously welcome wherever it went and few soldiers had to pay for their drinks in local pubs. A huge crowd turned out for the procession on May 17 which took place in glorious sunshine."[6]

They then advanced to Edinburgh where they were to furnish a Captain's Escort for the Thistle ceremony and a Sovereign's escort for the Opening of the Assembly. "We stayed in Redford Barracks, which is a fair hack from the centre of Edinburgh. A long day in the saddle certainly, but what a magnificent city to ride through – Arthur's Seat, Holyrood Palace, the Royal Mile,

Prince's Street, back to Holyrood for a rank past, and then the slow ride back to Redford Barracks. On our arrival we were horrified to find the whole of the massed pipe bands of the Scottish Division rehearsing on the square where we were hoping to dismount. One or two horses took grave exception to this intrusion."[7]

Now it was the turn of the Service Regiment for some Silver Jubilee ceremonial, which is to say the part they took, with the 4th Division, in the Queen's Review of Rhine Army at Sennelager. The Blues and Royals paraded no fewer than fifty-six fighting vehicles, in addition to finding two Ferret Scout Car escorts, the Queen's being commanded by the adjutant, Captain Peter Rogers, with Regimental Quartermaster Corporal Stephenson carrying the Guidon. The escort for the West Germany President was under command of Captain H. P. D. Massey, with a Squadron Standard held by the Technical RQMC, Regimental Quartermaster Corporal Hill. Colonel Peter Rogers looks back on that day:

"There was some debate as to whether the crews should parade in their vehicles or in front of them. It was felt that if they remained in their crew positions during the review, the Queen would not see them, but if they paraded in front of their vehicles there would be an ugly moment when they all had to scramble on board before starting up and driving past. One of the options was for crews to stand on the bins above the tracks for the review. The first time this was tried all officers, etc, took part, and the Commanding Officer, Hugh Pitman, whose tank was out in front of the Regiment, had placed the RCM (WO1 Peck) in his crew to have him nearby as a trouble-shooter if necessary. Normally of course the RCM had his own landrover and Mr Peck, being an ex-Blue, was not very familiar with tanks. When all the tanks had driven on to parade from the central dais word came for crews to come out of the turret and stand on the bins. The order then came:

'Crews, stand at ease!'. Mr Peck, a Guards Depot instructor, lifted his left leg the regulation height and drove it down in the usual manner, quite forgetting that he was already standing on the edge of the left side bin. The net result was that the RCM collapsed in agony on the ground beside his tank and the whole Regiment, with a ringside view, was unable to contain its mirth.

"Commanding the Sovereign's escort for the Queen's review was no

Blues and Royals Ferret car mounted with Vickers Vigilant

easy task. My 4 ferrets had to wait at a pre-arranged cross-roads in the middle of a German forest off the training area. As the Queen's Range Rover approached we moved off something in the manner of a relay runner, picking up the Range Rover on the move and falling in around it. At another pre-arranged spot I had to surreptitiously radio ahead to the RHA battery firing the Royal Salute, to tell them to begin in such a way that the 21st gun fired at precisely the moment the Queen stepped out of her car. As we drove onto the parade ground I realized that the street liners of Royal Military Police were slightly too close together, with the result that the off-side wing of my Ferret grazed their presented rifles, knocking several to the ground. I do not think the Queen saw and to the best of my knowledge no damage was done. Indeed I have often wondered whether the spacing was quite as critical as it appeared or whether my driver was using his privileged position to settle a few old scores!"[8]

Then it was back to Hohne and Soltau, returning to Detmold just in time for another visit from Colonel Gerald. He presented nine Long Service and Good Conduct medals, remarking that "it is the

Field Marshal Sir Gerald Templer greeting HM The
Colonel-in-Chief at Combermere Barracks

largest group of Warrant Officers and senior NCOs parading for
this particular medal that it has ever been my pleasure to present.
I've never seen so many good senior NCOs on one parade."[9]

1977 was also marked by the Army's restructuring, which
increased the Regiment's complement of tanks from 47 to 66,
thus prompting the temporary formation of "D" Squadron.
Despite Northern Ireland it was not a bad year for sport either.
The Blues and Royals staged another Weser Vale hunter trials,
which included, for the first time in BAOR, a cross-country team
race. And they won, not only the inter-regimental polo (with

Royals herald trumpets and banners, Wolfenbuttel, 1948

The Royals marching through London on 22 October 1963, to mark their being granted the Freedom of the City. *Artist: John King*

Household Cavalry quadrille, 1981. *Photo: Mike Roberts*

Lieutenant Colonel Pitman, Lieutenant Nigel Haddon-Paton, Lieutenant Somerville Livingstone-Learmonth and Lieutenant Martin Horsford), but the Captains and Subalterns too (with the same three subalterns joined by Captain Rogers).

Major Hugh-Smith had reported for duty as Second in Command in 1976, having gone to Detmold straight from Balmoral where he completed his appointment as Equerry to the Duke of Edinburgh. Taking the Commanding Officer's chair in January, 1978, he was to be confronted by a similarly arduous BAOR programme as Colonel Pitman had experienced. The first 1978 Canadian commitment being for an armoured, rather than an infantry, battle group, the whole Regiment, less "A" Squadron, exercised on the Alberta prairies with a company of the Duke of Wellington's Regiment with the necessary supporting arms under command. Later in the year, while "A" Squadron carried out their Canadian training, under command of the "Duke's" battalion, "B" and "C" provided border patrols, an SAS (nuclear) guard, a troop to appear in a film on fighting in built-up areas, and three relief troops for the Berlin squadron of the Scots Dragoon Guards. Before going on Christmas leave all ranks knew they were in for another tour on foot in Ulster, starting in February, 1979. It was Belfast this time – Andersonstown. And it was "D" Squadron's swansong:

"Despite the size of the Squadron there was no time for anyone to stand idle, and we were kept very busy with large-scale searches, guarding ballot boxes, covering marches from the Busy Bee and reacting to the various incidents that occurred in Belfast. Mr Horsford's Troop, while patrolling the Lenadoon, were rudely interrupted one day by a burst from an Armalite rifle fired at them from a range of 60 yards. It was remarkably poor shooting, for the only damage was a hole in a pair of lightweight trousers and a slightly singed Cpl Hanin (Royal Corps of Transport). When at last it was all over and our plane touched down at Wunstorf it was sad to see "D" Squadron disband as the 16th/5th Lancers set off for Wolfenbüttel and the "A" and "C" Squadron Corporal Majors set about sorting out who belonged to who. Quite a few of us had entirely forgotten that we had not always been just "D" Squadron."[10]

It had not been an unequivocally successful tour. In two separate

Royal Wedding, 1981. The Prince and Princess of Wales leaving
Buckingham Palace for Waterloo Station with their Travelling Escort,
commanded by Lieutenant Colonel A. H. Parker Bowles, with (*right*)
Captain N. Hadden-Paton. *Sun*

tragedies Squadron Quartermaster Corporal Tucker and Troopers Dykes and Thornett were killed. "By the time June came we
were only too happy to hand over to the Queen's Own Hussars
and disappear on leave for three weeks," a "B" Squadron cynic
remarked. "Four months living behind walls is enough. Only
Corporal Major Clayton was unhappy about leaving because he
likes ... walls, as they act as an amplifier for his voice. No one
could escape!"[11]

Meanwhile there had been a regimental loss of a different order
to be mourned. Field Marshal Sir Gerald Templer, who had been
Colonel of The Blues from 1963 to 1969, and since then of The
Blues and Royals, died in October. Due credit must be given to
the Blues, 16 years previously, for having secured as their Colonel

not only the most prominent and illustrious of all postwar soldiers, but one who was also widely regarded as the greatest Englishman – or Briton – of the postwar era. He was a man deeply immersed in the military tradition, he held an unshakeable faith in the regimental system, and had been an ardent admirer, throughout his career, of the Household Troops. Colonel Gerald proved to be very much more than a mere regimental figurehead. From the very start he made a close study of The Blues; and, without ever interfering directly in the running of either that regiment or, later, of The Blues and Royals he made it his business to keep himself fully and regularly informed of both Regiments' activities and their problems. His was the principal guiding hand behind the success of the amalgamation. He was someone who incited affection in people in all walks of life. No wonder his death was so keenly felt.[12]

However, as Colonel Hugh-Smith then said in an address to Blues and Royals past and present, "As 1980 dawns there is much to which to look forward. The Queen has been pleased to appoint General Sir Desmond Fitzpatrick to be Colonel of the Regiment and Gold Stick. This appointment, which will give the greatest pleasure to all Blues and Royals, will be particularly welcome to those of us who were serving at the time of the amalgamation and who know how much the new Colonel did to ensure that the new Regiment got off to an excellent start."[13] They were back at Combermere in March and were honoured with a three-hour visit by the Queen within a fortnight of their return.

Troop dialogue at Stapel, near Detmold, 1977. (*Left to right*) Cornet M. J. Macauley, Lance Corporal Jervis and Troopers Elliott and Manning

NOTES AND REFERENCES

1. In a letter from Colonel P. B. Rogers
2. Ibid
3. *The Blue and Royal*, 1977
4. In a letter from Colonel J. H. Pitman
5. *The Guards Magazine*, Silver Jubilee Number, 1977
6. *The Blue and Royal*, 1978
7. Ibid
8. In a letter from Colonel P. B. Rogers
9. *The Guards Magazine*, Winter, 1977–78
10. *The Blue and Royal*, 1980
11. Ibid
12. His memorial plaque was duly placed in the Household Cavalry section of the Guards Chapel. The dedication service was on 2 May, 1981
13. *The Blue and Royal*, 1980

BLUES AND ROYALS

November 1979

Commanding Officer: Lieutenant Colonel H. O. Hugh-Smith MVO
2 i/c: Major J. D. Smith-Bingham
Adjutant: Captain J. Mc M. Carr-Ellison
RSO: Captain M. H. Lingeman
IO: Captain F. G. S. Lukas
RCM: WOI W. MacDougall
Chief Clerk: WOII Sproats

A Squadron
Sqn Ldr: Major G. N. Smith (United States Army)
2 i/c: Captain W. R. Rollo
SCM: WOII O'Halloran

B Squadron
Sqn Ldr: Major D. M. Reed-Felstead
2 i/c: Captain C. C. Bucknall
SCM: WOII Clayton

C Squadron
Sqn Ldr: Major G. H. Tweedie
2 i/c: Captain T. P. E. Barclay
SCM: WOII Fortt

HQ Squadron
Sqn Ldr: Major H. T. Hayward
2 i/c: Captain (QM) R. B. Yates
Medical Officer: Surgeon Lieutenant Colonel J. P. A. Page
Quartermaster: Captain (QM) R. R. Giles
Tech Quartermaster: Major (QM) W. R. Marsh
RQMC: WOII Howick
TQMC: WOII Anslow

Mounted Squadron
Sqn Ldr: Major H. P. D. Massey
2 i/c: Captain H. St. J. Holcroft
SCM: WOII Patterson

Band
Director of Music: Major B. T. Keeling
Trumpet-Major: WOII Mansfield

Chapter IV

GLORY AND INIQUITY

(1980–1983)

Bidding farewell to Germany early in 1980, under their new Commanding Officer, Lieutenant Colonel James Hamilton-Russell, and converting once again to their armoured reconnaissance roles, the Regiment looked forward to much the same Windsor-based activity as they had enjoyed during the early 1970s. For the most part they were not to be deceived. The AMF(L) role for the NATO flanks had passed from the Household Cavalry to a battalion group at Tidworth. But there remained the Heathrow anti-terrorist commitment, and there was still the Ferret-borne task with the United Nations' force in Cyprus, this being the destination of "C" Squadron for the next six months.

"A" Squadron, temporarily under command of an exchange officer from the United States Army, the popular and very competent Major Gale Smith, was reorganized with five sabre troops, each of six vehicles, their primary mount for combat being the wheeled Fox armoured car whose main armament was a 30 mm Rarden cannon. (The Squadron prided themselves on being "the largest armoured squadron in the army"!) In 1980 "B" Squadron was placed under command of Major T. J. Sulivan, who had transferred from the Royal Artillery. In April, 1981, he took his soldiers to Fort Bragg, North Carolina, where they trained with the Sheridan, the light tank of the 82nd United States Airborne Division, while The Blues and Royals played hosts to one of the American Airborne companies at Windsor. July had "B" Squadron on Salisbury Plain, just about the time the Mounted Squadron were glamorously busy helping to furnish three escorts for the wedding of the Prince of Wales to Lady Diana Spencer.

271

And so to the melodramatic year of 1982, the spring of which saw "A" Squadron in Cyprus, "C" on block leave, and only "B" at Combermere. On 2 April half "B" were on Easter leave, while squadron headquarters and two troops were loaded up for a Warminster exercise when the news was broadcast of the Argentine invasion of the Falkland islands. On 4 April Colonel Hamilton-Russell was instructed to have two reconnaissance troops, each with two Scorpions and two Scimitars, and a REME light aid detachment (a Samson recovery vehicle under a sergeant), standing by, the vehicles to be ready for embarkation at Southampton on 6 April. The constraints of availability reduced the choice to two. They were those commanded by Lieutenant Lord Robin Innes-Ker (3 Troop) and Lieutenant M. R. Coreth (4 Troop). On 5 April Lieutenant Coreth flew by helicopter, with his Squadron Leader, to Plymouth for orders, then "returned to Windsor where," he said, "we found that even the paymaster had burned the midnight oil and kindly produced our mess bills!".[1]

En route for the Falklands, 1982; Testing the guns on Ascension Island

Two other Blues and Royals officers were to be engaged in Operation 'Corporate', both as watchkeepers, that is to say with the task of manning radio sets at headquarters – Major H. St J. Holcroft at the Joint Force Headquarters, at Northwood, and Captain R. A. K. Field with 5 Infantry Brigade in the Task Force.

OPERATION CORPORATE

The Blues and Royals detachment sailed on 9 April, the vehicles, with Corporal of Horse Thomson, Lance Corporals Mitchell and Lewis and the REME NCOs on *Elk* and the remainder on board *Canberra*, where, said Lieutenant Coreth, "3 Para became our guardians [who] didn't understand why we didn't run round the deck 25 hours a day . . . [our men] had hysterics over the waiters in the dining-rooms, most of whom wore three earrings and called us 'Ducks'." They stopped at Freetown, Sierra Leone, and next at Ascension Island, where they practised firing their weapons out to sea, though not without strong influence on the higher commanders by the troop leaders, "to persuade the hierarchy that we needed to get ashore to test fire and boresight was a major battle which lasted several days and involved numerous signals". Lieutenant Coreth remarks:

"We had not bore-sighted the main armament and had not fired since the previous annual firing in November. To add to this problem we had never fired the new armour-piercing discarding sabot round for the 30 mm cannon. For those that do not know, the APDS is a high-velocity chunk of tungsten steel that penetrates armour through kinetic energy. The problem involved with this round amounts to it having a higher velocity than the APSE or HE rounds, thus a different flight path."

Then they said goodbye to *Elk* and *Canberra* and went aboard HMS *Fearless*. On 10 May the Task Force pointed for the South Atlantic (their mail being dropped by parachute, "a great morale booster"). On 15 May, while Lieutenant Coreth, the senior of the two subalterns, was among the commanders receiving orders for the landings from Brigadier Julian Thompson, the Royal Marines commander of 3 Commando Brigade, news came of the sinking of the Argentine warship *Belgrano*. On 20 May *Fearless* entered the Exclusion Zone and the alarming roll of the ship told of the "roaring forties". 3 Troop were to land at San Carlos. The Blues and Royals' fighting vehicles were prepared for wading and the crews rehearsed in the skill of firing their main armaments (76 mm for the Scorpion, 30 mm cannon for Scimitar) from the bows of landing craft in a rough sea, in case of an opposed landing. Initially their tasks on the beachhead were to provide fire support for the battalions clearing the area, and then to occupy defensive observation positions on the surrounding hills.

Fearless, approaching from the north-east, dropped anchor at 0400 hours on 21 May. 3 Troop, pre-loaded in their landing craft, slipped towards San Carlos and, accompanied by naval gunfire, landed 200 metres from the shore, Lance Corporal of Horse Fisher leading. 4 Troop made it, unopposed, just west of Port San Carlos. "With the port secure," says Lieut Coreth (who now describes himself, jocularly, as "DRAC South Atlantic"):

"I sent Corporal of Horse Stretton and Lance Corporal of Horse Ward up to the aptly-named Windy Gap to help protect the north-east flank. The air raids began and became a feature of daily life. Two days later I replaced Corporal of Horse Stretton at Windy Gap. On the way there we proved our point for the first of many times. 'Inexperts' had said that [our vehicles] could not move on the Falklands terrain, we said they

River crossing, East Falkland

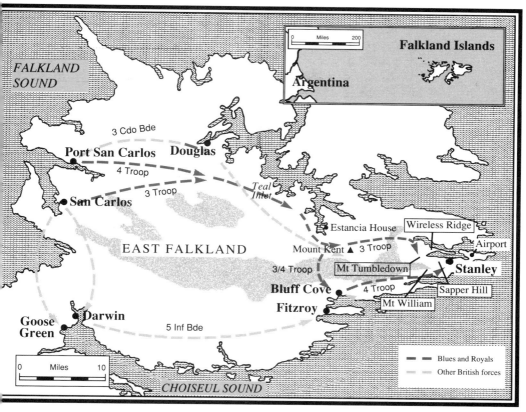

ampaign map: Operation Corporate

could. On the way we found a tractor up to its axles in a bog. Using our incredible kinetic energy rope we catapulted him out with the greatest of ease; all this with [our vehicles] on a thin film of peat with almost liquid bog beneath. For the remainder, by day we shot at aircraft which we enjoyed, and by night we froze.

"We then hit a logistical problem that was to dog us throughout the campaign – fuel. We were to support 3 Para on their advance to Teal Inlet. It was discovered that there were not enough jerry-cans for our fuel. Ordered to stay behind we went on a hunt. The vehicles rolled at 1400 hours and the Engineers discovered they were missing 28 jerry-cans."

The first trouble was that the troops did not enjoy the advantage of their own logistical back-up. What they needed was a command element to coordinate their action, with a small administrative echelon to supply them. The second misjudgment of the higher commanders and their staffs was in failing to appreciate the cross-country capability of The Blues and Royals' tracked vehicles, which proved to have the most remarkable facility for traversing the boggy terrain. The third error was in underestimating the fire-power and accuracy of their weapons. In hindsight it was generally agreed that, if the whole of "B" Squadron had been dispatched, the campaign might have been considerably abbreviated. However, "theirs not to reason why."

Using their "innate cavalry enterprise" they acquired fuel wherever they could find it – petrol given by Falklanders, petrol left behind by retreating Argentines. Arriving at Teal Inlet and hearing of the triumph and tragedy of Goose Green, Lieutenant Coreth's reaction was that, if the Parachute Battalion had been lent the support of The Blues and Royals, many lives might have been saved. Lt-Colonel H. Jones, commanding 2 Para, had in fact requested the support of the troops, but that was refused.

Crossing the San Carlos River, with paddles out and snorkels up, 4 Troop, having spent 10 days in the beachhead, advanced with 3 Para, eventually reaching Estancia Hill, where they established an observation post, from which, says the troop leader, tongue-in-cheek, "we could observe Stanley with its famous nightlife, discos, bars and hundreds of pretty girls".

3 Troop, who had found some buildings, were in for an air raid:

"Suddenly it came over the air the Argy 'jets' were only 10 miles away and closing," said Lieut Innes-Ker. "There was a mad rush for the door. I don't think I have ever run so fast for my vehicle. Lance-Corporal Mitchell was outside pondering on life . . . He nearly had a heart attack, I gave him such a shock. We just managed to get to a fire position before four jets came in from the west to attack the LSLs. It was a stirring sight. The air was full of missiles and bullets, big and small, of both ours and theirs. I never saw so much fire power being put into a small area in a such a short space of time. It was all over in a matter of seconds."

The Troop was then ordered to escort the tracked articulated oversnow vehicles of brigade headquarters on the 30 kilometres to Teal Inlet. Many of those vehicles got bogged or broke down in the dark, but were mostly saved by Lieutenant Lord Robin Innes-Ker and his men with their kinetic tow-ropes. The journey, described by the troop leader as "resembling the M4 westbound on a Friday evening," took nearly eighteen hours. (Apart from similar recovery tasks The Blues and Royals, being sometimes at the beck and call of sub-unit commanders on the spot, were frequently to be used for casualty evacuation, lifting ammunition and all sorts of "taxi" services, such as helping infantry patrols forward.) Once 3 Troop linked up with 4 both were ordered south over the mountains to join 5 Brigade which had advanced through Fitzroy to Bluff Cove. ("The 'experts' thought that would take 48 hours," comments Lieutenant Coreth, who had managed to organize guides; "we made it in six.")

It was now 7 June. 3 Troop were in Fitzroy, 4 Troop hull-down with the Welsh Guards in a quarry, where 3 Troop joined them next day:

"As they approached, Lance Corporal of Horse Fisher and Trooper Hastings waved cheerfully to two Harriers as they flew low overhead. Their hearts jumped when the saw they were Skyhawks ... nearly every weapon fired at the second wave. Trooper Fuggat even managed to empty two sub-machine gun magazines at them ... Trooper Tucker hit a Skyhawk with his 30 millimetre cannon, as did Trooper Ford back at Fitzroy. [Corporal-of-Horse Dunkley's Scimitar had returned to Fitzroy for a replacement gearbox.] This was the day of the tragedy of *Sir Galahad* and *Sir Tristram*. 23B and the Samson helped carry casualties."

3 Troop, who were to support 2 Para, pointed north. Lieutenant Innes-Ker describes the journey:

"We set off for 2 Para's position, full up, Lance Corporal of Horse Fisher carrying an extra 135 30 mm rounds. The only thing we were short of was food; 3 Para QM was very tight and wouldn't give us any. After about a mile a chopper came up on the air asking for work. There was little response so I asked him if he could get us food, so off he went back to 3 Para QM, took rations off him, which earlier he wouldn't give me, and flew them back to me! I felt very pleased with myself.

"After another 4 miles we got to Murrell Bridge. I had been warned that we may be too heavy for it so I got out and tested it. I didn't like it at all and wasn't going to cross it, but Lance Corporal Mitchell assured me he could do it so off we went and by God, the bridge bent; it was being pushed to its limits and there was no way 28 would be able to cross it, with its extra weight; it would be about 2 tons heavier than us, about 10 tons . . .

"Off we set again hugging the shoulder of the hill to hide from the artillery shells and to keep away from the bogs. Once I had to go down and we decided to chance having a go at a major bog, and it so nearly ended in disaster, we only just got out in time. Without Lance Corporal Mitchell's good driving I think we would have sunk. I feared not only sinking up to the tracks but all the way, with us inside; we were very, very lucky."

They linked with 2 Para near Estancia House, where preparations were being made for the assault on Wireless Ridge, maximum fire support being required from the troop. Lieutenant Innes-Ker reconnoitred fire positions within 300 metres of the enemy. The passive night sights of his vehicle acted as the eyes of the battalion and were most effective at locating enemy positions. At one point Lance Corporal of Horse Dunkley drove into a pothole and was knocked unconscious with much loss of blood. His crew, Troopers Ford and Ground, both 17-year-olds, worked wonders. Driving through the night they found their way with their injured NCO to the Regimental Aid Post, then reported back to their troop without the least mishap. Lance Corporal of Horse Dunkley was evacuated to the hospital ship. Captain Field, whose place as watchkeeper had moved up to battalion headquarters, immediately asked permission to take command of Dunkley's Scimitar, which he did. "I asked the gunner, Trooper Ford," Captain Field recalls,

"for a quick revision of 30 mm misfire drills; he pointed out that it was I who had taught him gunnery in the first place! If Callsign 23B's gunnery was not good, I had only myself to blame.

"It was a bright moonlight night, with a deep frost as we moved back to the battle – quite eerie with the distant chatter of machine guns and bursting illuminations. The only movement was that of small groups of stretcher-bearers, dark against the white carpet, carrying their sad loads. Exhausted, they put down their stretchers to exchange a brief word of greeting as we passed. It was as one imagined a First World War battlefield, not one of the 1980s. The constant whine of artillery shells,

The Scorpion that succumbed to an Argentine mine

the harsh backdrop, small groups of men huddled together for shelter and warmth, others moving gently forward for the next attack...

"We moved from the ridge line to join in the shoot onto the main part of Wireless Ridge. The Troop was doing a good job. Callsign 23A seemed to be playing a little game. A short burst of machine-gun fire; the Argentinians usually fired back. The cars would hit the source of the enemy tracer; that particular position would not fire again. Anything that moved or fired at us was 'zapped' and the real star was the Rarden 30 mm gun. The Rarden with its flat trajectory, its 6-shot capability and incredible accuracy could neutralize a target very quickly. The HE (High Explosive) and APSE (Armour Piercing Secondary Effects) rounds were used.

"We stood off at about 800 m from the enemy and with our GPMGs were able to put sustained bursts of fire into their positions. Trooper Round, my driver, while not on his stomach trying to replace the accelerator pedal which had decided that this was an excellent moment to fall off, played a crucial part in target acquisition. The prize though must go in this respect to the incredible night sight."

"On the third bound they [3 Troop] came across heavier resistance and returned fire," says another report. "They satisfactorily filled their game books for the season. 23C, with Lance Corporal of Horse Fisher and Trooper Hastings, even managed to fire at Stanley on the last bound, hitting a fuel and ammunition dump with spectacular effect. They pressed on in the dawn and, when the white flag went up, they, with some of 2 Para sitting on the vehicles, were among the first into Stanley."

Returning to the final battle on the southern front, 4 Troop were with the Scots Guards, the objective being Mount Tumble-down. "We moved forward to give fire support," says Lieutenant Coreth.

"About one kilometre short of my intended position there was a huge crater in the road. Since we were under artillery fire I knew this could be a shell hole, so I decided to risk the possibility of mines. There followed the most incredible explosion – we had hit a mine. The wagon flew into the air and Lance-Corporal Farmer failed his flying test for he crashed on landing. Shaken but not stirred, we all had roaring headaches for the next few days. The smell of smoke and burning cordite helped speed up our evacuation of the vehicle. The wagon was a shambles; the driver's hatch was blown off, as were the sprockets and some road wheels, the hull was buckled and the turret a mess. With shells falling and little point in hanging about, I sent Lance-Corporals Lambert and Farmer back to the Regimental Aid Post. The other vehicles pulled forward and we began to fire as best we could onto the enemy positions. This involved the invention of new techniques, untaught at Gunnery School. Lance

3 Troop heading for Stanley (showing the peaks of Wireless Ridge behind)

The head of the Household Cavalry Musical Ride, 1992. The officer in command is Captain G. V. de la F. Woyka, Blues and Royals

Blues and Royals in saddle and turret. Cavalry *en masse* and (*below*) manning a Challenger machine gun

Lieutenant M. R. Coreth (in front, on the turret) with a captured
Argentine Panhard

Corporals of Horse Ward and Meiklejohn used the previously unheard
of '30 mm High Explosive at 4000 metres' technique and Corporal of
Horse Stretton the '76 mm Indirect Night Shoot'. I corrected fall of shot
from the outside of the vehicles and awarded 'A' grades to all. The
battered patrol reappeared, most of them wounded, and were flown
back. We settled down for the remainder of the night. An engineer came
forward next morning. In a 25-metre radius around the crater he cleared
57 anti-tank mines. Having discovered that the Welsh Guards were now
advancing I took over 24B and, leaving A and C to help the Scots Guards
pick up their dead, set off in pursuit.

"The columns of men marching hell-for-leather up that road were an
amazing sight. We found the colonel who said that he believed the white
flag was flying but wanted me to recce forward to confirm it. We pushed
on past endless articles of abandoned equipment, artillery pieces, and
dead. Finally, we arrived on top of Sapper Hill, the key to Stanley. The
war really was over. We were elated. Elation turned to dismay when we
were ordered back to the mudhole that was Fitzroy. I and Lance
Corporal of Horse Meiklejohn stayed with my vehicle while the others

went back to make a camp. While we waited the minefield was marked with the help of the Argentinians who had laid it."

Then came the moment when the Chinook helicopter arrived to recover the mined Scorpion:

"Whoops of joy went up when that amazing two-rotor helicopter came into view. It is vast, fast and can carry, I believe, in the region of 22,000 lb more than its own weight. I had already prepared an LS for it and so signalled it in in a very professional manner. It flew away leaving a member of A's crew to put straps onto the vehicle, and returned half an hour later. A Scorpion weighing eight and a half tonnes seemed almost like picking up a beach ball. The poor wagon went off to Stanley to be dejected, a fate ill-deserved for such a loyal machine.

"The Whirlybird returned from Stanley and whisked us over to Fitzroy to join the rest of my team. B drove back via Bluff Cove where he stayed the night. I found our happy gypsy's encampment in a field, the wagons surrounding a roaring fire and a pot of boiling water. The Corporal of Horse had stripped down trench systems to collect firewood. It was peacetime."

Lieut Innes-Ker was by now settled with his troop in Stanley where he

"ran into Prince Andrew. What a surprise! I had written to him at San Carlos giving him the army war stories and had guessed that I would meet up with him. On the way down, while on *Canberra*, I had had a bet with a leading doctor, Ric Jolly, that Prince Andrew would not be allowed to go down to the Falklands. Obviously I had lost, but Ric had told this to him so he pulled my leg about it. He stayed most of the day. I offered him some coffee in the house but once the press got hold of him that was it. I didn't see him again. All I did do was to get him an FN rifle. Sadly I was seen by the press giving it to him so God knows of the consequences."

Lieutenant Innes-Ker had acquired a motor bike with which he took his troop's mail to the airport, finding en route

"a road barrier manned by Marines where the Argentinians handed in all their firearms, spare clothing and ammunition. There were massive weapon piles. They just walked past throwing their belongings on to the piles as they went. The clothing was being burnt and there were small groups of Argys clearing the area up. From the burning clothes there was a layer of smoke covering the whole area. All the way from Stanley various sized guns lay on the side of the road, all of which had shot at us

The Falklands troop leaders welcomed home by the Colonel of the Regiment. (*Left to right*) General Sir Desmond Fitzpatrick, Lieutenant M. R. Coreth and Lieutenant Lord Robin Innes-Ker

on Wireless Ridge. There was at least one triple A which I am sure was firing at us!

"What I didn't know was that once I was through the barrier, there were no more English soldiers, only 11,000 Argys! Thank God I was on the bike, at least I could drive away from them, but I hadn't even got my gun!

"All the way along the road the Argys sat huddled around fires trying to keep warm. Others were formed up on the road waiting to be moved to the awaiting boats to take them home. Thankfully they moved off the road when I came.

"The first impressions of the airfield were staggering. There were thousands of lost, disinterested, sad soldiers wandering around. Again they were burning what they could find to keep warm. Tents scattered the landscape blowing in the wind, mostly ripped or damaged. Again there was this odd layer of smoke which hung over the entire area. As I arrived at what was the air terminal it became more apparent to me that I was the only English person there; they all started to look at me, and the bike. Some started to walk towards me, then to my great relief I saw Max Hastings and a few other press just close by."

After spending a week in Stanley, and having, with commendable initiative, arranged to take two captured Argentine Panhard armoured cars[2] aboard, the two troops were back on *Fearless* again. On 24 June "we kissed the Falklands goodbye; we had all our vehicles with us, but, most important, we had not lost any men." Having enjoyed little more than two or three hours' sleep a night during the campaign they passed much of their time on the 8,000-mile voyage home in repose. They reached Portsmouth on 14 July. "The reception at Portsmouth was mind-blowing . . . but little could surpass the more personal welcome that Windsor put on for us. The crowds were almost covering our route and their banners were aimed at us alone . . . We were home at last."

Brigadier Julian Thompson wrote to Colonel Hamilton-Russell:

"I was most impressed by both troops. They took to the rather curious environment of an amphibious operation with great enthusiasm. As they will no doubt have told you, we put them right in the front of the leading landing craft to give us some ability to fire back with a bit of punch at anyone on the actual beaches. Not ideal perhaps, but in the hope that any enemy on the beach would be disinclined to argue with a 76 mm or Rarden.

"For the remainder of the campaign they did all that was asked of them with great style and were not deterred by anything. It was entirely my fault that I did not use them in the direct support role of infantry earlier. I just did not realize how good they would be across that appalling terrain until they motored across from San Carlos to Mount Kent. I then immediately lost them to 5 Bde – to my great chagrin.

"I got Robin's troop back with 2 Para for my Bde attack and subsequent operations. They supported the battalion very well and undoubtedly contributed greatly to the success of the attack on Wireless Ridge. When I saw them on the morning after the attack their tails were well up and they were, rightly, very pleased with themselves.

"I found everybody in both troops well mannered, well turned out in all circumstances, calm and collected – which is, if I may say so, what I would expect of Household Cavalrymen."

284

And the Major General commanding the Household Division heard from the Chief of the General Staff as follows:

"The two troops of the RHG/D seem to have been used in a multitude of tasks, ranging from reconnaissance and fire support to casualty evacuation and load carrying, and in doing so answered every call that came their way throughout the campaign, and crossed the most remarkable country. They deservedly earned themselves a very high reputation."

Those involved in Operation 'Corporate", apart from the watch-keeper officers, were:

3 Troop, "B" Squadron
Lieutenant Lord R. Innes-Ker*
CoH S. Thomson
Lance CoH G. Dunkley†
Lance CoH J. Fisher
Lance CoH M. Brown
L/Corporal M. Mitchell
Trooper G. Birch
Trooper H. Ford
Trooper C. Hastings
Trooper J. Holdsworth
Trooper S. Round
Trooper J. Pilchowski

4 Troop "B" Squadron
Lieutenant M. Coreth*
CoH P. Stretton*
Lance CoH S. Meiklejohn
Lance CoH S. Ward
L/Corporal G. Farmer
Trooper M. Flynn
Trooper P. Fugatt
Trooper T. Maxwell
Trooper E. Tucker
Trooper D. Voyce
Trooper A. Widdowson

Light Aid Detachment REME
Sergeant S. Reid
Lance Sergeant A. Hill
Lance Sergeant A. Watts
Lance Corporal A. Lamblein

"The Falkland Islands 1982" was soon to be added to the Regiment's roll of Battle Honours.

* Mentioned in Despatches.
† Commander-in-Chief Fleet Commendation

The Falklands troops back at Combermere. Standing: (*left to right*) Sergeant Reed (REME), Corporal of Horse Stretton, Trooper Fuggat, Lance Corporal of Horse Ward, Lance Corporal of Horse Dunkley, Trooper Maxwell, Trooper Voyce, Lance Corporal of Horse Meiklejohn, Trooper Flynn, Lance Corporal Birch, Trooper Round, Corporal of Horse Thomson, Trooper Brown. Sitting: L/Corporal White (REME), Trooper Mitchell, Lieutenant Lord Robin Innes-Ker, Lance Corporal Farmer, Trooper Lambert, Lieutenant M. R. Coreth, Trooper Ford, Craftsman Taylor (REME), Trooper Widdowson

OUTRAGE IN HYDE PARK

It was at 10.40 am on 20 July that the horror of the IRA attack on the Queen's Life Guards occurred. That was also the occasion of a remarkable coincidence. Lieuts Coreth and Lord Robin Innes-Ker, home from the South Atlantic for not much more than a week, were debriefed that morning at the Ministry of Defence. After the meeting, as Lord Robin drove along Knightsbridge, heading for Hyde Park Barracks, he was alerted by the explosion which was set off on the south side of the South Carriage Road at the precise moment that he drew parallel with the Guard. He immediately pulled into the side of the road and dashed across to see what help he could offer among the carnage. He naturally remarked how ironical it was that all twenty-eight members of the Regiment who had served in the intensely hazardous Operation 'Corporate' should return safe and sound while, in the same summer, four Blues and Royals, on duty in the middle of London, should be murdered by an enemy more treacherous, far more iniquitous than the Argentines. But Lord Robin had been hardened to the sight of the dead and dying.

Scene of the carnage of the South Carriage Road after the IRA bomb outrage in Hyde Park in 1982. *Press Association*

The IRA bomb – 25 lb of gelignite-based explosive, surrounded by 30 lb of nails, placed in a car and detonated by radio control – struck the Guard with devastating effect, as they rode to take over from The Life Guards at Whitehall. Lieutenant Colonel Parker Bowles, then commanding the Mounted Regiment, recalled that

"the last time I heard anything like that ominous explosion was in Londonderry in 1972. At 10.45 on 20 July soldiers were running back and forth, helter-skelter, below me. Everyone's instinct was 'Oh, my God, the Guard!' Then I heard one of the farriers say, 'The bastards have got the horses!' and I ran through the gate and down the South Carriageway as fast as I could. The first thing that caught my eye, through the smoke, was a tree in flames. I saw Pedersen standing, half-conscious, with a nail pierced through the gauntlet of his right hand and through his little finger, but still holding Sefton, from whose jugular the blood was visibly pumping. A Life Guards Corporal of Horse, O'Flaherty, who had doubled up to the scene, had his fist on the wound, feeling for the pressure point. He was covered in blood. I told him to get a shirt, or something, and stuff it into the hole, which he did."[3]

The murdered soldiers were Lieutenant Anthony Daly, commanding the Guard, Corporal Major Roy Bright, who carried the Standard, Lance Corporal Jeffery Young and Trooper Simon Tipper. Three other members of the Guard were seriously wounded, but it was stated that "jack boots, cuirasses and gauntlets gave a high degree of protection". Seven horses were killed or put down: Yeastvite, Epaulette, Rochester, Waterford, Falcon, Zara and Cedric. Three more horses, although dreadfully wounded, made a remarkable recovery, largely owing to the skill of The Blues and Royals vet, Major Noel Carding. Those were Sefton, Copenhagen and Eclipse. Sympathizers, including a great measure of the British public, wanted a symbol upon which to focus their pity and admiration. Sefton, a remarkable equine character with an unusually chequered career behind him, became the nation's hero. He was seen to epitomize the courage and fortitude of the Household Cavalrymen themselves. Nominated 'Horse of the Year' Sefton duly took his place centre stage at Wembley that autumn, led in by the man who had ridden him on the awful morning of 20 July, Trooper Pedersen. Having spent a couple of months recuperating at Melton Mowbray, hardly a

SQMC Roy Bright, who was killed in the incident

visible mark remained by then from the horse's dreadful injuries.

Following the outrage the Mounted Regiment received a vast number of presents and messages of condolence. Although they did not set up an appeal fund they received nearly £100,000. The two largest donations came from the band of the Second Battalion of the Parachute Regiment, who raised £18,000 from concerts;

Sefton, as Horse of the Year, with his rider, Trooper Pedersen, at Wembley. Sefton's miraculous recovery after the bombing was greeted with plaudits and presents from all around Britain. *Leslie Lane*

and the Royal Dublin Society, who, appealing for subscriptions from all over Ireland, received donations of over £30,000. The money was shared between the four widows and their respective four children, with a small amount kept back for a memorial in Hyde Park which was, in due course, placed opposite the spot where the atrocity occurred.

The Standard carried on 20 July and tattered in the explosion was defiantly carried, unrepaired, when the next Blues and Royals Guard rode down to Whitehall two days later. The Queen's Life Guard have brought their swords down from the 'slope' to the 'carry' and given the memorial plaque an 'eyes left' and an 'eyes right' ever since.

After the euphoric jubilation greeting the return of the Regiment's South Atlantic heroes this tragedy struck a bitter blow to morale, not only to The Blues and Royals Mounted Squadron, but to the whole of the Household Cavalry.

Given the Regiment's resilience, however, they were soon on a cheerfully even keel again. The Falklands men scarcely had time for their well-earned leave before they were off to Cyprus on the United Nations mission, relieving "A", who were hardly settled in at Combermere before they joined the remainder of the Regiment on a Salisbury Plain exercise, a warm-up for two weeks in Schleswig-Holstein where

"the Germans were most hospitable and the local Panzer battalion looked after our needs very well ... On our return to Windsor we bade farewell to Lt-Colonel J. G. Hamilton-Russell and welcomed, as the new Commanding Officer, Lt-Colonel J. D. Smith-Bingham. For the remainder of October and November we prepared for gunnery camp. We went to Castlemartin on 26 November. It was extremely cold."[4]

PRESENTATION OF STANDARDS, 1983

Colonel Hamilton-Russell, now Silver Stick, commanded the parade for the 1983 Presentation of new Standards to the Household Cavalry by the Queen. And what a spectacular parade it was, with a Life Guards squadron in Fox reconnaissance vehicles (got ready for them by The Blues and Royals!), "B" Squadron of the Regiment (home from Cyprus in January) and the panoply of the Mounted Regiment (with the tattered Blues and Royals Standard of 20 July 1982, included with the others) – a total of 196 horses, 46 armoured vehicles, 58 officers and 457 NCOs and troopers. The Queen having presented the new Standards and addressed the parade, Colonel Hamilton-Russell turned to the Chaplain-General: "Venerable Sir, on behalf of the Household Cavalry, we ask you to bid God's blessing on these Standards." To which the Chaplain-General replied, "We are ready to do so," and led the prayers:

"that [these Standards] may be an abiding symbol of our duty towards our Sovereign and our Country and a sign of our resolve to guard, preserve, and sustain the great traditions of bravery and self-sacrifice of which we are the proud inheritors ... O Lord Jesus Christ who ... hast called us to put on the armour of God and to take the sword of the Spirit, give thy grace, we pray Thee, to The Blues and Royals that we may fight manfully under Thy banner and … may mount up with wings as eagles."[5]

There was a different ending from that of previous Standards Presentations. Instead of leaving her Household Cavalry at Horse Guards the Queen drove at the head of the Squadrons to Buckingham Palace, taking leave of them there. In the afternoon Her Majesty attended a garden party for past and present members of the Regiments in the grounds of Burton Court, Chelsea.

Household Cavalrymen taking part in the film *The Last Cavalry Charge*

BACK TO DETMOLD

"It was apparent two years ago," Lieutenant Colonel Jeremy Smith-Bingham was writing in 1985, "that The Blues and Royals would not have an easy first year in Germany and therefore steps were taken to ensure that, during 1983, conversion training was carried out well above the basic guidelines which the Regiment had been set ... We had only been in Germany a short time before it became obvious to all how essential this additional training was going to be."[6] How aptly that underlines the anxiety and precaution of a commanding officer taking over an armoured reconnaissance regiment of the Household Cavalry and faced with the prospect of leading them into the exacting tank role in Rhine Army. The Blues and Royals arrived at Detmold in February, 1984, and, within weeks, were back on the familiar stamping-grounds of Soltau and Hohne. They would remain in Germany for the next six years.

REFERENCES

1. All the quotes concerning Op 'Corporate' given in this chapter are from one or other of the troop leaders unless otherwise stated
2. One was kept by the Regiment at Windsor, the other by the Tank Museum at Bovington
3. In a letter from Brigadier Parker Bowles, previously related on p 92 of *Sefton: The Story of a Cavalry Horse*
4. *The Blue and Royal*, 1983
5. From the parade programme
6. *The Blue and Royal*, 1985

BLUES AND ROYALS

October 1982

Commanding Officer: Lieutenant Colonel J. D. Smith-Bingham
2 i/c: Major I. M. D. L. Weston
Adjutant: Captain W. T. Browne
RSO: Captain P. J. Tabor
IO: Lieutenant (QM) J. A. Livingstone
RCM: WOI M. Patterson
Chief Clerk: WOII Sturrock

A Squadron
Sqn Ldr: Major P. B. Rogers
2 i/c: Captain T. P. E. Barclay
SCM: WOII Villers

B Squadron (UNFICYP)
Sqn Ldr: Major T. J. Sulivan
2 i/c: Captain A. J. Miller-Bakewell
SCM: WOII McKenna

C Squadron
Sqn Ldr: Major G. T. R. Birdwood
2 i/c: Captain R. A. K. Field
SCM: WOII Sayer

HQ Squadron
Sqn Ldr: Major H. St J. Holcroft
Medical Officer: Surgeon Lieutenant Colonel J. P. A. Page
Tech Quartermaster: Major (QM) J. G. Handley
Quartermaster: Captain (QM) J. Peck
RQMC: WOII O'Halloran
RQMC: WOII Birt
SCM: WOII Holt

Mounted Squadron
Sqn Ldr: Major J. Mc M. Carr-Ellison
2 i/c: Captain F. G. S. Lukas
SCM: WOII Brown

Band
Director of Music: Major B. T. Keeling
Trumpet-Major: WOII Whennell

Chapter V

CHIEFTAINS AND CHALLENGERS

(1983–1990)

Household Cavalry commanding officers anticipating the prospect of leaving Combermere for the contrasting and exacting Rhine Army role were, as stressed at the close of the preceding chapter, at pains to have as much tank conversion as possible prepared in advance. Colonel Smith-Bingham set the necessary crewmen training in motion early in 1983 although the Regiment did not return to Detmold until January, 1984; and while the sabre squadrons had been familiarizing themselves once more with Chieftain, Headquarters Squadron added guided weapons and reconnaissance troops to their establishment.

Regimental field training was by no means confined to Soltau and Hohne. Colonel Peter Rogers, The Blues and Royals' last Commanding Officer, is to be thanked for these graphic and exuberant reminiscences:

"For the more military among us the highlight of the year was the formation size field training exercise, of which there was normally one each autumn. The excitement of deploying by road or rail or even driving to virgin farmland East of the Weser River was enormous. It must partly have stemmed from the prospect of operating as a troop relatively unsupervised by one's squadron leader. But even better was the opportunity to live on, and drive across, civilian farmland and forest. Not only was this of far greater and more realistic training value than the normal training area at Soltau, but also I found it great fun hiding up in villages and barns or in the depths of some ancient forest, recceing on foot and waiting to be called forward to battle positions.

"The last major FTX I did was 'Lionheart' in 1984, when I was commanding "A" Squadron. We started with a long rail move to the exercise area. There followed about 3 days living in a forest with myself and the troop leaders doing detailed recces. We then deployed forward to near the East German border and covered all entry points into our TAOR. It was very exciting, particularly at night, sitting in my headquarters awaiting the first enemy contact. After this had come the business of conducting the squadron withdrawal. With all the attendant problems of cheating enemy, lack of umpires, broken-down vehicles, civilian traffic accidents, etc, that was a real adrenalin trip. Then followed a clean break and long road move on radio silence back to a pre-recced secondary defensive position, with a running replen at night en route. I remember on 'Lionheart' being in my command vehicle near the rear of the Squadron as we withdrew, overseeing the final enemy contacts. As a result I tasked Cornet Christian Ward-Thomas, a recently

In aid of the civil power. Spartan and Range Rover at Heathrow for 'Operation Woodshed'

arrived new troop leader, to lead the Squadron packet up the withdrawal route. I knew that behind us the rest of the Brigade were to follow.

"It was at night and we were on radio silence. Most of the route was marked by military police traffic sentries but at one critical cross-roads there was none, and as I reached the point I realized that Christian had taken the Squadron the wrong way. Not only could I not contact him to put him right, but also I knew that the whole Brigade was hot on our tail. Christian must have realized his error because we then proceeded like some vast snake to weave our way cross-country doing, presumably, untold damage to many fields and tracks. Eventually we got back onto the right road and I did intimate to RHQ that we had not taken precisely the laid down route, wondering whether this might be the end of a promising career. However, having heard no more about it for two days I concluded that nobody else had been reading their maps. The lesson I learned was always lead the Squadron personally, and certainly do not get stuck at the back when on radio silence.

"Parking up in German villages and visiting gasthofs for a drink was very much part of the fun, even in tanks but particularly on recce. When I was a troop leader exercises were very alcoholic affairs with the ready-round bin and external turret baskets being filled with cases of bottled Heineken ("stubbies") for the soldiers, and a bottle of whisky for the troop leader. Most crewman had an open "stubby" on the go permanently ... When I returned to Germany as a squadron leader BAOR had virtually gone dry, with spirits forbidden and beer rationed 'at commanding officer's discretion'. This was probably right, both because of the far greater volume of civilian traffic on the roads and because of the increased sophistication of tank turret services which needed a clear head to operate.

"I used to enjoy night moves both on tanks and in recce. Usually in the autumn exercise period it could get quite cold at night. One would stand with one's head out of the turret with the cold air rushing against one's face frequently bringing with it marvellous autumn country smells. Every so often one would drop down into the turret, into a warm atmosphere with the turret lights glowing and the bodies of one's crew just discernable. The gunner normally slept immediately in front of one's knees propped against his sights, while the operator sat with his head-set on a pad on his knee and the coffee-making kit at his elbow. It was so cosy that it took quite an effort to force oneself back out into the cold night air, particularly if one was in a large convoy and map reading was not really required.

"I can remember one occasion when my driver fell asleep. We had

Night firing, Hohne

come to a T junction and instead of turning left, the tank just went straight on. I had to jump out and climb in the dark down the front of the turret to tap him on the head and wake him up. In fact fatigue was the greatest problem on exercises, particularly for commanders and officers who were not only fighting that day's battle but also planning and recceing subsequent phases. For this reason it was essential that the troop leader's crew was thoughtful enough to look after him. Some soldiers were very good at getting out the troop leader's sleeping bag, etc, and organizing it for him on the back decks so that he could come back from his orders without worrying about anything. Other soldiers were not so good and made his life much harder.

"I know, as a squadron leader, I used to drive my crew pretty mad by never being with the tank when they cooked food and then asking for something when everything had been packed away. Actually it was much easier for a squadron leader because he also had his Land Rover following along: and, in the end, I usually went to a guest house for feeding and shaving etc. One tended to have, at every rank, a marvellous relationship with one's crew, partly because they were hand-picked to be compatible and also because of the long hours one spent in very close contact with them. Any officer worth his salt would either produce, or give the money to his operator to buy, a lot of additional culinary goodies to add to the rations from which the whole crew benefited."

A Blues and Royals Fox CRV (W)

Colonel Rogers follows with a note on life in the officers' mess:

"One of the major advantages of Lothian Barracks was an excellent outdoor swimming pool. All ranks were able to take advantage of this facility. There was a tennis court beside the Mess and it was wonderful to be able to play until about 7 pm and then have a swim before having dinner on the lawn. At weekends half the Regiment sometimes seemed to be lying in the sun on the grass around the pool...

"Although I was horribly old to be living in the mess, almost every night was really good fun. Dinner as usual was in black tie and the food was generally good ... Sadly, towards the time when I left, BFBS Television had arrived plus videos. These had a disastrous effect on mess life as I had known it, which was compounded by the opening of a MacDonalds Hamburger chain in Detmold. Subalterns found it easier to slop in front of the television in sports kit rather than change into black tie and have a proper dinner. The absurdity of this was brought home to me when I saw a subaltern drive to MacDonalds in his Porsche to collect an armful of burgers and french fries."[1]

By then the Lothian days were strictly numbered. During 1986, the year in which Lieutenant Colonel Hywel Davies assumed command, it was announced that The Blues and Royals were to be one of three Rhine Army regiments to be equipped with the new main battle tank, the Challenger. Coincidentally, the Regiment was transferred from 4th Armoured Division to 3rd Armoured. All this came at the same time as the decision to move them from Detmold, which had been the Household Cavalry's German station for seventeen years, their new home being Athlone Barracks, Sennelager, where they relieved the Royal Scots Dragoon Guards. Lieutenant Colonel Davies takes up the thread:

"The barracks in Detmold were being rebuilt; one squadron was living about 20 minutes away while their block was refurbished, and the tanks were parked in rows on the square while the hangars were rebuilt. As winter set in the square, which had become a rutted mess, took on a nightmarish aspect like the forecourt of Gormenghast Castle while the Regiment, trying to maintain tanks in temperatures well below zero, lit coal braziers in a brave attempt to produce a little heat. All this would have been bearable if at the end the reward was a modern barracks. Unfortunately the Ministry of Defence had embarked on one of those periodic reorganizations designed to produce greater efficiency but in reality creating a close resemblance to chaos, and threatening the morale of considerable sections of the Army. As part of this the Regiment had been told that they would have to move to a new barracks about thirteen miles away and the move was scheduled to coincide with the completion of the barrack rebuild. This rationalizing move was into a larger barracks as the Regiment became smaller but was justified on operational grounds although no one ever managed to state these in very precise terms ... Having arrived in Sennelager the Regiment set about its new role with considerable vigour and success, but it was clear that a number of basic facilities were missing.

"One cause of concern was the lack of suitable stables for the 'blacks' which suffered an appalling first winter in bitter conditions and in unsuitable stabling. The stables had been for polo ponies, really designed for summer use only, and were little more than a tin shed with

Members of the Mounted Squadron off the south coast from their summer camp at Sopley, New Forest, 1984. (*Left to right*) Lance-Corporal Yorke, Troopers Nichols, Edgington, Chalmers, Willis, Watt and Liddle

loose-boxes. It was unfortunate that on 12 December the temperature fell below 20 degrees Centigrade and effectively stayed there until the middle of March. Water buckets froze very quickly and horseshoes tended to freeze to wet ground if a horse stood still for a long period. It was impossible to exercise the horses properly because there was no riding school and the outside was frozen solid. After a second horse (Amos) was put down because it was too old to cope with the intense cold a meeting was convened by the Commander-in-Chief who, after hearing the full story, said, "We were right to move The Blues and Royals, weren't we?" The Corps Commander looked the other way with a rather embarrassed expression, and the new Divisional Commander hummed and hawed and said it had not been thought through properly, but it had happened, so everyone would have to make the best of it...

"The Regiment settled into Sennelager well but it was never quite the home that Detmold had been, although new stables and a riding school[2] were built in time for us to get some use from them prior to handing them over to The Life Guards. The curious thing is that morale stayed remarkably high and the premature voluntary release figures were amongst the best in the Army. It is undoubtedly true that adversity brings out the best in us."[3]

Before adopting their Challengers they were to complete a year on a four sabre squadron basis, and for that purpose they took a squadron of the 14th/20th Hussars under command. The hectic task of conversion began in May, 1987, although they did not receive their fleet until early the following year, after which the 14th/20th soldiers duly returned to their parent regiment. Lieutenant Colonel Tim Sulivan, who took command that August, looked forward enthusiastically to the advent of the new tank. "The greatly increased speed of reaction possible with Challenger," he said, "will require us to look carefully at our battle procedures and drills. Now we can produce some real dash and élan on the battlefield."[4] But they had not seen the last of Chieftain, for, in July, 1989, their regimental battle group, which included a company of the Queen's Own Highlanders, proceeded to the plains of Alberta in Canada again, to BATUS (British Army Training Unit, Suffield), and Exercise Medicine

"A" Squadron pacesticking team, 1987. (*Left to right*) Corporal of Horse Miller, Lance Corporal of Horse Robertson, Corporal of Horse Sandercock, Squadron Corporal Major Evans

Man 4, except for "C" Squadron who went to Soltau to join the infantry battle group, (who, they complained, "completely upset the [first] exercise timetable by a series of rapid and unorthodox manoeuvres".[5])

Just after Colonel Sulivan's arrival a WRAC officer was posted, more or less straight from Sandhurst, to be assistant adjutant. "The first female cornet," the Regiment recorded. This was Second Lieutenant Diane Mawby who remembers settling into the job

"remarkably quickly, but initially I found it difficult to say 'Corporal Major' and 'Corporal of Horse'. I was nominated as Unit Fire Officer and whilst attending the course, every Warrant Officer would look at me agog when I started calling them 'Corporal-Major'. People outside the Regiment found it harder and still do, to accept that the WRAC have infiltrated The Blues and Royals. On answering the telephone, I am greeted with either the receiver being rapidly replaced or hearing a shocked voice saying 'That's not The Blues and Royals is it?'

". . . On carrying out various adjutantal tasks I have discovered that the subalterns are all overworked. I only have to walk into the mess and ask one what he was doing the following Thursday and within seconds I am given the entire timetable for that day! This timetable is very flexible and can change rapidly if, for example, a trip to the Hague is offered!"[6]

New Year 1990 saw not only the end of their six-year tour with the Rhine army, it also fell just short of the 21st anniversary of the amalgamation of the two Regiments, a landmark which was to be celebrated in due style in the Warrant Officers and Corporals of Horse mess at Combermere on 29 March, when eleven out of thirteen of those who had held the post of Regimental Corporal Major were the guests of honour.

Just before The Blues and Royals left Sennelager for home Lieutenant Colonel Sulivan[7] was relieved of command by Lieutenant Colonel Peter Rogers, a third generation Royal who was one of the last officers to be commissioned into the Royal Dragoons. "We can now very truly be said to have come of age as a Regiment in our own right," he said that spring. "Recruits joining today were not even born when amalgamation took place . . . And 1990 holds another significance for us. It is now 50 years

Members of the Regiment with their Challenger tanks at Soltau in 1989

since our predecessors in the two Regiments handed over their horses and, for the first time, learned the art of gunnery, the science of radio and the skill of driving armoured vehicles." The Commanding Officer continued as follows:

"It should not be forgotten that today the complexity of equipment and range of skills which all ranks are required to master is greater than ever before. At the same time, while many are better educated, most come from softer backgrounds than their predecessors, and we live in a civilian world where old-fashioned standards have frequently slipped. However, I feel confident that, as we enter the last decade of the 20th Century, those Blues or Royals who gave up their horses some 50 years ago will find in their successors in the Regiment today young men with the same motivation, professionalism and comradeship which was the hallmark of previous generations."[8]

NOTES AND REFERENCES

1. In a letter from Colonel P. B. Rogers
2. The new Rhine Army (Sennelager) Equitation Centre was opened on July 7, 1989
3. In a letter from Lieutenant Colonel H. W. Davies
4. *The Blue and Royal*, 1988
5. Ibid 1989
6. Ibid
7. Brigadier Sulivan then underwent the Higher Command and Staff course prior to going as Commander 7 Armoured Brigade Group. His appointment coincided, however, with the opening of the Gulf War which found 7 Bde in Saudi Arabia. In the event he spent an interim as British Liaison Officer on Gen Schwartzkopf's staff; and, while establishing a significant rapport with the Americans, he was able to provide Gen de la Billière with invaluable advice on the use of armour during the campaign. This service earned him a CBE
8. *The Blue and Royal*, 1990

BLUES AND ROYALS

December 1988

Commanding Officer: Lieutenant Colonel T. J. Sulivan
2 i/c: Major G. T. R. Birdwood
Adjutant: Captain M. R. Coreth
Operations Officer: Captain R. J. Onslow
RSO: Captain G. V. de la F. Woyka
RCM: WOI T. Quinn
Chief Clerk: WOII Reeve

A Squadron
Sqn Ldr: Major A. J. Miller-Bakewell
2 i/c: Captain C. B. B. Clee
SCM: WOII Wendon

B Squadron
Sqn Ldr: Major F. G. S. Lukas
2 i/c: Captain W. R. B. Jowitt
SCM: WOII Evans

C Squadron
Sqn Ldr: Major W. R. Rollo
2 i/c: Captain J. S. P. Swayne
SCM: WOII Guest

HQ Squadron
Sqn Ldr: Major T. P. E. Barclay
Medical Officer: Surgeon Captain A. Y. D. Moss
Quartermaster: Captain (QM) S. Sibley
Tech Quartermaster: Captain (QM) D. O'Halloran
RQMC: WOII Buckle
TQMC: WOII Harkness

Mounted Squadron
Sqn Ldr: Major B. W. B. White-Spunner
2 i/c: Captain J. W. Johnsen
SCM: WOII Sackett

Band
Director of Music: Major R. J. Tomlinson
Trumpet-Major: WOII Brammer

Chapter VI

TOWARDS THE UNION

(1990–1992)

The contrast between life at Combermere and that in Rhine Army must, in 1990, have seemed greater than ever before. Whereas a tank regiment in Germany was subject to intensive centralization by regimental headquarters, the armoured reconnaissance role in the strategic reserve involved, as we have already seen, considerable squadron independence or detachment; and the return to squadron autonomy was naturally welcomed.[1] But it was the additional contrast in vehicles which rendered such a fresh difference this time round. Crews missed the power and punch of Challenger, so greatly superior to Chieftain. By comparison the combat reconnaissance vehicles – the Fox wheeled armoured car for "A" Squadron, the tracked Scorpion for "B" and "C" – seemed positively mild.

They had first taken over the Windsor tracked fleet in the early 1970s. Little wonder, considering the buffetings those vehicles had received on the training areas during two decades, that they were showing their age. And the main armament, the 76 mm, was virtually the same as that of the Saladin of the 1950s. As for the Fox, "it proved to be a tricky beast", was "A" Squadron's verdict, "particularly when moving cross-country at night ... 2 Troop had several narrow escapes, with Corporal of Horse Tapsell providing some interesting new ideas on track discipline when travelling some distance on two wheels."[2] Notwithstanding the facts that there was a great deal less maintenance to contend with than on tanks and local roads could be used for driver training, many crewmen imagined the ideal combination to be Combermere with Challengers!

The transition from tanks to armoured cars being completed in

309

Riding school in the new manege, Hyde Park, 1990. *Mike Roberts*

March The Blues and Royals, who had taken the precaution, before leaving Germany, of having eleven men parachute-trained, were in 5 Airborne Brigade's order of battle. And there was now a sprinkling of red berets to be seen at Combermere. By November the outgoing brigadier was writing fulsomely to Colonel Rogers that "your Regiment has tackled the new airborne role in exemplary fashion and I was delighted to find such a positive and enthusiastic approach to life in every quarter. You command a very fine Regiment and can be justly proud of them."[3] But, indirectly, the Gulf War was to have an adverse effect on airborne training, because RAF Transport Command was to be materially and physically exhausted from its efforts in the campaign for many months to come.

Although 5 Airborne Brigade were on standby for that operation, and the Regiment fully expected to go, in the end they were considered to be too light for the task in hand, and were stood down. Which is not to say that the Regiment was not involved. Besides the increased vigilance necessary at Combermere, "A" and "B" Squadrons were on a continuous rotation of 8-hour patrols, in conjunction with the police, at Heathrow. "C" Squadron flew to Cyprus for their six-months United Nations tour on the very day that the ground battle on the Saudi-Kuwait border began. And considering that the island was within Scud range of Iraq there was much concern for their safety.

Salisbury Plain demonstration during the Royal Review of 5 Airborne Brigade in May, 1990. Recovery of a "C" Squadron Scorpion by a Chinook helicopter. *Soldier Magazine*

It was an especially successful UNFICYP tour, quite apart from "C" Squadron's highly commendable work there. To name one of several "flag-showing" enterprises the Squadron Leader (Major White-Spunner) arranged for the regimental band to be flown out, the highlight of their visit being the sunset concert they gave at Kyrenia harbour, a full-dress affair which delighted the Turkish Cypriots. Then the Squadron Corporal Major (Corporal Major Manning) organized a most venturesome visit to Egypt for the senior NCOs. When the Squadron left, the Commander of the island's British contingent said it "was probably the best anyone could remember since "A" Squadron of the same Regiment was here in 1982."

There were several other foreign adventures in store for The Blues and Royals during this Windsor sojourn. "B" Squadron enjoyed exercises in Cyprus, while "A" (with two troops from "B") flew to Australia, with stops in Bahrein and Singapore on the outward journey and in Hawaii and Seattle on the way home. In the outbacks of the Northern territories "when the rain finally turned to drizzle and after being a cat's whisker away from participating in the flood relief we set off for Crocodile Dundee country . . . Our exercise area was a block of 6,000 square miles . . . After many a farewell in true Aussie style in Darwin, back in Sydney we were airborne once again." Meanwhile a squadron of Australia's 2nd Cavalry Regiment "sampled the delights of Salisbury Plain and Thetford Training Area," said *The Blue and Royal* ironically. "The Australians departed in shocking style having eaten a goldfish from the aquarium at The Lord Raglan. *The Sun* and *The Mirror* had a field day." The sight of one of their comrades plucking an inmate of The Lord Raglan's goldfish bowl from its water and eating it alive may have given the Australians great amusement, but the bravado was not so well appreciated by the pub's Blue and Royal clientele, since the landlord banned all military personnel from the premises thereafter.

In September, 1990, Lieut Scott and Cornet Hamilton-Russell led two "B" Squadron troops to Belize (Honduras) where, living primarily in the jungle with the Glosters battle group, they assisted the local defence force in the control of drug-smuggling.

This tour also included much imaginative training and many adventurous expeditions.

"Join the Household Cavalry and see the world!" The late 1980s and early 1990s seemed to have been remarkable, despite the heavy training programmes, for the numbers of Blues and Royals who managed to get away on extra-regimental attachments and adventurous trips. There were, for instance, several secondments to infantry battalions in Northern Ireland. Parties accompanying HMS *Broadsword*, which had helped provide the British presence in the Falklands Protection Zone, took in a series

"C" Squadron at the United Nations Medals parade, Nicosia, Cyprus, 1991

313

of alluring ports of call. Others went trekking in India or Corsica, or working for the wildlife services in Kenya, or paddling dinghies along the English canals, while Lance Corporal of Horse Hastings led a party over the Pyrenees and back, and Lance Corporal Hagan secured a place on the Operation Raleigh expedition in Zimbabwe.

Nor were home schemes, or expeditions to fire the vehicle weapons at Castlemartin or Lulworth, ever dull. Far from it. The Regiment's tactical swansong (Exercise Last Legend) was unique. After 10 days on Salisbury Plain the Commanding Officer ordered his Squadrons – some 170 tracked and supporting wheeled vehicles – to move by convoy to harbour areas in Somerset. With regimental headquarters based on Melbury House[4] and the squadrons covering a front that reached from the Bristol Channel to the south coast, they spent the next 24 hours manoeuvring back to the Plain on advance to contact. These were the very last manoeuvres for the Regiment as such.

Before discussing the reduction of the Household Cavalry in 1992 let us take a look at some aspects of The Blues and Royals at sport during those years immediately prior to it. Their rugby team, trained by Lieut Davies, a former Mounted Regiment Regimental Corporal Major, and Corporal Major Kilvington, won, first, London District's Prince of Wales Cup, then the Cavalry Cup. And three members of the team went on to play for the Army under-21s. The skiing team (half officers, half troopers) reached the Army final. On the two occasions that the Regiment entered a military go-karting competition they won it, contributing £1,000 in prize money to the PRI. Lieut York was selected for the Army cricket XI and Lieut Brietmeyer to captain the British under-25 rifle team. The Regiment won the Captains and Subalterns Polo Cup and were runners-up in the inter-regimental.

In 1991 the Household Cavalry scored the remarkable distinction of taking four of the first five places in the Grand Military Gold Cup. The winner was Captain Ward-Thomas, Blues and Royals on Brunton Park, with Captain Wingfield Digby, Blues

The last Ferret scout cars held by the Regiment being loaded at Combermere Barracks for return to the Command Ordnance Depot, 1992. The curator of the Household Cavalry Museum, Major A. W. Kersting (*right*) who stands next to the Technical Quartermaster, Captain M. R. Brown, saw the first Ferret arrive at the barracks in 1955 when he was a trooper

and Royals second (Golden Friend) Captain Ogden, of The Life Guards fourth (Bob Tisdall) and Captain Woodward, Blues and Royals fifth (Elvercore).

The cold war was over, NATO was contracting and looking in other directions; BAOR would soon shrink to a shadow of its former self; and the dreaded words "options for change" resounded in the ears of the British regiments. It appeared, on precedent, as though The Blues and Royals, having amalgamated as late as 1969, would be safe.

However, it soon became apparent that the reductions in armour were to be as much as 40 per cent, a far greater cut than the Army had expected. In those circumstances it was inevitable that the Household Cavalry would become fully involved. The

The first parade of the Household Cavalry Regiment at Combermere Barracks. Life Guards and Blues and Royals Squadrons formed up on the square for Remembrance Sunday, 8 November 1992. Behind Lieutenant Colonel P. S. W. F. Faulkner, LG, the Commanding Officer, are Major F. G. S. Lukas RHG/D (Second in Command), RCM J. Lodge, LG (*left*) and Captain G. C. N. Lane-Fox RHG/D (*right*). Major N. E. Hearson (late LG) leads the Comrades. The Blues and Royals squadrons are front right and rear left. The officer wearing the dark uniform and beret behind Major P. J. Tabor, the Blues and Royals Squadron Leader (*right*), is Captain A. L. Coxhead (on attachment from the Royal Canadian Dragoons). *Kingsley-Jones*

Queen had expressed a wish that if one of the two Regiments were to be reduced in size or amalgamated with a Line Cavalry regiment at least their identities should be retained. After much discussion by all concerned the Army Board recommended that there should be a "Union" within the Household Cavalry. Accordingly, the Chief of the General Staff wrote to the Commanding Officer in July, 1991:

"I have to inform you that the Army Board, chaired by the Secretary of State, recommended to Her Majesty's Government that The Life Guards and The Blues and Royals (Royal Horse Guards and 1st Dragoons) are to form two combined regiments retaining their individual identities. One of these two regiments will be in the armoured reconnaissance role. The other will form the Household Cavalry Mounted Regiment. This recommendation has been accepted.

"This letter, in advance of the announcement in the House of Commons, will allow you the opportunity to inform your Regiment of this decision in the most appropriate manner."[5]

The effect of this decision was that the Mounted Regiment was to remain unchanged and that the armoured reconnaissance regiment at Windsor would consist of two sabre squadrons of Life Guards and two of Blues and Royals with a mixed regimental headquarters and headquarter squadron. "This most unusual organization will undoubtedly raise problems", said General Sir Desmond Fitzpatrick, "but the good will and determination to make it work displayed by all ranks of both Regiments will surely produce an excellent result."[6]

"For anyone who labours under the misapprehension that life in the Mounted Squadron is a rest cure our programme for the past year will give the lie to it."[7] That recent assertion has been echoed, in so many words, for 45 years or so. And, although the highlights of the Squadron's annual programme remain much the same as each season passes we know that the steady tempo of work at Hyde Park Barracks stays at a relentlessly high pitch. The Mounted Squadron isn't just the shop window of the Blues and Royals, it is the *sine qua non*. And the Household Cavalry Mounted Regiment is the pride of Britain and the envy of the world. It would be no exaggeration to say that there are thousands of people outside the Household Cavalry who sense that if ever the Queen's Life Guard was suspended, or even if the character of it was radically altered, or if any of the other pageantry provided by the Household Cavalry were to be extensively reduced it would be a very ominous portent for Britain. For many thousands of Britons the Household Cavalry is the first symbol of the nation.

As for The Blues and Royals at large, past and present, any member of the Association who attended the At Home day at Combermere on 27 September, 1992, a little over three weeks away from the union with The Life Guards, would agree that the celebrated aura of regimental fraternity which has been mentioned more than once in these pages is at least as alive as ever. Therein lies great hope for the future of the Regiment.

After dark, Horse Guards

NOTES AND REFERENCES

1. Colonel Rogers referred to this as "the rent-a-squadron nature of Windsor soldiering"!
2. *The Blue and Royal*, 1991
3. Ibid
4. Melbury House, Dorchester, home of the Hon Mrs Morrison, only child of the late Major Viscount Galway (LG) and a granddaughter, on her mother's side of the late Captain Lord Stavordale (RHG). Her uncle, Hon Stephen Fox-Strangways, was killed on active service with The Blues in Cyprus in 1958 (see p 89)
5. One of the principal ironies of this regimental misfortune was that The Blues and Royals had rarely, if ever, been better recruited. Much of the credit for that had to go to Major Lane (who had been Regimental Corporal Major during the early 1970s) for his tremendous industry in touring the country with the recruiting team.

   Thanks largely to the efforts of Colonel Parker Bowles, when he was Silver Stick, the Regiment was way over strength with young officers, too. (As a consequence of that Colonel Rogers was able, during his tour of command to send officers on individual postings and attachments to fourteen different countries in five continents.) The Blues and Royals claim to field more officers who are second or third generation representatives than any other regiment in the army.
6. In a letter from General Sir Desmond Fitzpatrick
7. *The Blue and Royal*, 1992

BLUES AND ROYALS

June 1992

Commanding Officer: Lieutenant Colonel P. B. Rogers
2 i/c: Major F. G. S. Lukas
Adjutant: Captain G. C. N. Lane-Fox
RSO: Captain C. M. Daly
Operations Officer: Captain W. R. B. Scott
RCM: WOI N. Sackett
Chief Clerk: WOII Tomkins

C Squadron
Sqn Ldr: Major P. J. Tabor
2 i/c: Captain W. R. B. Jowitt
SCM: WOII Manning

D Squadron
Sqn Ldr: Major J. S. P. Swayne
2 i/c: Captain A. J. P. Woodward
SCM: WOII Rogers

HQ Squadron
Sqn Ldr: Major S. H. Cowen
Medical Officer: Surgeon-Major C. M. Stone
Quartermaster: Major (QM) J. A. Livingstone
Tech Quartermaster: Captain (QM) M. R. Brown
RQMC: WOII Harding
TQMC: WOII Partis
SCM: WOII Gimblett

Mounted Squadron
Sqn Ldr: Major J. Shaw
2 i/c: Captain J. B. Poole
SCM: WOII Dunkley

Band
Director of Music: Major C. R. C. Garrity
Trumpet-Major: WOII Brammer

INDEX

Note: Where no regiment is given after regimental names the person concerned is, or has been, a member of The Blues and Royals. The reader will find no reference, as such, here to The Life Guards, the Royal Horse Guards, the 1st Dragoons or The Blues and Royals. Ranks, in the case of all the three regiments concerned, are intended as the highest reached within the Household Cavalry or the Royals. I apologise to anyone finding themselves 'demoted'! J.W.

321

328